Āṇḍāḷ and Akkā Mahādevī

Feminity to Divinity

Āṇḍāḷ and Akkā Mahādevī
Feminity to Divinity

Alka Tyagi

PRINTWORLD
Publishers of Indian Traditions

Cataloging in Publication Data — DK
[Courtesy: D.K. Agencies (P) Ltd. <docinfo@dkagencies.com>]

Tyagi, Alka.

Āṇḍāḷ and Akkā Mahādevī : feminity to divinity / Alka Tyagi.
p. cm.
Includes bibliographical references (p.).
ISBN 13: 9788124607169

1. Bhakti. 2. Āṇṭāḷ – Criticism and interpretation. 3. Akkamahādēvi, fl. 1160 – Criticism and interpretation. 4. Bhakti in literature. I. Title.

DDC 294.54 23

ISBN 13: 978-81-246-0716-9

First published in India in 2014

Printed and published by:
D.K. Printworld (P) Ltd.
Regd. Office : *'Vedaśrī,'* F-395, Sudarshan Park
(Metro Station: Ramesh Nagar)
New Delhi – 110 015-11
Phones : (011) 2545 3975, 2546 6019; *Fax* : 2546 5926
e-mail : indology@dkprintworld.com
Web : www.dkprintworld.com

In humility, I offer this
to the source of my being

Swami Satyasangananda Saraswati,

Peethadeeshwari of Rikhiapeeth,
the Tapobhumi of
Swami Satyananda Saraswati

वन्दे बोधमयं नित्यं गुरुं शङ्कररूपिणम्।
यमाश्रितो हि वक्रोऽपि चन्द्रः सर्वत्र वन्द्यते।।

vande bodhmayaṁ nityaṁ guruṁ śaṅkararūpiṇam ।
yamāśrito hi vakro 'pi chandraḥ sarvatra vandyate ।।

— *Śrīrāmacaritamānasa*

Preface

Women, Bhakti and Poetry

IN medieval India, emotion of *bhakti* evolved into a pan-Indian socio-spiritual movement. There have been saints and sages from all over India whose lives are supreme examples of *bhakti*. The myths that are woven around their lives and the literature left by them still inspire popular imagination of common Indian masses. The socio-cultural and also political transformation that this movement could effect by the sheer force of its poetry and performances is remarkable. The way it challenged the feudal system, the caste system and the gender inequalities is unparalleled in pre-modern history. My interest in myths, literatures, performances and the arts of *bhakti* is a small step in my journey to arrive at a more culturally-rooted answer to prevailing problems of the self and society.

Bhakti movement began in Tamil Nadu in the sixth century, spread all over India and continued well into the seventeenth century. In terms of popularity and significance, no other pan-Indian movement has been as lasting as Bhakti movement. It is very much a living tradition in modern India also. The main reason for its widespread appeal may be that except for promising the liberation (*mokṣa*), the highest achievable goal in Indian way of life, it also extends a democratic attitude towards all people and life forms. Bhakti movement, that had *bhakti* poets as its major exponents, could cut through the callously rigid *varṇa*[1] structure which had a strictly compartmentalized caste system. It was not possible for an individual born in a certain caste to go up or down the four rungs of the caste ladder. However, *bhakti*'s view considered "love" to be the highest *dharma* and looked at book-learning, status and wealth associated with higher castes of brāhmaṇas, kṣtriyas and vaiśyas respectively, as rather impediments in the complete self-surrender to God. With this kind of perspective, Bhakti movement could defy brāhmanas' exclusive right to knowledge (*jñāna*) and to attainment of the highest "Truth".

By expositing, that God dwelt in all the hearts and by denouncing all major knowledge bodies, the movement opened its doors not only for the lower castes, poor and illiterate people but most importantly for the women.

In addition, the shift in the means of expression from Sanskrit to vernacular unleashed the creative potential of women *bhakti* poets. These poets played a very significant role in the development of regional languages and literatures also. For instance, in all the major regional languages, one or the other *bhakti* poetess attained prominence; Āṇḍāḷ in Tamil, Akkā Mahādevī in Kannada, Lal Dêd in Kashmiri,[2] Mīrā in Rajasthani and Gujarati are only to name a few. By making the vernacular the medium of their expression, these poetesses helped to make it more flexible and more suitable for conveying simple colloquial wisdom which usually contained profound philosophical thought.

Though it is a remarkable aspect of our culture that

---

1 *Varṇāśaram dharma* inscribed in the "Dharmaśāstras" reinforced the caste structure based on birth and divided the society into four castes namely brāhmaṇa, kṣatriya, vaiśya and śūdra in hierarchical order.

2 Lal Dêd from Kashmir is remembered as the mother of the mother-tongue in the region.

women's poetry survived not only in oral forms but in written forms also, it should be noted that *bhakti-mārga* was not an easy choice for women of medieval age. It was certainly a very difficult path for women *bhakta*s than it was for men *bhakta*s. While *bhakta*s like Kabīr and Tukārām could continue to be the householders it was not possible for women *bhakta*s like Akkā Mahādevī or Mīrābāī to remain in ever dominating and ever threatening patriarchal set-up. Except for Bahinābāī, women *bhakti* poets had to struggle their way out of social norms and marital forms that were too oppressive to contain their aspirations for personal spiritual growth. These women saints did not begin as rebels or social reformers as such but were simply individuals searching for a spiritual space free from tyrannies of institutionalized social and religious systems. Since similar hierarchical tyrannies prevail even in contemporary society and culture, these women poets' lives continue to inspire women today.

Literary value of their poetry is also unique. The kind of poetry they wrote was neither *śravya-kāvya* (epic-poetry) nor *dṛśya-kāvya* (dramatic-poetry). It was both and much more. Expression of their mystical experience took such forms, which cut across the genres of literature and those of art.

Bhakti poetry is in fact a rich inter-fertilization of forms of art and literature. It emerged as an amazing culture that amalgamated art, music, literature; philosophy, politics, soteriology and mysticism in its fold.

Present Study

This study focuses on two medieval women, Āṇḍāḷ, a eighth-century Āḻvār saint-poetess from Tamil Śrīvaiṣṇavite tradition and Akkā Mahādevī, a twelfth-century Kannaḍa saint-poetess from Vīraśaivite tradition. This choice is motivated primarily by the fact that though both the poetesses are studied under the common rubric of *bhakti* phenomena; there are very subtle differences in their perception of life and that of the God. Their perception manifests in their poetry and this in turn has influenced the way they were received by the community to which they belonged and also by the society on a larger scale. While Akkā Mahādevī was considered as a revolutionary and a rebel, Āṇḍāḷ was very much a part of the tradition and the community structure. Akkā Mahādevī could never be integrated into the mainstream religion; Āṇḍāḷ always occupied the central place in Śrīvaiṣṇava religion. Akkā Mahādevī's image posed a threat to the perceivable image of the Goddess in Hindu iconography,[3] Āṇḍāḷ had been raised to the status of a Goddess in her lifetime itself. In fact, major thrust of the study is on the journey and reception of these women *bhakta*s by the society in their own times and the times that followed. This is done by looking into how the works of these poetesses and the legends about their lives have been adapted into various art forms including films, songs, processions, temple architecture, calendar art and painting.

This book is divided into three sections. Section One serves as the background. It focuses on the understanding of *bhakti* in historical, philosophical and social perspective. It explains the idea of *bhakti*, the ancient religions, the phenomenon of *bhakti* and the evolution of *bhakti* in south India.

Section Two focuses on the lives and works of Āṇḍāḷ and Akkā Mahādevī. This is the main body of the text and is a detailed study of the saints' lives and their chosen path of *bhakti*. It contains:

- Life sketches of Āṇḍāḷ and Akkā Mahādevī.
- Textual analysis of the poetry of Āṇḍāḷ and Akkā Mahādevī from religious, literary and socio-political angles.

---

[3] A temple near Shikaripura in Udutadi district in Karnataka was dedicated to Akkā Mahādevī in the last century.

- Study of *Tiruppāvai* ritual performance in Śrīvaiṣṇavite centres like Śrīraṅgam in Tamil Nadu and Melkoṭe in Karnataka.
- Analysis of classical and neo-classical musical renderings of Āṇḍāḷ's *Tiruppāvai* and *Nachiar Tirumoḻi* and Akkā Mahādevī's *vacana*s with the help of interviews with scholars, dancers and singers.
- Analysis of representations of the two poetesses in rituals, literature, theatre, cinema, dance, painting and other arts.

Analytical tools that are used to critique the textual material from the saints' lives and works are borrowed from the field of semiotics and is referred to as "Intersemiotic Transformations" in order to address questions of transformations between *bhakti* compositions and verbal, performing and visual arts that follow from it. The idea is also to understand specific ways in which these culturally significant women's texts are represented in other genres of art and to look into the extent to which this process is socio-historically mediated and subjected to further transformations. It should be made clear here that use of the term "semiotics" is more as a word with a specific meaning than as a category of Western literary theories. "Semiotics" is simply defined as "study of signs". To this extent, we can use this term when we refer to a specific language register which has its own signs. And hence extendedly I use the term "Intersemiotic Transformations" as it is very conducive to explain the interchangeability happening within various art forms that build up their base on *bhakti* literatures. The subsequent chapters deal with how these transformations are working within as well as outside the works of the chosen saint-poets and how they filter into forms of expression other than their poetry.

Section Three reflects on how the works of saints have sieved into the living patterns in modern India. It contains interviews with individual scholars, painters, dancers, performers, musicians and spiritual seekers. In other words, this section is dedicated to living traditions in *bhakti*.

Finally, in the Appendices Section, Appendix, A is an attempt to understand *bhakti* from the psychological perspective. Here *bhakti* is being placed in a context that is devoid of all religious paraphernalia. It is an attempt to extricate *bhakti* experience from its mystical aura and to make it more accessible to our perceptive faculties. Appendix B provides the translation of "the Sacred View" by Aṇḍāḷ in Tiruppāvai and Appendix C features the translation of ten selected *vacana*s of Akkā Mahādevī.

Contents

Preface vii

Acknowledgement xv

Section One

1. Ancient Religions and Emergence of Bhakti 3
2. Evolution of Bhakti in South India 13
3. Āḻvār Bhakti and Śrīvaiṣṇavism 18
4. Nāyaṉmār Bhakti and Vīraśaivism 33

Section Two

5. Bhakti Poetry: Intersemiotic Transformations 57
6. Āṇḍāḷ: Śrīvaiṣṇavite Woman Āḻvār Saint 68
7. Transformations in Āṇḍāḷ's Life and Work 74
8. Akkā Mahādevī: Vīraśaivite Woman Saint 114
9. Transformations in Akkā's Life and Work 123

Section Three

10. Living Bhakti Traditions 173

Appendices

Appendix A: Bhakti Poetry and Bhakti Experience: A State of Mind and a Way of Being 215

Appendix B: Tiruppāvai: The Sacred Vow by Āṇḍāḷ 234

Appendix C: Akkā Mahādevī's Vacanas 243

Bibliography 247

Index 253

Acknowledgement

FIRST thanks are due to Prof. R. Satyanarayana, renowned musicologist and one of the greatest living scholars on Indian philosophical and spiritual traditions, for keeping me focused and providing me with his valuable insights all the time. Then I would like to thank Prof. H.S. Shivaprakash who helped me with primary texts in Kannada and Tamil. He has helped in filling the loopholes in the argument and has translated Akkā Mahādevī's *Yoganga Trividhi,* specially for the sake of this study.

I would like to register my gratitude to Swami Satyasangananda Saraswati of Bihar School of Yoga for giving me time and discussing with me important concepts of tāntric traditions.

My thanks are also due to some very sincere and unassuming scholars as well as students living in the City of Mysore, Karnataka. They are: Dr V.S. Sampathkumaracharya, Prof. T.R.S. Sharma, Mr Ramu, M.A. Jaishree, M.A. Narsimhan Dr Lakshmitatacharya, Dr Vasundhara Filliozat and Prof. Pierre-Sylvan Filliozat. I would also like to thank classical dancers Nandini Eswer, Rohitha Eswer and Rashmi Eswer who gave me their valuable time and allowed me to have a glimpse of their devoted life. Another renowned Bharatanatyam dancer Vasundhara Doraswamy deserves my sincere appreciation for sharing her ideas on Akkā's *vacana*s and their potential for a dramatic performance. Mysore-based Carnatic classical singer R.S. Nandkumarji has helped me in more ways than can be mentioned here. I thank him for leading me to some of the scholars mentioned above and also for his valuable insights into the tradition of *vacana* singing.

I would like to thank A.J. Thomas as he translated Prof. K. Satchidanandan's poem on Āṇḍāḷ for this work. I thank Prof. Satchidanandan for allowing me to use his poems on Akkā Mahādevī and Āṇḍāḷ.

I am grateful to Prof. C.N. Srinath from Dhvanyaloka, Mysore, for allowing me a comfortable stay at the premises and also for allowing me to use the library there.

Thanks are also due to Mr Anil Dharurkar who kept my chapters safe in his computer and helped in creating the soft text. I thank Ms Victoria Gerner for looking at the structure and formatting of the text and helping me in making it presentable, and Mr Bernd Fellner for sustaining my spirits by constant human connection–compassion.

I would like to express my gratitude to *saṁnyāsī*s living at the headquarters of The Divine Life Society at Sivananda Ashram, Rishikesh, especially to Swami Shanmukhananda, Swami Devbhaktananda and Swami Padmanabhananda for giving me time to discuss Akkā Mahādevī, Nārada's *Bhakti-Sūtra*s and the concept of *avatāra,* respectively, from their perspective.

I would like to place on record my acknowledgement to Sreenivasa Rao, Secretary, Sahitya Akademi, New Delhi, for allowing me to use H.S. Shivaprakash's translation of *Tiruppavai* for this book. I am also thankful to the Librarian Dr Vijayalakshmi, and her associates Mr Padmanabhan, Mr Khanna, Ms Usha and Mr Ashok Choudhary from Sahitya Akademi Library, New Delhi. I am also thankful to Mr Jnanendra, Mr Meena, Sriji and all the staff at Dyal Singh (Evening) College Library.

Special thanks are due to Shri Deepak Malhotra, the Principal, Dyal Singh (Evening) College, and the UGC for granting me leave from active teaching for two years without which this text would not have appeared in print. I would also like to thank my publisher Shri Susheel Mittal for his diligence and dedication in bringing out this book.

Finally I would like to thank my daughters Sanya and Lavanya who represent love and duty, in other words inspiration and discipline needed for any kind of work.

Guru Pūrṇimā, 22 July 2013 **Alka Tyagi**
New Delhi

Section One

1

Ancient Religions and Emergence of Bhakti

Ancient Religions

Two of the most popular Indian religions — Vaiṣṇavism and Śaivism — have flourished together, sometimes conflicting, sometimes coalescing with each other as part of basic Hindu religious tradition. It is interesting to note, how the two streams that originally belonged to two different cultures altogether, finally became a part of the mainstream Hindu religious culture. Śiva has often been established as a Draviḍian God and Draviḍian culture was an agrarian culture. They lived a settler-farmer life and Śiva originally could well have been a fertility god. *Liṅga* (phallus symbol), associated with Śiva, is a primitive symbol and conforms to this idea of fertility. This indicates that the concept of God with a manifest form possibly came first to the Draviḍians who lived a settled life. Also related to this is the idea of house of the God, i.e. temple. Thus concept of "temple" is also a Draviḍian contribution. Later, when both Aryan and Draviḍian cultures co-mingled, Śiva attained the status of prime God in the whole of the subcontinent.

VAIṢṆAVISM

Vaiṣṇavism places Viṣṇu along with his *avatāra*s as the Supreme God. Viṣṇu, however, was an evolute of the Aryan god Indra. Aryans were originally a nomadic tribe; hence their gods were generally without a form and were generally abstract. They depicted the forces of Nature. Thus Viṣṇu, primarily an abstract Supreme God of the Vedas, was originally associated with

Indra (god of rain and thunder), who is conceived amongst the most powerful deities in the *Ṛgveda*. Kṛṣṇa's association with Viṣṇu was also probably a result of the complete merging of the Draviḍian and Aryan cultures. Kṛṣṇa (lit. the Dark One) could have been a regional Draviḍian deity, who was later integrated into the Aryan fold. This might be one reason for the innumerable efforts seen throughout the Vedic, Upaniṣadic, Purāṇic and Epic literatures, to project the oneness of both Śiva and Viṣṇu and finally the supremacy of both in the larger cosmic structure. Invocation from *Ṛgveda* — *ekam sat viprā bahudhā vadanti*, which means "the God is one, though the wise call him by various names" is the driving force behind the spirit of polytheism in the Hindu culture. Therefore, there is harmonious coexistence of Śaivism and Vaiṣṇavism. While Viṣṇu devotees conceive Viṣṇu as the ultimate cause of creation, Śiva devotees consider Śiva to be the causal principal in the creation. Viṣṇu is said to have ten *avatāra*s. Two of these *avatāra*s are Rāma and Kṛṣṇa. *Bhakti* saints established a personal relationship with these *avatāra*s in particular and sang songs to celebrate their love for them.

ŚAIVISM

Religion in its primitive form was an obeisance to the terrifying and incomprehensive aspects of nature. Gradually, as man started understanding the cosmic forces, he learnt to celebrate them. Religion constituted the ways of understanding and appreciating these cosmic principles. Śaivism is a religion of this stage in human journey of evolution. In other words, it is there from the beginning. This religion promotes a life lived in harmony and in rhythm with nature as these manifest in creation. Śaivism is a religion of celebration of life and its mysteries. Alain Danielou, in his celebrated text *While the Gods Play*, traces origins of Śaivism and declares it to be one of the most primitive religions in the history of mankind dating back at least 6,000 years.

Emergence of Bhakti

More recent research in historical studies confirms that Draviḍians entered the Indian subcontinent much before Aryans did.[1] They came to India in 9000 BCE after the first ice age came to an end. M. Sakhare confirms that Draviḍians migrated from a continent called Lemuria, which later got drowned into the sea. They spread from Kanyā Kumārī (Cape Comorin) to the Himalayas, evolved and reached the peak of their civilization between the sixth century BCE and the second century BCE. According to Alain Danielou:

> It was the Draviḍians who built, among others in the Indus Valley, the cities of Moheñjo-Dāṛo and Haṛappā, considerable traces of which have recently been discovered. The influence of the Draviḍian civilization was very extensive. It affected the whole continent, but also extended to the Sumerian cities with which the people of the Indus were definitely in contact. Sumerian deity called the Lord of the Animals corresponds to the Indian Paśupati (Lord of the Animals). The Sumerian Goddess, the Lady of the Mountains, is called Pārvatī (Lady of the Mountains) in India. The Sumerians were called "Black Faces". The followers of the old religion, throughout the course of history and still today, called the Kālāmukhas (Black Faces) in India.
> — Danielou 1987: 7

He further says, "Śaivism," the religion of the ancient Draviḍians, had always been a religion of the people. Śiva had been the central deity of the pre-Aryan cultures in India. A famous stone image from Haṛappan sites that depicts a lean

---

[1] H. Thipperudra Swamy, *The Vīrasaiva Saints: A Study*, tr. S.M. Angadi, Mysore: Rao and Raghavan, 1968.

yogī sitting in lotus pose is recognized as an image of Śiva.[2] Metaphysical, cosmological and ritual conceptions of Śaivism were preserved by communities of wandering ascetics living on the fringes of the official society, whom the Aryans scornfully called *yati*s (wanderers), *vrātya*s (untouchables), or *ājīvika*s (beggars) [Thipperudra Swamy 1968: 15]. Āgamas, Purāṇas and Yoga are the sources where the major principles of Śaivism are laid down. Śaivāgamas are the ancient texts that deal elaborately with the rituals and tenets of Śaivism.

Āgamas contain the rites of worship of the deities — Śiva, Śakti and later of Viṣṇu. Aryan's sacred scriptures, the Vedas, contain the deities that are representations of powerful aspects of the Nature like Varuṇa (Air), Indra (Rain and Thunder), and Sūrya (Sun). As Sakhare says,

> the Vedic religion was a system of propitiation or conciliation of those Nature powers by means of sacrifices and offering into the fire, . . . while the Āgamic deity was a personal deity that controlled the forces of nature.
>
> — Sakhare 1978: 173

Probably this was the reason why the path of devotion was an inherent and natural way of attaining *mokṣa* in Śaivism. However, later both Agamic and Vedic streams merged into each other and *bhakti* evolved as the highest path to attain liberation in Hinduism, where both Vaiṣṇavism and Śaivism flourished together.

---

2 "On a seal found in Moheṅjo-Dāṛo, a divine figure seated in *yoga-mudrā* surrounded by wild animals is found. Experts have guessed it to that of Śiva Himself. Its head-dress in the shape of a trident has confirmed this belief. Here Śiva is depicted as the great *yogī* and Paśupati. The *liṅga*s that are found in Haṛappā and Moheṅjo-Dāṛo are eloquent evidences to prove that the worship of Śiva, not only in the form of idols but also of Śivaliṅga, was already in vogue even at that period." — Thipperudra Swamy 1968: 24

It is worth noting here that due to Aryan influence and resultant supremacy of Vedas, scholars until recently held the view that Āgamas are a part of the Vedas only. However it was in 1050 BCE (approx.) that Aryans invaded the Gangetic plains and destroyed the ancient cities of Indus. They conquered the natives and subjugated their culture, philosophy and religion. But the southern and eastern parts of the subcontinent could preserve their culture and religion for a long time. The natives were derogatorily called as "Dasyus" and were accorded a servile status by the Aryans. By 600 BCE Aryans had carved a very strong foothold over the entire land. Vedas, Upaniṣads and Epics, which hitherto were being transmitted orally as a part of the Brāhmanical education system, now started assuming a kind of standard form as the Vedic writing happened during this period.[3] Writing was however subject to change and the palm-leaf manuscripts needed to be copied after a stipulated time. In fact, it was only after some thousand years after the Aryans first came to

---

[3] Renowned Indologist Malati J. Shendge has an interesting point to support the thesis that Draviḍians were a highly civilized race and it were Aryans who are indebted to them for everything that comes down to us in the name of "Refined" or "Śreṣṭha" (lit. the best) as they call themselves. She says:

"On the other hand during the centuries that followed the conflict between the Āryas and *asuras*, the Āryas who settled down in the new home, adopted this culture which was definitely more advanced than their own, and also adopted the language. It must be remembered that the Indus civilization, i.e. the *asura* culture was literate, having a script for the language and naturally with a greater awareness of the process of civilization itself. Whereas the Aryans were defeated, dispossessed of their land and driven out of their home. The adoption or absorption of the *asura* culture by the Aryans was total so that no difference between them and the *asuras* remained. This "symbiosis", if it could be so named was given the name of Aryan culture". — Shengde 1997: 72

India that the process of consolidation of texts began to happen and it kept on happening well into the Common Era.[4]

It was the brāhmaṇa scholars, *ṛṣis* and *munis*, who started writing down classical texts on palm-leaf manuscripts. This required copying at regular intervals. This copying of texts often provided ample scope for revision and for integration of native and contemporary knowledge systems. New additions were often inadvertently autochthonous and received ideas from native wisdom. In fact, Aryans couldn't but integrate elements from these native traditions, which later became a part of a broader phenomenon called Hinduism. In *Ṛgveda*, for instance, Rudra appears as a terrifying, howling god responsible for destruction. This was certainly a Draviḍian god, who later interestingly got integrated into the Aryan culture. In fact, by the time of *Yajurveda*, Rudra-Śiva is established as Paśupati the Lord (Pati) of all the gods who are beasts (*paśus*) before Him. Gradually, in *Śvetāśvatara Upaniṣad* Rudra-Śiva is raised to the status of theistic Brahmā, the Supreme God of the universe[5] (Sakhare 1978: 110). It is important to note that while other major Upaniṣads talked

---

[4] "The first inscriptions date from the third century BCE. The Vedic language had evolved, giving birth to various vernacular languages, the Prākṛt, Pāli and Apbhraṁśa.

Writing allowed the Aryans to fix the religious and philosophical texts until then passed on orally. It was on this basis that great scholars forged an artificial language called Sanskrit, the 'refined language' devised to last forever, which little by little, became the universal language of the culture.

In the fourth century BCE, the grammarian Pāṇini, summarizing earlier works, established in his famous grammar, the definitive form of Sanskrit, which has not changed since."

— Danielou 1987: 13

[5] M.R. Sakhare, *History and Philosophy of Lingayat Religion*, Dharwad: Karnatak University, 1978, p. 110.

about non-theistic Absolute *Brahman*, *Śvetāśvatara Upaniṣad* conceives Rudra-Śiva's dual form of "protector–destroyer" as the Supreme. Hence, the idea of a personal God in the form of Śiva, which basically comes from the Āgamas, sieves into the Upaniṣads thereby attesting the presence of *Śiva-bhakti* much before *Viṣṇu-bhakti* appeared in *Bhagavad-Gītā* in the epic period to which beginnings of *bhakti* are generally associated.

Śaivism, however, was preserved in its mystical form by secret communities of ascetics, who were wanderers and who preferred to live away from the social milieu and generally remained at the outskirts of civilized society. These ascetic wanderers passed on their esoteric wisdom, mystical rites and religious cults to closed groups of disciples. Many such non-Aryan sects like Pāśupata, Kālāmukhas, Kāpālikas and Daśanāmī Nāgās were able to preserve and sustain their mystical and occultist theological traditions.

Makkhali Goṣāla (560–484 BCE) and Lakulīśa (100 BCE) are two important figures which relate to these ancient streams of Śaivism. Goṣāla was a contemporary of Buddha and Mahāvīra. The two princes actually followed Goṣāla and lived with him as ascetic-wanderers for a substantial period of their lives. Initially, they were attracted to the freedom and joy of living without inhibitions offered by Goṣāla's religion. This religion contrasted with the excessive Vedic ritualism and Brāhmanical oppression, which was not overt but covert. And for kṣtriyas and the aristocratic classes, it manifested generally in the form of moral obligations indoctrinated by the brāhamaṇas in religio-political atmosphere. Performances of elaborate rites such as *havana*s and *yajña*s like "Aśvamedha Yajña", sacrificial *yajña*s and *yajña*s for the *pitṛ*s, i.e. the ancestors, etc. had great financial bearings and the outcome was often a futile effort. More financial burden on the royal treasury actually meant more taxes on the subjects which more often than not had the danger of causing feeling of dissent in people against the ruler.[6] A similar situation in twelfth-century Karnataka was one major reason for the rise of Vīraśaiva movement. Vedic *karma-kāṇḍa* (ritualism) had reached a kind of saturation and was already on decline, when these two princes emerged on the religious scene. Later they separated ways from Goṣāla and also from each other to move on to lay the foundation of two great atheistic religions of Jainism and Buddhism, which also like Śaivism, influenced all world religions in some way or the other and particularly through their tenet of non-violence. However these two religions are poles apart from Śaivism (Danielou 1987: 29).

After Goṣāla in sixth century BCE, it was an *ājīvika* saint called Lakulīśa, who brought Śaivism into the forefront of Indian religious culture and helped in finding for it a central place in the civil society. Lakulīśa was probably a contemporary

---

6 A classic example of this dissent is the Vīraśaiva movement in twelfth-century Karnataka, where Brāhmanical pressure on the King Bijjala of Kalyāṇa to perform an elaborate *yajña* led to levying of extra taxes on people. This was certainly one of the causes of the murder of Bijjala among other more stronger reasons like *anuloma vivāha* which was not acceptable to the brāhmaṇas as they found it against the Śāstras.

At the time, the families of the warlike aristocracy were in revolt against the authority of the brāhmaṇas and the rigid ritualism of the Vedic religion.

Immense sacrificial ceremonies, such as the sacrifice of the horse (Aśvamedha), through which the brāhmaṇas imposed their power, ruined the states financially. Gautama was at first attracted to the anti-social mysticism of Śaivism. For a time, he was also a disciple of Goṣāla and very close to Mahāvīra, who was three years younger. For several years he practised the austere and free life of a wandering monk. He eventually left them, however, and soon became their rival (Danielou 1987: 23).

of John the Baptist and lived in around 100 BCE[7]. Lakulīśa belonged to a non-Aryan priestly class called "Jaṅgama" and "Kālāmukha" sect which had been active in the south uptil the thirteenth century CE and probably later.[8] His major contribution to Śaivism was that he expounded the ancient religion of Pāśupata and revived practices of *haṭha-yoga*, Tantra and also cosmogonies of ancient Sāṁkhya philosophy. Mādhāvacārya in his famous *Sarvadarśana Saṁgraha*, refers to a certain book about Pāśupata religion which seemed to have been written by Lakulīśa. During Lakulīśa's time Kuṣāṇas were the major rulers in the north. To quote M.R. Sakhare:

> In the early centuries of Christian era, Śaivism prevailed during the period of Kuṣāṇas. The earliest coins bearing

---

7 In the fourth century, Candragupta, an adventurer of Scythian origin, who had married a princess of the ancient Śiva tribe of the Licchavi, assassinated the last monarch of Pāṭaliputra and ruled from CE 319 to 330. It is from this period on that representations of Lakulīśa are to be found in India. These portray him as a naked *yogī* with a staff (*lakula*) in his left hand and a citron (*mātu-liṅga*) in his right, with his penis erect and either standing or seated in lotus posture. At about the beginning of the eleventh century, the Lakulīśa cult seems to have shifted its activities to southern India (Danielou 1987: 29).

8 There are evidences in literary texts and inscriptions found in various *maṭhas* and Śiva temples in Karnataka's Belgaum, Hassan, Halebiḍ and Arsikhere regions, which mention activities of Kālāmukha priests. It seems that this ancient sect was gradually absorbed by Vīraśaivism.

According to H. Thipperudra Swamy:

"Though Vīraśaivism and Kālāmukha Śaivism, principally differ from each other, yet it may be said, the Vīraśaivism of Basavanna's time was ready to absorb the influential Kālāmukha sect. Several Kālāmukha *maṭhas* were converted into Vīraśaiva *maṭhas*. Pandits have admitted that the conversion of the Kālāmukha *maṭha* at Puvalli of Belgaum district into a Vīraśaiva *maṭha* is a living testimony." — Thipperudra Swamy 1968: 40

> Śiva emblems, an image of Śiva with trident in hand on obverse and his bull on reverse are those of Kuṣāṇa. Wema Kaḍphises, a powerful prince of Kuṣāṇa race, styles himself on the reverse of his coins as a devotee of Maheśvara or a member of the Maheśvara sect. — Sakhare 1978: 132

According to K.P. Jaiswal, it was around CE 150 after the rule of imperial Kuṣāṇas that Baraśivas started expanding their kingdom in the north and took over Bihar, United Provinces of Agra, Oudh, Bundelkhaṇḍ, Central Provinces, Mālwā, Rājpūtānā and Madra republics in Punjab. They declared Lord Śiva as the presiding deity of their kingdom. This spirit was sustained by the Vākāṭaka dynasty that ruled between CE 284–348. However, after the coming of Gupta kings, Vaiṣṇavism spread in the north as most Gupta rulers were ardent Viṣṇu devotees including Samudragupta, the last of Gupta kings. After this period, prominence of Vaiṣṇavism and Śaivism rose and fell in north India according to the political conditions prevalent in the country. For instance, during the reign of Harṣavardhana in the seventh century CE Śaivism gained prominence again while after the Muslim invasions and under British colonial period, both Vaiṣṇavism and Śaivism grew and sustainably remained a strong silent religious force in the country.

It is important to note here that in the history of Bhakti movements, there have been two important offshoots of Vaiṣṇavism and Śaivism. They are Śrīvaiṣṇavism and Vīraśaivism, respectively. Āṇḍāḷ was a Śrīvaiṣṇavite saint-poetess and Akkā Mahādevī was a Vīraśaivite saint-poetess. They lived during a specific religious upsurge of these two sects in Tamil Nadu and Karnataka in tenth and twelfth centuries, respectively.

2

Evolution of Bhakti in South India

ONE of the most ancient of world cultures, Tamil culture is said to have its beginnings some 3,000 years before Christ. However, indigenous natives of this extreme southern part of the subcontinent must have undergone the Palaeolithic, Mesolithic and Neolithic stages of evolution, before they established themselves in the region as a cultured and refined race with elements of a well-developed civilization. Due to specific geographical features like mountains, rivers and plateaus, this part was protected from political invasions from the north. There is also no evidence of cultural transmigration from the north till about 600 BCE. Vedic literature from the north seldom reveals any knowledge about the region lying to the south of Vindhyas. A later hymn of *Ṛgveda* suggests, that someone expelled from the Aryan-fold took up "Dakṣiṇāpatha", i.e. way to the South. On the pattern of *āśrama* life of Aryan sages as seen in Vedas and Upaniṣads, several natural caverns adapted for human inhabitation have been found in southern Tamil districts also. These caves depict Tamil inscription in Brāhmī script, which belongs to second century BCE. A Buddhist text *Sutta Nipāta* mentions a Vedic scholar and teacher, who left Kausala and moved to a village on the bank of River Godāvarī. These above-mentioned evidences are first few to indicate a slow, peaceful penetration of Aryan's Vedic culture into the southern region including the Tamil land.

However, the most lucid account of ancient Tamil culture comes down to us through the literature of the region in

Saṅgam period. The dates of this period are debated and are supposed to range anywhere from 200 BCE – CE 250 or 500 BCE – CE 200. According to a legend first recorded in a ninth-century commentary to a grammatical treatise,[1] there were three Saṅgam periods in succession which lasted for about 10,000 years. However some 30,000 lines of poetry, that have become extant clearly belong to the last and third Saṅgam period. Synchronism referred to in the Saṅgam literature, especially poetry, suggests a span of 150 to 200 years including some six successive generations. Out of the three important kingdoms of the region namely Cera, Coḷa and Pāṇḍya, only some Cera genealogies find mention in the poetry of Saṅgam period.

Two important epics, *Cilappadikāram* and *Maṇimekalai*, which were earlier ascribed to Saṅgam period, are now considered as works of post-Saṅgam age (Nilakanta Sastri 1963: 11-12).

Cilappadikāram, which is believed to have a Jaina authorship, the author being Ilaṅgo Aḍigaḷ (prince ascetic), nevertheless reflects Tamil culture in its rich variety. The legend of a chaste wife Kannagi and her trader husband Kovalan, *Cilappadikāram* is a telling account of people's beliefs, customs, rituals and other religious practices. It reveals, how many faiths silently mingled and coexisted with each other in this period. In *Cilappadikāram* religious concepts of sin, its expiation, those of charity and of receiving gifts find different manifestations in different characters that are portrayed in the epic. These characters come from a wide spectrum of caste, class and religious systems. Buddhists, Jainas, brāhmaṇas and Aryans are portrayed as living together in mutual respect and recognition.

---

1 This treatise is named *Iraiyanar Ahapporul* which suggests that the author of the work is Lord Śiva himself.

On the other hand, *Maṇimekalai*, is pre-eminently a Buddhist work, which recounts the story of *Maṇimekalai*, daughter of Kovalan and his chaste paramour Madhavi.[2] In this epic, the heroine *Maṇimekalai* in the role of a nun is certainly used as a mouthpiece to propagate the Gospel of Buddha. It is however very significant that a woman nun is portrayed as a liberated soul (Buddha), considering the fact that official Buddhism denies *nirvāṇa* to women.

In fact, in both the epics women are reverentially portrayed. This is true not only of the heroines but also of other women characters such as Mādhavī who is a courtesan and paramour. Tamil culture has always afforded the respect due to women as human beings. This is clearly reflected in the literature of various eras.

These epics also indicate an ascendancy of Jainism and Buddhism. *Maṇimekalai* in particular propagates Buddhism in exclusion of other religions. Scholars believe that while in Saṅgam age these two religions coexisted in harmony with other faiths, in post-Saṅgam age, they become powerful and oppressive. It was in reaction to the fear of extinction, that traditional religious leaders started consolidating what we now know as Hinduism. Buddhism and Jainism emphasized upon asceticism and other life-negating values. In these religions human desires are considered as the root cause of suffering. Tamil land, which exuberated in nature's bounty and sense of prosperous fulfilment, acknowledged and accepted human desires and passions. Basic man–woman relation, understood as the source of *ānanda* (bliss) in this world, later transforms into the *mādhurya* or *nāyaka–nāyikā bhāva* between an individual devotee and God. This is the clue to

---

2 It is interesting to note that author of Maṇimekalai, Sattanār, a grain merchant and a Buddhist by faith, was a contemporary of Ilaṅgo Aḍigaḷ, a Jaina monk. Sattanar hailed from Madurai.

the origin of *bhakti* in Tamil Nadu. Composition and singing of hymns and songs in praise of God in vernacular in the beginning led later to more organized devotional expressions like debating, competition in miracle performances, tests of truth of doctrines, etc. Devotees would gather together, sing, dance and would wander from one place to the other spreading this enthusiasm through this new kind of passion for none else but God Himself.

Although south India assimilated Vedic culture from the north, it contributed the aspect of *bhakti* to Indian religion and philosophy. *Bhakti* existed in earlier times but this element of passionate love for God came only from Tamil Āḻvār and Nāyaṉmār saints. In *Rāmāyaṇa, Mahābhārata* and in Upaniṣads, *bhakti* or devotion has a very serene and detached face. Lakṣmaṇa, Hanumān and Arjuna are not emotional in their respective devotion. In *Bhagavad-Gītā*, Lord Kṛṣṇa talks about *sambhava* (equanimity), *sākṣībhāva* (witness attitude) and *sthitaprajñayatā* (steadfastness), all of which indicate a very controlled and disciplined living. In fact, in the north of India these qualities are celebrated as the premium qualities of an ideal human being with a very controlled, evolved and detached view of life. The sources of these values are Vedas, Upaniṣads and epics.

However, in south India, be it due to the need to drive away or resist the spread of ascetic and life denying Jaina and Buddhist religions or due to the presence of a life affirming sincerity inherent in the Tamil culture, there is this projection of common human passion into relationships between individuals. And personal love, which is an experiential aspect of all existence, has very extensively and comprehensively touched the living and cultural aspects including the religious expressions of people in this region.

There are many theories about the origin of *bhakti*, but I believe that the accessibility of this kind of experience at all levels with no prerequisite qualification, is the most important factor in development of an attitude of *bhakti* or intense love for a personal god.

This spirit of *bhakti* found expression in the efflorescence of devotional verses composed by devotees of Viṣṇu and Śiva, in the period from the sixth to the ninth century CE in Tamil Nadu. Devotees of Viṣṇu are revered as Āḻvārs and those of Śiva as Nāyaṉmārs. Works of twelve Āḻvārs were compiled in the tenth century CE by Nāthamuni, the first Śrīvaiṣṇava *ācārya*, under the rubric of *Nālāyira-Divya-Prabandham* (The Sacred Book of Four Thousand). The word Āḻvār traditionally means "one who is deeply immersed" in the love of God. This title was conferred on the twelve poet-saints at a later date by the Śrīvaiṣṇava community.

3

Āḷvār Bhakti and Śrīvaiṣṇavism

THE framework of all the Āḷvār poetry compiled in *Nālāyira-Divya-Prabhandham* including that of both of Āṇḍāḷ's poems, *Tiruppāvai* as well as *Nachiar Tirumoḷi,* is based on the concept of Vaiṣṇava *bhakti* which has its origin in the classical forms of *bhakti* that were prevalent much before the Ālvār saints. Within this context, we must refer to classical *bhakti* as defined in the ancient texts of *bhakti.*

Classical Background: Concepts Associated with Bhakti

The phenomenon of *bhakti* always had a theological base supported by ancient religious texts like *Bhagavad-Gītā,* and an emotional base supported by Viṣṇu mythology as given in major Purāṇas like *Harivaṁśa Purāṇa,*[1] *Viṣṇu Purāṇa* and *Brahma Purāṇa,* and epics like *Rāmāyaṇa* and *Mahābhārata*. Two other classical texts associated with phenomenon of *bhakti* are Nārada's *Bhakti-Sūtras* and Śāṇḍilya's *Bhakti-Sūtras*. However following three stanzas from the *Bhagavad-Gītā* are significant

---

[1] *Harivaṁśa Purāṇa* and Hālā's *Sattasai* (Skt. *Saptaśatī*) are two important texts that were known to south Indians. *Harivaṁśa* with its typical beginning appears to be a later addition to epic tradition of *Mahābhārata*. Probable dates for *Harivaṁśa* are considered to be before fourth century CE, much before *Bhāgavata Purāṇa,* which is supposed to have been composed in CE 920 or so. *Sattasai* was a second-century Prākṛt text compiled by a Sātvavāhana ruler Hāla. These two texts, i.e. *Harivaṁśa Purāṇa* and *Sattasai,* were well rooted in the south Indian culture by the time Āḷvārs began singing their songs of Kṛṣṇa. All the chief motifs of mythical landscape that colour their poetry were supplied by such texts much before *Bhāgavata Purāṇa* came into picture.

from the theological viewpoint and from the point of view of later evolution of Kṛṣṇa *bhakti*:

> *yadā yadā hi dharmasya glānir bhavati bhārata* ।
> *abhyuthānam adharmasya tadātmānaṁ sṛjāmy aham* ॥
> — 4.7
>
> O! Bhārata! Whenever the righteousness is on the decline and unrighteousness is in ascendant then I take upon a body.
>
> *paritrāṇāya sādhūnāṁ vināśāya ca duṣkṛtām*
> *dharam-saṁsthāpanārthāya sambhavāmi yuge yuge* । —4.8
>
> For the protection of the virtuous, for the extirpation of the evildoers, and for establishing *dharma* on a firm footing, I am born from age to age.
>
> *janma karmaca me divyam evaṁ yo vetti tattvataḥ*
> *tyaktavā dehaṁ punar-janma naiti mām eti sorjuna* ॥ —4.9
>
> Arjuna my birth and actions are Divine. He who knows this in reality, is not reborn after leaving this body, but comes to Me.

Above verses from *Bhagavad-Gītā* are the classic reference points, which are inherently present in the collective unconscious of all the *bhaktas*. These verses point at the concept of *avatāra* (lit. descension). God takes an *avatāra* whenever there is need to protect the virtuous. The idea of God coming down to earth and live among human beings is at the centre of all *bhakti* literature. Nevertheless, this scriptural reference to *bhakti* as found in *Bhagavad-Gītā* is more of an intellectual nature and is very different from the emotional *bhakti* that prevails in Āḻvārs' poetry. Intellectual *bhakti* as expounded in *Bhagavad-Gītā* has its roots in Upaniṣads and presupposes *yoga*. *Yoga* here is understood as withdrawing all the senses from their objects and focusing them along with mind (*manas, buddhi, cit, ahaṁkāra*) on to the Supreme Being. This process is supposed to be instrumental in attaining the state of *mokṣa* (liberation).

This process of withdrawal of senses, presupposed in intellectual *bhakti* is certainly a yogic state named as *pratyāhāra* in Patañjali's *Yoga-Sūtras* and is exactly in opposition to emotional *bhakti,* which involves intense participation of the senses. A.K. Ramanujan attributes "Being in Touch" among the chief characteristics of *bhakti*:

> The Āḻvārs (and the Nāyaṉmārs) thrive on contagion, communion in community. Nammāḻvār says that all the five senses are "the bodies of God" and he strains all of them to realize god. Yet the sensory modes he favours in his poetry are the "near senses": touch, taste, smell. The Vedic poets were "seers"; philosophy is a "seeing" (*darśana*); and the word "see" occurs in the *Gītā* scores of times. The Vedas are "heard" (*śrutis*), as earlier classical Tamil poems were "things heard" (*kelvi*). Both sight and hearing are senses of distance. But the favourite *bhakti* sense is the sense of touch; *bhakti* is contact, contagion. The devotee's heart or hands touch, not just the feet of god, but his entire body.
>
> — Ramanujan 1981: 146-47

Senses require objects to engage themselves. In *bhakti,* the senses are focused intensely on one single object, a personal god. In the final stage of *bhakti,* however, this focus becomes so intense, that all other objects are dropped off automatically. This state in *bhakti* is similar to the other classical form of *yoga* known as *rāja-yoga*. In these stages, senses are withdrawn completely from everything else and are brought to focus on one's *iṣṭa* (chosen deity). These processes of complete withdrawal and then intense focus are in fact advance stages of *yoga* defined as *dhāraṇā, dhyāna* and *samādhi* by Sage Patañjali in his text *Yoga-Sūtras*. Therefore *bhakti* in the beginning serves as the stepping stone to *bhakti-yoga* and *iṣṭa* serves as a stimulus to attain those heights of *bhakti-yoga* which lead to *samādhi* (a complete union with the Absolute).

The idea of a personal god, which is the founding stone of emotional *bhakti*, is coloured by Indian mythological tradition. Indian mythology is based on the concept of God's *avatāras*. The word *avatāra* is related to *avataraṇa* (to descend down). As observed in the *śloka* from *Gītā* quoted above, God takes birth in the form of a living being on earth to protect the world when evil begins to pervade it or when the cause of the good is annihilated by the evil ones. *Viṣṇu Purāṇa* relates twelve *avatāras* of Lord Viṣṇu and *Bhāgavata Purāṇa* relates no less than twenty-two *avatāras* of the Lord. Most famous Indian epics are legends of God's *avatāras* and their feats on earth. The *Rāmāyaṇa* is story of *Rāma avatāra* and *Mahābhārata* relates the story of *Kr̥ṣṇa avatāra*. It is the life story of Kr̥ṣṇa, which captured the imagination of a whole civilization that witnessed generations and generations of poets and saints singing and writing about marvellous multifaceted Kr̥ṣṇa — the God in a man's body.

The concept of *avatāra* is very significant for understanding the evolution of Vaiṣṇava *bhakti* poetry. The whole of Āḻvār saints' poetic corpus refers to human form, *avatāra* of the Absolute God (here Viṣṇu) especially as found in the Purāṇic lore. Among the important Purāṇas of Viṣṇu are Viṣṇu, Harivaṁśa and Bhāgavata. All of them narrate the story of Kr̥ṣṇa from his birth to human parents and his divine play on earth through various stages of his life — as a child (in Gokula), as an adolescent (in Vr̥ndāvana), as a youth (in Mathurā), as a man (in Kurukṣetra) and as a king (in Dwārkā).

It should be noted that the historical authenticity of Purāṇic literature is debatable. Yet it is quite probable that Kr̥ṣṇa was a historical figure whose deification in later eras could have strengthened popular faith in his *avatāra* status. However, the question of whether the character of Kr̥ṣṇa is historical or mythical, is besides the point, as the image of his character, which emerged through Purāṇic lore provided highly intense material for poetic imagination. The idea of a God, who came down to earth and lived among the mortals as one of them, who was loving and could be loved as a mischievous son, a mysterious lover, a brave warrior, a divine friend and a kind king, is thoroughly fascinating. This visibility of the Absolute Supreme in human form is almost necessary for any kind of emotional relationship with Him.

Āḻvār saints imagined this God in various relations to themselves — sometimes He is a little child, sometimes a lover, sometimes a friend and sometimes Lord and the master. Their poetry is an attempt to establish a relation with God in human form in order to experience His Divine Being with human urgency.

While theology and religion make an attempt to comprehend the Supreme Being through intellect and faith, respectively, *bhakti* is a way to comprehend the Supreme Being with all human faculties — be they higher (relating to mind) or lower (relating to senses). *Bhakti* is a complete surrender of the whole being, intellect as well as emotion, mind as well as senses, to God and works through faith and wisdom. Thus, while theology uses only one faculty, that of the mind, to connect to God, *bhakti* path uses the mind, body and emotion — all three aspects of the human being to experience Him. Hence, the path of *bhakti* is considered as superior to the path of *jñāna* (knowledge) and that of *karma* (detached action). *Sūtra* 25 of classical Nārada's *Bhakti-Sūtras* describes this supremacy of *bhakti* over other paths of attaining the Divine:

Sa tu karmajñānayogebhyopyādhikṛta

> The Supreme Devotion (*bhakti*) is indeed, as a technique even superior to Path of Action (*karma*), the Path of Knowledge (*jñāna*), and the Path of Disciplined Contemplation (*yoga*). — Chinmayananda 1968: 41

Elevenfold Bhakti

Śāstras on *bhakti* prescribe many ways of relating to God. Narada's *Bhakti-Sūtras*, one of the classic texts on *bhakti*, puts down not less than eleven ways of reaching God. These are depicted in *sūtra* 82 as:

> *guṇamāhātmyāsakti rūpāsakti pūjāsakti smaraṇāsakti dāsyāsakti sakhyāsakti vātsalyāsakti kāntāsakti ātmanivedanāsakti tanmayāsakti paramavirahāsaktirūpa ekadhāpyekadaśadhā bhavati* ||
>
> Love for glorifying His Qualities; Love for His Divine Form; Love for worshipping Him; Love for remembering Him; Love for doing service for Him; Love for friendship in Him; Love for the Lord as one's own child; Love as that to a beloved; Love for a total self-offering at His Feet; Love for complete absorption in Him; Love as expressed in the pang of separation from Him — thus though Love is one only, It is expressed in eleven different modes.
>
> — Chinmayananda 1968: 159

If we look at this *sūtra* closely, we will find that some of the attitudes mentioned here overlap each other.

Ninefold Bhakti (Navadhā Bhakti)

Navdhā bhakti, mentioned in the *Bhāgavata Purāṇa*, which gives nine ways of *bhakti*, seems to be a re-ordering of the eleven ways given by the ancient Sage Nārada. *Navadhā bhakti* is the most popular form of *bhakti* which is prevalent in modern times also. The stages of *navadha* (ninefold) *bhakti* are depicted as follows:

> *śravaṇaṁ kīrtanaṁ viṣṇoḥ smaraṇaṁ pādasevaṇaṁ* |
> *arcanaṁ vandanaṁ dāsyaṁ sakhyamātmnivedanam* ||
>
> Listening to the names of God; singing the names of God; continuous remembrance of God; serving at the feet of God; worshiping the God; praying to the God; relating to Him as

> a servant; relating to Him as a friend; (finally surrendering the ego to Him).[2]

However, in the context of Āṇḍāḷ and other Āḻvār saints, it might be true that their *bhakti* poetry was composed much before the theorization happened in Śāstras. Āḻvār saints might not have been familiar with any of the above-mentioned texts at all. They might not have known eleven ways of *bhakti* given by Sage Nārada or the nine ways of *bhakti* (*navadhā bhakti*) expounded in the *Bhāgavata Purāṇa* as *Bhāgavata Purāṇa* is later than Āḻvārs. To quote Vidya Dehejia:

> It appears certain that the *Bhāgavata Purāṇa,* which is the main text for the legend of Viṣṇu, is later than Āḻvār poetry since it makes selective use of themes from the poems of these saints. The relationship between Tamil Āḻvār poetry and the Sanskrit *Bhāgavata Purāṇa* has been explored by Friedhelm Hardy, who points out that the Purāṇa was composed in south India in the ninth century, and that it combined themes from the poems of Āḻvārs (600–900) with the input of the northern Sanskrit *Brahma* and *Viṣṇu Purāṇa* (500–700).

She further relates:

> From the perspective of Āṇḍāḷ's (Āṇḍāḷ's) poetry, an important reason for concluding that the songs of the Āḻvārs must predate the *Bhāgavata Purāṇa* is the fact that two episodes prominent in the Purāṇa are not mentioned by Āṇḍāḷ (Āṇḍāḷ). The celebrated *rāsa* dance of Kṛṣṇa with the *gopīs*, and the theme of their intense longing for Kṛṣṇa combined with the pain of separation from him once he

---

2 *Navadhā bhakti* as mentioned in *Bhāgavata Purāṇa* involves nine ways which are:

śravaṇaṁ kīrtanaṁ viṣṇoḥ smaraṇaṁ pādasevanaṁ |
arcanaṁ vandanaṁ dāsyam sakhyamātmnivedanam ||

— *Bhāgavata Purāṇa* vii.5.23-24

> leaves Gokula for Mathurā, are given specific treatment in independent chapters of *Bhāgavata Purāṇa*. . . . If Āṇḍāḷ had known of these two Kṛṣṇa themes through the *Bhāgavata Purāṇa*, she would undoubtedly have made use of them in her poems. With Kṛṣṇa as her chosen lord, and the anguish of separation as the personal theme of her *Nachiar Tirumoḻi*, Āṇḍāḷ would surely have made reference to the agony of the *gopī*s when Kṛṣṇa departs. — Dehejia 1990: 21-22

Vidya Dehejia's statement about Āṇḍāḷ, relating that Āṇḍāḷ does not use episodes of *gopikā*s' ecstasy in *rāsa* dance and their pining anguish when Kṛṣṇa departs to Mathura from the *Bhāgavata Purāṇa*, is true only to the extent that *Bhāgavata Purāṇa* was not compiled in Āṇḍāḷ's time. Although as we see that in the poem *Tiruppāvai*, Āṇḍāḷ recreates the spectacle of a Gokula street and the cowherd girls (*gopī*s) living there as its chief motif, it is very clear that Āṇḍāḷ was familiar with the earlier Purāṇas (*Viṣṇu* and *Harivaṁśa*) and knew about the *gopikā*s' intense love for Kṛṣṇa.[3] Another significant point in this context

---

[3] Also I do not agree with Vidya Dehejia when she says:

"The subject matter of *Nachiar Tirumoḻi* suggests that it might have been her later work, since the *Tiruppāvai* is written in a much lighter vein, showing Āṇḍāḷ as a carefree girl surrounded by companions".

— Dehejia 1988: 121.

In fact, *Tiruppāvai* is not written in lighter vein at all. It is a very serious work. The only place, where one finds humour, is in the dialogue between the *sakhī*s or *gopikā*s. Here we have to remember that this dialogue is a part of the technique which helps the poetess to unfold some nuances of a very mature undertaking. For instance, it is in *Tiruppāvai*, that one witnesses a range of *rasa*s — *karuṇa, hāsya, vātsalya, mādhurya, vīra* and *adbhuta* — all in the thirty stanzas, while *Nachiar Tirumoḻi* focuses exclusively on *mādhurya bhāva* (and corresponding *rasa* called as *śṛṅgāra*). Also the images and metaphors used in *Tiruppāvai* are pregnant with a range of references that encompass a whole cultural and religious tradition. *Nachiar Tirumoḻi* also presents a spectacular imagery but the metaphorical framework is not as rich as that of *Tiruppāvai*.

is that seventeenth canto of famous Tamil epic *Cilappadikāram* from Saṅgam period, that certainly predated Āḻvārs, contains an entire episode on the *rāsa-nṛtya* enacted as the "Round Dance of the Herdswomen". To quote from the canto:

Among them, Pinnai (Rādhā) puts the garland of rich basil.
On Mayavan and begins the flawless round dance.
It is our own Pinnai, her arms ringed with bangles,
that turned the gaze of the lord, renowned for striding.
All the three worlds, away from his consort, Lakṣmī, ensconced
on his chest, hā! hā! — R. Parthasarthy 1993: 173

There is very high probability that Āṇḍāḷ knew this episode from the epic, which was like a popular cultural document of the Tamil land.

At the same time it is interesting to note that in their way of worship (*bhakti*) the Āḻvārs make use of almost all the *bhakti bhāvas* (sentiments) mentioned in the classical texts referred above in relation to their chosen God.

Fivefold Bhakti

Later theologians and scholars of *bhakti* precipitate down these nine sentiments in classical *navadhā bhakti* to five important sentiments (*bhāvas*).

P. Jairaman, in his study on Tamil Āḻvār saints and Hindi Kṛṣṇa *bhakti* literature, brings out five modes of relating to the God which he says are very commonly used by Āḻvārs in their poetry. These, according to him, are: *dāsya, sakhya, vātsalya, mādhurya* or *kānta,* and *nirveda* or *śānta bhāvas.*[4]

---

[4] P. Jairaman, *Bhakti ke Āyāma: Kṛṣṇa Bhakti Sāhitya*, New Delhi: Vani Prakashan, 2003, pp. 339-40 (Hindi text).

Here I would like to propose that *nirveda* or *śānta bhāva* need not be taken up and pointed out in exclusion. According to Ācārya Abhinavagupta, *śānta rasa* pervades and underlies all the other *rasas* and that the experience of all *rasas* in their intensity finally →

Dāsya bhāva is a way of relating to one's Lord and Master. In feudal set-up and monarchy, the status of the king and the feudal lord is considered to be next only to God and it is the *dharma* (religious obligation) of all the subjects to serve their sovereign and the master. This same sentiment when projected towards God becomes *dāsya bhakti*. Almost all the Āḷvārs use this sentiment to express their intense love for the *iṣṭa*, the chosen one. Nammāḷvār calls out, probably to his own self, to surrender at the feet of none else but Kṛṣṇa:

> Quick, think of the fragrant *tulsī*-wreathed Kṛṣṇa's feet. They who ruled over other kings who touched their feet, with great kettledrums rumbling in their porticos, have become pulverized to dust. — Srirama Bharti 2000: 487

Sakhya bhāva is a way of relating to God as a friend, where sharing, sacrifice and surrender all are involved. Kṛṣṇa relates to Arjuna in *Mahābhārata* as a *sakhā* (friend). And Arjuna also takes Him to be his most intimate friend and shares every desire and aspiration with Kṛṣṇa. In Āḷvār poetry *sakhya bhāva* is mentioned in relation to other *bhāvas*. This is not found as a dominant *bhāva* in any of the poems by Āḷvār saints. Viṣṇucitta Āḷvār or Periyāḷvār refers to Kṛṣṇa's support to Arjuna as a *sakhā* in the battlefield as follows:

> If you are in search of him, there are many who saw him by Arjuna's side where he hid the sun with his discus, when

→ leads to an experience of the *śānta rasa*. What the Ācārya says about *śānta rasa* should be true of *śānta bhāva* as well. *Śānta bhāva* is a *bhāva* which lingers behind all forms of *bhakti bhāvas*. In fact, this *bhāva* can be described as a prerequisite or preparation for *bhakti*. *Śānta bhāva* has its source in the feeling of *vairāgya* (detachment) from the transitory situations of life and a developing sense of omnipresence of the Divine. Rise of this *bhāva* leads to a sense of calm in all situations and the *bhakta* surrenders his/her self completely to the will of God. Except for *śānta bhāva*, the other four *Bhāvas*, viz. *dāsya, sakhya, vātsalya* and *mādhurya* have their source in common human relations.

> Arjuna rained arrows that rolled Jayadratha's head into a pit.
> — Srirama Bharti 2000: 65

Vātsalya and *mādhurya* are the two most frequently used *bhāva*s in *bhakti* poetry.

In the attitude of *vātsalya*, the *bhakta* adores the God as his/her own child in order to experience the wonder of His *bāla līlā*s (i.e. His divine childhood). Viṣṇucitta Āḻvār's songs elaborately deal with Kr̥ṣṇa's childhood, adopting the perspective of mother Yaśodā, Kr̥ṣṇa's earthly (foster) mother. There are cradle songs,[5] lullabies, songs about giving bath to child Kr̥ṣṇa, songs of gentle chiding, songs about sending the child to cow grazing for the first time and so on.[6]

Mādhurya bhāva is considered to be the most intimate and mystical relation between the *bhakta*, the devotee and the *Bhagavān*, the God. Here God is conceived as the beloved or as the husband regardless of the gender of the *bhakta*. Kr̥ṣṇa's relation to *gopikā*s and vice versa is the ultimate example of *mādhurya bhakti*. *Mādhurya bhāva* can be experienced in the state of separation from the beloved or in the state of union with the beloved. Love of God experienced as a state of separation

---

[5] *O, Great Moon! My dark hued little child, my sweet ambrosia, my master calls and beckons to you with his wee hands. If you wish to play with him, do not hide behind the clouds. Come running here happily.*
— Srirama Bharti 2000: 11

[6] *If you catch insects and let them into the calves' ears, they will go helter skelter and run away. Let me see how you gobble butter thereafter. O Lord who shot through seven trees, it is your birth star, śravaṇaṁ today. You must have your bath. My master, do not run away, come hither!*
— Srirama Bharti 2000: 29

from Him is called as *viraha bhakti* and Love of God experienced as complete union with Him is called as *mādhurya bhakti*. The term "bridal mysticism" is popularly used for this same concept. *Saṁbhoga śṛṅgāra* also refers to this relationship in classical poetic vocabulary.

In this same framework of *mādhurya bhāva* in *bhakti*, Āḻvār saints fondly take on the role of Kṛṣṇa's beloved to express their deep longing to unite with Him in an eternal embrace. They express their *bhakti* through their songs in state of *viraha* (separation) as well as in state of *saṁbhoga* (union). Though all the eleven Āḻvārs use this *bhāva*, Tirumaṅgai Āḻvār, Nammāḻvār and Āṇḍāḷ stand out in their use of *mādhurya bhāva* also known as "bridal mysticism". As a result, a unique urgency and intensity runs through their songs.[7]

Śānta or *nirveda bhāva* is a sentiment which signifies a sense of peace and serenity in the individual consciousness. It is an effect of an evolved state of mind. It can be associated with *bhakti* as *bhakti* leads to this state of mind. Bharata Muni, the second century aesthetician had enumerated eight *bhāvas* in the *Nāṭyaśāstra*, his famous text on dramaturgy. These eight *bhāvas* are: *śṛṅgāram, raudram, hāsyam, kāruṇyam, bībhatsam, bhayānakam, vīram* and *adbhutam*. *Vātsalya, śānta* and *bhakti* were added at a later period to the classical eight *bhāvas* and *rasas*. *Śānta bhāva* was first mentioned by the tenth-century philosopher Ācārya Abhinavagupta in his commentary on the *Nāṭyaśāstra*. He called it the "*bhāva* of the *bhāvas*". It is said that *śānta bhāva* is the underlying *bhāva* of all other *bhāvas*.

---

7 Saint Nammāḻvār sings:
O Gregarious bees go drink the nectar from
the tulasī flowers worn by the lord, —
he steered the chariot for the Pāṇḍavas against
the great army in war — come back quickly and
blow his fragrance over my coiffure flowers.
— Srirama Bharti 2000: 539

Saguṇa Bhakti and Nirguṇa Bhakti

In *bhakti* philosophy and Bhakti movement two basic streams of *bhakti* emerged. They are *nirguṇa bhakti* and *saguṇa bhakti*. While most Vaiṣṇava and all Śrīvaiṣṇava poets are steeped in *saguṇa bhakti* (*bhakti* of God with a specific form), Vīraśaiva poets from Karnataka were steeped in *nirguṇa bhakti* (God without any specific form). For *bhakti* in *mādhurya bhāva* which involves thinking of God as one's lover, *saguṇa bhakti* is the natural way of being. However, there have been saints who could relate to the Divine principle without subscribing to a specific form. Saint Kabīr is the foremost example in this category. The poets under study belonged to both the *saguṇa* as well as *nirguṇa* kind of *bhakti*. That is to say, while Āṇḍāḷ was mainly a *saguṇa bhakta*, Akkā Mahādevī was mainly a *nirguṇa bhakta*.

Bhakti as Conflict and Reconciliation Between Saguṇa and Nirguṇa

The two aspects of the supreme reality simultaneously, viz. an awareness of the Absolute as a mystical state of being and a perception of it as a personal god are visible in the entire *bhakti* tradition. In other words, the Absolute is perceived both as *nirākāra* as well as *sākāra* (formless as well as in a form), *nirguṇa* as well as *saguṇa* (without attributes as well as with attributes). The Śāstras and classic religious texts like the Vedas and the *Bhagavad-Gītā* project supreme reality in both the aspects. However, the Upaniṣads primarily focus on the *nirguṇa*, and epics and later *bhakti* literature focus on the *saguṇa* aspect of the Supreme. This does not mean that there is a complete absence of the elements pointing at the mystical and incomprehensive Absolute in *bhakti* literature. On the contrary, *bhakti* poetry, throws up a wonderful amalgamation of mystical and personal features of the Divine. *Bhakti* poetry often, for instance, while making the personal God its subject, transcends it and foregrounds the mystical aspect in all its intensity. A.K. Ramanujan makes a significant observation in this context. In his essay on "The Myths of Bhakti: Images of Siva in Saiva Poetry", he says:

> All devotional poetry plays on the tension between *saguṇa* and *nirguṇa,* the lord as person and the lord as principle. If he were entirely a person, he would not be divine, and if he were entirely a principle, a godhead, one could not make poems about him. . . . The Vaiṣṇavas, too, say that the lord is characterized by both *paratva* (otherness) and *saulabhaya* (ease of access); he is both here and beyond, both tangible as a person and intangible as a principle — such is the nature of the ground of all being. It is not either/or, but both/and; myth, *bhakti* and poetry would be impossible without the presence of both attitudes. — Dharwadkar 1999: 295

It is interesting to note that in Āḻvār songs, the *nirākāra* and *nirguṇa* (without form and attributes) aspects of god are not taken up at all. Their *bhakti* is *saguṇa bhakti.* And it is only in the doctrines of Śrīvaiṣṇavism that evolved later that the personal god and Absolute God merged into each other.

Often saints pour out emotional *bhakti* poetry and scholars create religious cults out of their poetry. History has witnessed this phenomenon in *bhakti* all along. All *bhakti* cults, be it Śrīvaiṣṇavism, Vīraśaivism, Caitanya Sampradāya or Kabīr Pantha, etc., are an outcome of this process of emotional outpouring by saints and later indoctrination by the scholars and critics and religious enthusiasts.

The Āḻvār saints' poetry makes use of classical forms of *dāsya, sakhya, vātṣalya* and *mādhurya bhāva* described above under the aegis of fivefold *bhakti*. But *bhakta* Āṇḍāḷ specifically subscribes to *mādhurya bhāva* in both of her poems *Tiruppāvai* as well as *Nachiar Tirumoḻi.*

Bhakti: The Path as well as the Goal

In order to understand the philosophy of *bhakti* it is important to understand that *bhakti* Śāstras like Nārada's *Bhakti-Sūtras,* Śāṇḍilya's *Bhakti-Sūtras* and *Bhāgavata Purāṇa* exposit *bhakti* not only as a means (*sādhana rūpa*) but also as a goal (*sādhya rūpa*).[8] This goal is worth pursuing for the eternal joy it ensues in the *bhakta*. The *bhakta* is not aiming to achieve anything else but *bhakti* itself.

8 This particular theme runs through the entire Āḻvār corpus also. Jīva Goswāmī in his famous text *Durgam Saṅgamni* distinguishes between *sādhana rūpa bhakti* and *sādhya rūpa bhakti*. *Sādhana rūpa bhakti* (relating to the means) is further divided into *vaidhī bhakti* and *rāgānuga bhakti*. In *vaidhī bhakti*, *bhakta* takes up the means as laid down in śāstras. *Śravaṇa, kīrtana, pūjana, arcana, pādasevan*, etc. fall under this category. *Rāgānuga bhakti* is marked by the fundamental human tendency to love. *Dāsya, sakhya, vātsalya* and *mādhurya* come in the category of *rāgānuga bhakti*. In this kind of *bhakti*, the *bhakta* is able to transform the base emotions of *kāma* (lust) and *vāsanā* (desire) into a pure re-motion towards *iṣṭa*, the chosen God. In a way, when a *bhakta* takes first steps of *vaidhī bhakti*, i.e. *śravaṇa, kīrtana, manana, arcana* and *pādasevana*, then these steps serve as a means to a higher form of *rāgānuga bhakti* which finally leads to *prema bhakti* which is a state of pure joy and love. Sage Nārada defines this *bhakti* as — *sa tvasmin param premasvarūpa*, which means that "it (*bhakti*) is of the nature of ultimate Love for the Divine". *Bhakti* is complete merging with the Divine and is also a state of self-realization (*mokṣa*).

4

Nāyaṉmār Bhakti and Vīraśaivism

NĀYAṈMĀRS saints were the Śiva devotees who flourished along with the Āḻvār saints in Tamil Nadu between fourth and ninth centuries CE. These sixty-three Nāyaṉmārs were strong devotees of Śiva. Prime saints among them were Sundarār, Appār, Sambandhar and Maṇikavasagar,. Their devotional songs are compiled in *Tirumurai*. Twelfth-century Vīraśaiva Bhakti movement found its base and inspiration in the poetry of Nāyaṉmār saints. In order to understand the evolution of Vīraśaiva movement, we have to go back to the time of Nāyaṉmār saints and how they challenged the existing forms of religion that became too oppressive.

Jainism and Buddhism were the ascendant religions after the Tamil Saṅgam period of the second century CE in south India. Under the rule of Kalabhras in the south, religious and cultural values of Tamils suffered oppression and excessive censure in the third and the fourth century CE.[1] In almost a reactionary mode, some of the pilgrim Nāyaṉmār saints moved along the sacred geography of southern land singing in devotional ecstacy and challenging the life-denying values of Jainism and Buddhism. They gathered support from common people wherever they went. They were majorly responsible for the re-establishment of Hinduism especially Śaivism. Initially in fact the rise of Śaivites as well as Vaiṣṇavite (Nāyaṉmār and Āḻvār, respectively) *bhakti* was a process of

---

1 Out of the two great epics in Tamil language, viz. *Cilappadikāram* and *Maṇimekalai* written towards the end of the Saṅgam period, the latter seems to have been written only to propagate the philosophies of Buddha and to prove Buddhist supremacy over other religions.

consolidating non-ascetic values of love and heroism already present in Saṅgam culture, but later these movements were used to channelize other dimensions of cultural traditions including questions of caste, class and gender.

When these Bhakti movements were able to create a strong social support and participation of the masses, then they automatically attracted royal patronage which led to consolidation of *bhakti* values. Like Bhāraśivas and Vākāṭakas in the north, Pallava kings also supported Śaivism as their state religion in the south. The Pallava dynasty ruled the southern land from CE 295 to 360. There are many examples in the Tamil history when the kings were converted into Śaivism and Vaiṣṇavism due to the influence of a saint-poet. Evidently Mahendravarman, an early seventh-century Pallava ruler was himself a convert from Jainism. His contemporary Nāyaṉmār saint Appār, also a Jaina earlier, successfully converted the king into Śaivism. Similarly another Nāyaṉmār saint Sambandhar (Campantar) transformed the Pantiya region by converting the king and his subjects to Śaivism. Writings of some of these saints were instrumental in shaping various Śaiva sects especially the philosophy of "Śaiva Siddhānta".[2] Though references to Śaivism go back to the *aham* and *puram* poetry of the Saṅgam period in Tamil literature, one of the most important Śaiva texts in Tamil is *Tirumandiram* by saint Tirumular (Sakhare 1978: 136). Tirumular was one among the sixty-three Nāyaṉmārs who lived in the land during the fourth and the ninth-century. Sambandhar, Appār (*c.* CE 650) and

---

[2] "Of all the religious works of Śaiva authors, *Tirumandiram*, the work of Tirumular, is the most authoritative; as it became the foundation on which the superstructure of Śaiva Siddhānta philosophy was raised later by Tirumular's successors. But it is mainly the Nāyaṉmārs that were greatly instrumental in the spread of Śaivism by their life of intense, sincere, exemplary devotion." — Sakhare, 1978: 138

Sundarār (*c.* CE 800-825) together with Maṇikavasagar, who wrote *Tiruvasagam*, are considered as four *samayācāra*s of Śaivism or teachers of Śaivism. Sundarār wrote songs about the lives of Nāyaṉmārs in his work *Tiruttoṇḍattogai*. However it was an eleventh-century Śiva devotee, Sekkizhār, who wrote detailed accounts of the lives of sixty-three Nāyaṉmārs in his celebrated text *Periya Purāṇam*. *Periya Purāṇam* is an interesting rendering of the devotional acts and miraculous incidents in the lives of Nāyaṉmārs. This text has assumed the status of a sacred scripture in south Indian Śaiva religious culture.[3]

Just as Śaivism established its roots in Tamil culture through devotional songs of Śaiva saints, Vaiṣṇavism re-established through the devotional songs of Āḻvār saints. Sixty-three Nāyaṉmārs along with eleven Āḻvārs are considered as seventy-five Apostles of south Indian *bhakti* as together they helped in the consolidation of Bhakti movements in the south.

When Āḻvārs and Nāyaṉmārs in Tamil Nadu were pouring devotional songs in praise of Viṣṇu and Śiva, respectively, they were somehow trying to counter the influence of religions of Gautama Buddha and Mahāvīra Jaina. These saints singing ecstatically used to wander from temple centre to temple centre thereby reviving the ritualistic temple lives in the whole land of Tamil Nadu. Compositions of these saints were integrated into temple rites which led to a new amalgamation of Āgamic rituals and the *bhakti* compositions, consequently initiating a whole new culture of inclusive, open, free-flowing expression of divine love in an otherwise exclusive Brāhmanical ritual context in the temple space. In Viṣṇu temples, songs of Āḻvārs from *Divya Prabandham* were sung and in Śiva temples, compositions of Nāyaṉmārs from *Tevaram* were sung in Śiva

3 It is a significant fact that Śaiva-devotionalism made popular by the Nāyaṉmārs in seventh century was also being practised earlier by women saint-poets like Karaikkal Ammaiyyar and Avvaiyar.

temple. This also indicates how *bhakti* compositions actually were harmoniously integrated into the already existing ancient system of Āgamic ritual worship, thereby making the whole system open to common masses. As the saints sang in vernacular and not in classical or courtly language, they held great mass appeal and their popularity increased manifold as the temple integrated the songs in its worship routines.

Gradually this new *bhakti* tradition found roots in the culture and conferred great powers on the temple space, which with time afforded more and more political bent to the temple administration. Another outcome of popularity of *bhakti* saints and through the *tīrtha-yātrās* (pilgrimages), their relation to sacred geography, was an upsurge in the building and development of temples. Wherever these saints went about singing, people thronged them and the places they touched during their journeys were transformed into sacred places. Whole cities and townships came up around temple structures during the period of Nāyaṉmārs for instance. The sixty-three Nāyaṉmārs saints in Tamil Nadu filled the whole land with their devotional songs, which carved a permanent place in the consciousness of Śiva devotees. These saints left their mark in public memory by visiting many cities. Using the colloquial language, they sang wandering through the land with a large following thereby creating sacred geographies (*tīrtha-sthalas*). Examples of Appār and Sambandar (Campantar) are particularly interesting. According to R. Champakalakshmi:

> Campantar's hymns (seventh to eighth centuries CE) are considered the most successful from the *bhakti* point of view, as they, apart from their emotional significance, also establish Śiva as the local god and the transcendent deity. Campantar's hymns are also significant as extolling the idea of pilgrimage. On his peregrinations to various Śaiva shrines composing melodious Tamil hymns, he is said to have been accompanied by crowds of fellow devotees. A

> *paṇar* (musician) called Tirunilakanta Yalppanar set his hymns to music (*paṇ*) and accompanied him on his journeys. Campantar also visited many Śiva shrines with his elder contemporary Tirunavukkaracar (Appār), both of them drawing a large following of devotees.
>
> — Champakalakshmi and Gopala 1996: 142

The power, these saints wielded over the populace, was not only due to the colloquialism of the songs but also due to their high emotional appeal and great music compositions. The idea of pilgrimage led to two important things — adaptation of temples of local deities into the Śiva-fold and construction of grand temple-structures on a large scale. According to K. Meenakshi:

> The construction of temples began roughly during the Pallava–Pantiya period, i.e. seventh to ninth centuries, and gained momentum and reached its culmination during the Coḷa period (ninth to twelfth centuries). The Coḷas are known to have constructed a large number of temples. Though the earlier ruling dynasties instituted grants for worship at and maintenance of temples, it was during the Coḷa period that temples were institutionalized, becoming thereby the centre of all social and economic activities. . . .
>
> — Champakalakshmi and Gopala 1996: 122

K. Meenakshi raises an important point while mentioning the role of temples in the socio-economic aspects of the medieval south. She says, that when *bhakti* led to construction of temples and revived Āgamic modes of worship, the brāhmaṇas, who were in the know-how of rituals and also supposedly more pure,

> acquired high ritual status and others, ritually less pure, came to be assigned lower ranking, leading to the emergence of a hierarchy around the temple based on Brāhmanical caste relations. — Champakalakshmi and Gopala 1996: 122

Dwelling on this point a little, one can easily infer that the Bhakti movements which were a reaction to the heterodox religions, had to counter at least one positive aspect of these religions, which was their position against *varṇāśramadharma* (caste-system). And probably it was to acknowledge this that *bhakti* followers had to be inclusive of all castes. However, caste equality proclaimed by various saints and *Ācārya*s never actually sieved down into the social set-up. There are many examples of saints from lower classes who were denied entry into the temples and who gave up their lives sitting at the temple gates (e.g. Nandanār, a Śaivite devotee, Tiruppanāḷvār, a Vaiṣṇavite saint).[4] Temples till this date protect this caste hierarchy. C.V. Narayan Ayyar argues:

> By feigning to admit the low born in their ranks and treat them on a par with the higher groups, these sects wanted to take the edge away from the Jaina propaganda that only Jainism stood for a society of equals. In practice, however, the śūdra Nayanar continued to suffer as ever, from social disabilities. — Narayan Ayyar 1974: 122

Institutionalization of Bhakti Culture

Nāthamuni in the tenth century compiled the works of Āḻvārs in *Nālāyira-Divya-Prabandham* and *ācārya*s like Yāmunācārya and Rāmānujācārya, putting the writings in philosophical perspective, created a whole new religion of Śrīvaiṣṇavism in the twelfth century.

---

4 Poignant story of saint Nandanār, who was a dealer in dead animal carcasses, appears in *Periya Purāṇam* by Sekkizhār. He had to walk through fire to purify himself before he could walk towards the temple in the city of "Thillai". Sekkizhār says:

The very moment he entered the fire,
His delusive false appearance lost its form,
And in the form of a great muni of great virtue, he rose from the fire
With the white thread shining on his body,
And matted locks to match. — Sekkizhār, 1985: 564

In the context of Śaivite faith, Nāyaṉmārs' writings were also consolidated by various authors like Sekkizhār, Tirumular and Appār. *Tevaram* is the collection of hymns of Nāyaṉmār saints. A major philosophy that arose from Nāyaṉmār saints' writings was Śaiva Siddhānta. *Nālāyira-Divya-Prabandham* and *Tevaram* contain the hymns of Āḻvār and Nāyaṉmār saints, respectively, which were integrated into the temple rituals in Vaiṣṇava and Śaiva *devasthānams* (temples). The strong theological base provided by Rāmānujācārya, where he successfully integrated Sanskrit Vedas and Tamil "Divyaprabandham" of Āḻvārs, helped in according a scriptural status to the Āḻvār literature, while Nāyaṉmār hymns served a limited function of ritual singing at the Śaiva temples and could never be raised to form a theology.

After the initial phase of *bhakti* euphoria in Tamil Nadu and later in Karnataka, *bhakti* culture received strong support from the royal patrons and became institutionalized in the processes of temple administration — its policies and politics by the eleventh and twelfth centuries. Temple administration gained enormous power, and centred itself in the hands of a few in the line of priestly hierarchy.

According to R. Champakalakshmi.

> In the medieval south Indian context, all the emergent institutions and urban forms, including the *nagaram*, "merchant guilds" and craft organizations, were merged in to a single systemic relationship. Diverse economic and ethnic groups were thereby accommodated as a substantial component within the same structure, i.e. the temple society, by seeking validation within the norms of the traditional order of ritual ranking.
>
> — Champakalakshmi and Gopala 1996: 163

However, in spite of its integration into the political systems of the times *bhakti* as a principle always propagated equality of all the individual souls in the scheme of creation.

Time and again the saints referred to this idea in their songs. Therefore, when the medieval temple ranking rituals excluded the commoners, saints from this era challenged the temple itself as house of God and posited the idea of body of the individual *bhakta* itself as the real house of God.

Therefore, within the Bhakti movement, there initially were phases of establishment of structure-like temple as a symbol of love and devotion for God and later those of revolt against these structures when they became too orthodox in their turn.

Tamil Siddhas and Kannaḍiga Vīraśaivas: Challenging the Temple Structure

R. Champakalakshmi has pointed out in the above-quoted essay that Nāyaṉmār hymnists had a close affinity with *siddha*s and some of them like Tirumular were from Siddha tradition, believers in Śaiva Siddhānta philosophy. Later *siddha*s incidentally proved to be a voice of dissent against the initial thrust of Bhakti movement on the sacred space (temple) and the manifest form of the deity (Champakalakshmi and Gopala 1996: 159). Early *siddha*s belonged to the early phases of *bhakti* (seventh–ninth century CE) but the later *siddha*s arose in the post-institutional phase of *bhakti*. These saints were adherents of ancient yogic practices and

> challenged the established religious and social order, and denounced the exterior manifestations of religious practices such as elaborate sacrifice, idol worship, and pilgrimage to holy places.[5]

*Siddha*s probably registered their voices of protest when they witnessed the temple space transform into oppressive centres of power and also into a space of caste politics and exploitation

[5] K. Meenakshi's essay in R. Champakalakshmi and S. Gopala (eds.), *Tradition, Dissent and Ideology: Essays in Honour of Romila Thapar*, New Delhi: Oxford University Press, 1996, p. 125.

of lower castes. In a way, it was a need of the times to defy this external temple structure and to relate back to the inner sacred space of true *bhakta* (devotee). This ideology was profitable to the ruling classes as it erased any threat of rebellion whatsoever from lower castes to acquire a more legitimate role in temple politics. Hence the voice of the *siddha*s was very relevant to provide a broader political base to the *bhakti* philosophy. To quote a song by Sivayakkiyar for example:

> *Brick, black stone, red liṅga,*
> *Copper and other base metals*
> *You say Śiva resides in these metals*
> *After you realize yourself*
> *The omnipresent god will sing and dance within you.*[6]

This song is an example of how *bhakti* impulse of freedom was already trying to go beyond the physical confines of the temple, which had become a centre for political power and which, still, excluded a large section of the society.

In the twelfth century, similar impulse of freedom gave impetus to the Vīraśaiva movement of Karnataka which sought to throw open its doors to all, irrespective of cast and gender. Vīraśaivites created an entire line of symbolism around the microcosm (the human body) and the macrocosm (the Cosmic Consciousness). They relegated the "Sthavara Liṅgam" (fixed *liṅga*) of the temple to adopt the "moving *liṅgam*" worn on the body by the Vīraśaiva devotee. Thus doing away with the need for external rituals and rites that were the forte of the temple priestly class. Vīraśaiva religion created its own praxis of *bhakti* that allowed for an expansive outlook on society and posited a philosophy that defied the *varṇāśramadharma*.

---

6 Quotation of the song from K. Meenakshi's essay in Champakalakshmi and Gopala (eds.), 1996, p. 131.

Vīraśaivism

Here we must discuss the important tenets of Vīraśaivism (Heroic Śaivism) as the saint-poetess, Akkā Mahādevī belonged to this sect of Śaivism. This is an offshoot of Śaivism and as said earlier was strongly influenced by Śaiva Siddhānta philosophy and Nāyaṉmār saints. It arose in Karnataka in the twelfth century. However some schools of thought consider it to be a very old religion. In spite of the debate, it is certain that the religion became consolidated after the Śaraṇa movement in twelfth century under the leadership of saint Basavanna.

Vīraśaiva philosophy emphasizes more on the means of attaining the goal of "Śiva Sāyujya" (Oneness with Śiva) than on organized metaphysics and theory of cosmogony. The cosmological expositions as found in other forms of Śaivism like Pāśupata, Tamil Śaivism, Śaiva Siddhānta and Kāśmīra Śaivism are reflected in *vacana* literature only indirectly.

Vīraśaivism conceives a system of faith and practice for its followers. This system centres around the concept of *ṣaṭsthala* (six phases or stages) in the spiritual journey of a *śaraṇa*. In fact, before *ṣaṭsthala,* three preparatory *sthala*s are mentioned. Hence in all, they become nine *sthala*s like the nine stages of *navadhā bhakti* as discussed with reference to Āḻvārs and Viṣṇu *bhakti*. In this context, A.K. Ramanujan observes:

> The *vacana* and later Vīraśaiva texts in Kannada and Sanskrit speak of the mystical process as a succession of stages, a ladder of ascent, a metamorphosis from egg to larva to pupa to the final freedom of the winged being. . . . Six phases or steps (*sthala, sopāṇa*) are recognized. The devotee at each stage has certain characteristics; each stage has a specific relationship between the *aṅga* (the soul) and the *liṅga* (the lord).
>
> — Ramanujan 1973: 169

Entry into the Vīraśaiva faith is reserved by initiation by a competent *guru*. *Guru* initiates the disciple by giving a *mantra* and an *iṣṭaliṅga* to the disciple. This *liṅga* is to be worn on the physical body. A more popular name of Vīraśaivism is Liṅgāyata, which comes from the practice of wearing the *liṅga* on the body. *Guru, jaṅgama* and *liṅga* are principally and practically important for a Vīraśaiva. Regardless of caste or class one can get initiated into the path by a *guru*. After *guru*, comes the *liṅga*. In the words of S.C. Nandimath:

> The *liṅga* presented by the *guru* functions as *ācāraliṅga* in the nose, as *guruliṅga* in the tongue, as *śivaliṅga* in the eyes, as *jaṅgamaliṅga* in the touch, as *prasādaliṅga* in the ears, and as *mahāliṅga* in the heart. The *liṅga* worn on the person is termed as *iṣṭaliṅga* and the *liṅga* meditated in the centre of the heart, *prāṇaliṅga*. — Nandimath 1965, vol. I: 37

In the initial stages, the seeker has to understand the first three *sthala*s and then through understanding has to proceed further on the spiritual path.

Ṣaṭsthala Scheme in Vīraśaivism

Sthala in Sanskrit means place. In Vīraśaiva faith, it represents the "stage" or phase in the journey of a *śaraṇa* to the Divine. Each *sthala* involves a level of awareness in devotional *bhakti*. The different stages of awareness in devotion sometimes need to be developed with spiritual practices but sometimes a highly evolved awareness is already there in the seeker due to *puṇya*s (good deeds) in the previous births.

There are three preparatory *sthala*s and six main *sthala*s. In all there are nine *sthala*s which remind of nine-fold classical *bhakti* (*navadhā bhakti*).

The three preparatory *sthala*s are *piṇḍa sthala, saṁsāraheya sthala* and *māyāvilāsaviḍambanā sthala*.

In *piṇḍa sthala, jīva* (individual) develops a pure heart with the consciousness of the divine principle working in the creation.

In the *saṁsāraheya sthala, saṁsāra* is the unending cycle of birth and death. To be bound in this cycle, without any hope for liberation, is *saṁsāra*. To understand the nature of the "Self", as being a part of "Paramaśiva" and meditate on this with a hope to finally cut through this cycle without getting disturbed by the play of *saṁsāra*, is the purpose of this stage in the life of the seeker.

In *māyāvilāsaviḍambanā sthala, māyā* is Śiva's own power that works to put up the play (*līlā*) of the Lord Himself in perfect conjunction with His Will (*ichā-śakti*). This *māyā,* which feeds the five senses with various kinds of foods, is varied and attractive. It entangles the mind of the seeker in its clutches if he/she is not aware. Therefore the function of this *sthala* is to make the seeker understand the true nature of *māyā* as illusion.

When the seeker has thus prepared him/herself after initiation by *guru,* in the form of receiving *mantra* and the *iṣṭa-liṅga,* by meditating constantly on the true nature of the Self, then he/she is ready to enter the next six *sthala*s known as *ṣaṭsthala*s. These follow as:

BHAKTA STHALA

At this stage, the seeker has to offer dedicated service to the *liṅgam* (*liṅgapūja*), *jaṅgama* (*jaṅgama dasoha*) and to the *guru* (*gurusevā*). This stage demands complete surrender of the self to the three principles of divinity in the form of *guru, jaṅgama,* and *liṅga*. Through the *karma-yoga* or *sarkayaka* the consciousness of the seeker becomes purer and purer.

MAHEŚVARA STHALA

At this stage, the faith in the Divine becomes more and more consolidated and becomes a living reality with the *bhakta*. Now the *bhakta* is still doing the external worship — *aṣṭopacāra, ṣoḍaśopacāra pūjā,* etc. but is no more dependent on it to feel the Divine consciousness pervading inside and outside him/her.

PRASĀDĪ STHALA

Prasāda actually means grace of God. Grace descends as we surrender to the Divine Will. The more the dedication, the more will be the grace. *Avadhāna* (attentiveness), *nirahaṁkāra* (egolessness) and *sujñāna* (right knowledge as opposed to ignorance) are the characteristics of the seeker at this *sthala*. The seeker makes the offering of the "ego" by removing ignorance and is called a *prasādī*. In his/her *arpaṇa-kriyā* (acts of dedication), he/she offers his/her body, mind and property to the *guru*, *liṅga* and *jaṅgama*, respectively. By making this offering, all these entities are purified of the *mala*s (impurities) and the seeker receives them back now as *prasāda*.

PRĀṆALIṄGĪ STHALA

Experience of the Self is the hallmark of this stage. Here the seeker, completely withdrawn from the outside world, turns inward and experiences the presence of *liṅga* in the very breath going in and out. Experience of the subtlety of the Divine is revealed through stirring of *kuṇḍalinī-śakti* within the central nerve *śuṣumnā*. This happens due to constant meditation upon the *linga* in the palm which brings about the synthesis of *dṛṣṭi* (subject) and *sṛṣṭi* (object) (Nandimath 1965: 40).

ŚARAṆA STHALA

In this stage, the seeker has become established in the light of the Divine and enjoys the bliss of divine consciousness. All the conflicts, which arise due to *avidyā* (ignorance), are dissolved and the seeker achieves a blissful state of tranquillity.

AIKYA STHALA

This is the last stage in the journey as propounded by the *ṣaṭ-sthala* scheme in Vīraśaivism. Here the seeker has become one with the divine and has achieved *Śivatva*. The *bhakta* now has no independent will or identity of his/ her own but has become one with the Divine Will.

S.C. Nandimath, in volume I of *Śūnya Sampādane,* writes about one more *sthala* called *jaṅgama sthala* with reference to Allama Prabhu's spiritual journeys, that were taken up by him purely in order to show the path of liberation or *jīvan-mukti* to deserving seekers throughout the land.

Interestingly Akkā Mahādevī talks about all these states and other characteristics of Vīraśaiva faith in detail in an unusually long *vacana* by her. This *vacana* is worth quoting in full:

Thinking that the animate and the inanimate
Are born of Śiva's Consciousness
And finding Śiva's soul in all creatures
And that of all creatures in Himself,
Due to the dual nature of Śiva,
The compassionate omniscient energy
Is to be obtained in the bhakta sthala
The energy of perfect satisfaction
Is to be obtained in the Maheśvara sthala,
Without losing heart on account
Of blame, obstacles and troubles,
And thinking that joy, sorrow, pain and pleasure
Come to one at God's behest.

The energy of eternal vigilance
That causes the propitiousness of eternal Paraśiva
Who is the cause of the temporal world including body,
Is to be obtained in prasādī sthala, mark!
The independent energy which creates
Awareness that Śiva is so independent
That though the motion of the whole world,
Including body, is subject to Him,

He is not subject to any,
Is to be obtained in prāṇaliṅgī sthala.
The manifest energy that creates awareness
That all manifest things including body,
That are subject to Paraśiva are ephemeral
And that Lord Paraśivaliṅga,
Who is the cause of the birth
Of all manifest things including body,
Alone is eternal,
Is to be obtained in the śaraṇa sthala, mark!
The infinite energy that causes
The complete union with Paraśivaliṅga,
By showing the union of aṅga and liṅga
Is to be obtained in the aikya sthala, mark!
Proof of this is in Śivarahasya.

O Śaṅkara, that which is supposed
To be bhakta sthala
Is called omniscience!
Maheśvara sthala is my satisfaction.
That which is supposed to be prasādī sthala
Is called unbridled vigilance,
And that which is supposed to be prāṇaliṅga
Is called Liberation
That which is supposed to be śaraṇa sthala
Is called manifest Śakti,

And that which is supposed to be aikya sthala
Is called infinite Śakti.
Unless they trample down the way to birth,
By knowing the state and nature of
Sixfold energy in the sixfold sthala
And embodying the sixfold liṅga
Through meditation and worship,
They cannot become sthalabrāhmīs.
But how can the wretched fellows

Who blame and censure blindly,
Enjoy other's wife, maidservants and prostitutes
Eat filth, and like poṭarāja, jogī and kṣapaṇa,
Go about begging for a loaf of bread,
Some by tying their hair into knots and buns
And some by shaving their heads,
Be ever called detached sthalabrāhmīs, sir?
I say "Hail" to the holy feet of Cennabasavanna,
Who by knowing the sixfold energy of such eternal
Sthalabrahma Nirabhari
Has become the detached jaṅgama
Sthalabalabrāhmī,
O Cennamallikārjuna![7]

This *vacana* is a very significant one not only in Akkā's oeuvre but in the entire corpus of the *śaraṇa* literature. Besides revealing Akkā's understanding of different stages of the spiritual path, it opens a good wide window to the tenets of *śaraṇa* philosophy in simple experiential poetry. The sixfold energy explained by Akkā can be realized only by serious seekers like Cennabasavanna. She staunchly criticizes the fake *śaraṇa*s and hypocrites! The last lines about the fake *sādhus* and licentious men are an indication of the corruption in the prevailing religious streams. Twelfth-century Vīraśaivism was a movement which opposed all those practices which had turned into empty, repetitious rituals devoid of the spiritual goal of self-transformation.

The above discussion indicates that the tenets of Vīraśaivism placed no ritualistic demands on the individual seeker. This new philosophy was directed at making the seeker free from the codified religious ideologies coming from Brāhmanical institutions like temples and *maṭhas*.

---

[7] C.R. Yaravintelimath (tr.), *Vachanas of Women Saints*, Bangalore: Basavasamithi, 2006, p. 149.

In fact the entire movement of Vīraśaivism was propelled by the contemporary needs of social reformation in twelfth-century Karnataka. The medieval kingdom of King Bijjala included a large territory of present-day Karnataka and Andhra Pradesh and had its capital at the city of Kalyāṇa. King Bijjala had given enormous freedom of action to his extremely radical prime minister Bāsaveśvara, who was the leader of the *śaraṇa* movement and finally also became instrumental in bringing the movement to an unexpected culmination. What is striking about this movement, is not so much the social upheaval that it created in the process of fighting the orthodoxy of the caste-system, that almost destroyed the city of Kalyāṇa, but the undying spirit of change that it could breathe into the orthodox religious orders of the day.[8]

Vīraśaiva movement, like the original spirit of its parent religion of Śiva, did not make any distinction between sacred and mundane. Therefore the movement sustainably maintained its focus on two important aspects of human

---

[8] According to C.R. Yaravintelimath:

The society, which the Śivaśaraṇas dreamt of, and strove to translate their dream into reality, was a casteless society, in which men and women enjoyed equal opportunities in all walks of life. They also strove to free women from the shackles of the Vedic family system, in which man's dominance over woman was unquestioned and man enjoyed equal opportunities in all walks of life. Hitherto woman was confined to the four walls of her house. The Śivaśaraṇas pulled down the walls of her prison, and extended the scope of her freedom beyond the four walls of her house to social, religious and spiritual worlds. She was made to realize her potential — both physical and spiritual, and to enjoy equal opportunities with men. So the principle of equality became the main pillar of the Śivaśaraṇa society. The lives of various Vīraśaiva women writers and their *vacanas* are a proof of the fact that the spirit of equality pervaded the atmosphere that prevailed in the twelfth-century Karnataka. — Yaravintelimath 2006: 3

existence — social and spiritual.[9] Both these aspects found central place in the socio-political and spiritual agendas of Vīraśaiva movement. Both the agendas therefore form the subject matter of the *vacanas*[10] composed by Śaraṇas and Śaraṇés. Their social agenda proved to be an important breakthrough in the socio-historical evolution of Hindu society in India especially in south of India. It challenged the caste and gender-based discrimination and floated some very positive alternative concepts for the society like *kāyaka* (lit. work done by the body) and *dasoha* (lit. service to men). The concept of *kāyaka* directly challenged the age-old menace of *varṇāśrama dharma* (caste distinctions based on birth of an individual). According to *Kāyaka* philosophy, no work is considered menial. All work is taken up as a sacred venture

[9] For details, see V.K. Javali's article on "Kayaka and Dignity of Labour" in *Eighth Centenary Comemoration Volume on Sri Basavesvara*, Bangalore: Government of Mysore, 1967.

A quote from the article:

"*Kāyaka* is a spiritual view of labour and not merely a materialistic view. According to *kāyaka* man has to sublimate his physical labour into a spiritual pursuit. The mercenary motive is sublimated into a spiritual motive.... Kannada saying is *kāyakave kailāsa*. Every labour is looked upon by *śaraṇa* with high honour, dignity and spiritual significance. . . . *Kāyaka* is to be done in the spirit of *dasoha*. The earning from *kāyaka* is to be dedicated to the preacher or *jaṅgama* who in his turn utilizes it for the good of the society. *Kāyaka* is a duty by which each one has to maintain oneself, and render its proceeds to the welfare of society as a whole." —p. 140

[10] *Vacana* form is a kind of free verse composition which became the hallmark of this movement. In literary history of Karnataka, this dialogic form holds a place of pride by the name of Vacana movement. *Vacanas* were recited or written down by *śaraṇas* and were used generally for propagation of *śaraṇa* philosophy, for self-analysis, and most often for contemplation. However, due to their dialogic nature (often they are an address to the *iṣṭa*), they are potentially performative texts.

and the fruits of the work are surrendered to the "service of other men" (*dasoha*) or to the community or for social welfare. For instance, woman *vacana* poet, Ayadakki Lakkammā lovingly chides her husband Śaraṇa Marayya in one of her *vacanas*, telling him, lest he should forget, that *kāyaka* in itself is the fruit and is not to be regarded as a means to a reward-physical or spiritual:

If you want to work to go to heaven
By doing work and rendering service,
Do you think heaven is a wage for your work?
If you stay absorbed in your work
Imagining no future and recollecting no past,
Where Marrayya Priya Amareśvaraliṅga is
There is heaven.

— Yaravintelimath 2006: 28

Another *vacana* by Śaraṇeya Akkammā reveals the essence of *Kāyaka* philosophy as it was conceived by Vīraśaivas:

One should go about doing one's daily work
As long as one can,
And thereafter one should go to see the guru,
To worship the liṅga and serve the jaṅgama.
As also to hold discourse with Śiva devotees,
And to spend time in their company.
It is proper for a devotee to know this rule.
He alone is the dynamic spirit
Rāmeśvaraliṅga
To whom right conduct itself is life-breath.
Nothing remained there
When the spinning cord broke
I did not embrace any vow-breaker.

— Yaravintelimath 2006: 28

Hence Śaraṇa movement was a reform movement in the social context and a reform movement in spiritual context also. *Vacana* literature refers to both these facets of Vīraśaiva movement and not always in exclusion to each other as is evident from the *vacana* quoted above.[11]

In fact, this movement for the first time in the religious history of India openly added the dimension of a personal spiritual path hitherto available only to the ones who left the material world and took to esoteric forms of *sādhanā*s (spiritual practices). Through this movement, choice of freedom from the available religious paths was made available to common people in their own social context (householder or ascetic-wanderer) and at their own social status (regardless of their caste and class).

Every individual was welcome in the *anubhava mantapa* (literally, the house of experience) set up in the great capital of Bijjalla's empire, Kalyāṇa, by his visionary prime minister Basavanna. The idea of *anubhava mantapa* and *mahāmane* (the great house)[12] was to allow a space for every *śaraṇa* to share

11 There were at least thirty-three Śiva *Śaraṇeyas* (women *śaraṇas*) who wrote more than a thousand *vacanas* (or we can say these many are extant now). Most women *vacanakāras* were housewives and shared with their husbands the concerns of treading a spiritual path.

12 C.R. Yaravintelimath says:

At Kalyāṇa, Basavanna founded two big houses — one was the *mahāmane* and the other, the *anubhava mantapa*. The concept of *mahāmane* and the *anubhava mantapa* was fluid and dynamic. It did not refer to any stone building, since both were *bayalu-ālayas* (houses of space). Every kitchen where *prasādam* was prepared and distributed was a *mahāmane*, and each place where devotees assembled and held mystic discourses was an *anubhava mantapa*. In fact, the home of every devoṭee housed the two houses where *dasoha* of some kind would go on perennially. Both the houses were complementary to each other — one took care of the body and the other, the soul. In *mahāmane*, *annadasoha* — distribution of *prasāda*, the sacred food meant for *guru*, *liṅga* and *jaṅgamas* was →

and discuss his own insights on a path to the Absolute Consciousness conceived as Śiva in this system.

The philosophical tenets of the Vīraśaiva sect were codified by its later followers. The king Prauḍhadeva Rāya (1419-47) of Vijayanagara empire took personal interest in the collection and systematic compilation of *śaraṇa* literature. However, a close look at the *vacanas* of Śiva-śaraṇas reveals that each one conceived their own path and moved independently on it. The idea of having one's own *iṣṭa* or a personal god validates this. Besides, it is a fact that every *vacanakāra* uses an *aṅkita*, a signature name which is nothing but his/her own conception of the Absolute Śiva Consciousness.[13] It is important to note that for *śaraṇas* the *aṅkita* used by them had no material manifestation of Śiva. This *aṅkita* was remarkably an individual conception of the metaphysical idea of Śiva. Thus the *aṅkita* in Vīraśaiva *bhakti* context, serves as the personal god for the *śaraṇa* just like the personal god found in the Tamil Āḻvār and Nāyaṇmār *bhakti*. However, the major point of difference is that personal gods of Āḻvārs and Nāyaṇmārs were chosen from specific temples in a specific locale while Vīraśaiva *aṅkitas* were truly metaphysical and experiential. Experience was the most important facet of spiritual life for *śaraṇas*. Allama Prabhu says in one of his *vacanas*:

> *Can the spark in the stone*
> *Kindle?*
> *Can the tree in the seed*
> *Rustle?*

→ going on; at the *anubhava mantapa* the dispersal of divine knowledge would take place. They were regular features of a *Śaraṇa*'s residence.
— Yaravintelimath 2006: 18

13 Akkā Mahādevī's *aṅkita* is "Cennamallikārjuna", Allama Prabhu's *aṅkita* is "Guheśvara" and Basavanna's *aṅkita* is "Kudalsaṅgamdeva" to name a few.

Guheśvara's majesty,
Being unapparent,
Does not shine out
For the common eye:
He only knows it
Who has tasted the joy
Of the experience!

— Nandimath, Menezes and Hiremath 1965, vol. I: 56

Anubhava mantapa, which was presided over by the mystics like Allama Prabhu, validated all experience if it stood the test of seeker — *śaraṇa's* own conviction.

This again leads to the fact that Śaraṇa movement actually defied all structures especially temple structures and institutions which had turned extremely exploitative by this time.

Finally it can be said that Bhakti movements were free from the religious doctrines and denominations. They kept on enlivening the essentially positive in the religious systems. These movements have kept on flourishing and have taken various turns down the centuries and are still impregnating mundane life with high inspiration.

Above discussion provides a context for our chosen poetesses Āṇḍāḷ and Akkā Mahādevī as they were put under the aegis of Śrīvaiṣṇavism and Vīraśaivism, respectively, by the interpreters of history and religion.

Section Two

5

Bhakti Poetry

Intersemiotic Transformations

BHAKTI poetry is a unique evolute of poetry which is an essential part of all cultures. In medieval times *bhakti* became a coherent aesthetic in its own category. But the form and diction of *bhakti* poetry did not arise in exclusion. *Bhakti* poetry was borrowing from the existing forms of poetry and later gave rise to many forms as it moved from language to language and region to region. In order to understand the transformations that *bhakti* effected in the existing forms and the transformations that itself undergone with time, I am using an analytical category which I call "intersemiotic transformations".

Semiotics is generally defined as study of signs. Signs can be words, images, sounds, gestures or objects, i.e. "everything that stands for something else" can be a sign. Signs are organized into specific structures to effect signification. All sign systems have their own codes or rules of organization. All of us are exposed to sign-systems without understanding the codes that go into their organization. Hence, we feel that the meanings conveyed to us are fixed, given and transparent. But semiotics helps us to understand that we can be active creators of meaning around us, if we are aware of the rules that govern the making of a semiotic system or a text. Semiotics provides us with a method of textual analysis to reveal peripheral layers of meaning and signification.

Semioticians and linguists after Saussure and Peirce have used this science to read socio-cultural phenomena and the belief systems that go into shaping up of the ideological bases of specific cultural traditions. Saussure's distinction of *langue* and *parole* in linguistic semiotics is now being used for other semiotic systems like media, film and cultural studies. Saussure uses the term *langue* for the system of language with its rules and conventions and the term *parole* for individual use of language as in speech. These terms have come to signify a general distinction between "system and usage, code and specific message, structure and specific event". While Saussure preferred *langue* over *parole*, contemporary theorists differ over whether the system determines and comes before the usage or the usage determines and comes before the system. While post-modernists go to the extreme view that no meaning exists beyond a text, Marxists propose that systems cannot be studied in isolation, as the signs carry out ideological functions in a society and its culture. In other words, social reality which is understood through signs is influenced by hegemony and is not pre-given or prefixed.

To take the Marxist view a little further, I would like to say that hegemony in itself is a very problematic concept and has to be defined and redefined in a context. Construction of hegemony is a complex phenomenon that needs to be studied. I personally believe that social realities are very volatile occurrences and changes in them are directed by many more factors than what can apparently be counted as a dominant ideology.

The *bhakti* trend that began in Tamil Nadu and took over India from the sixth century onwards provides a fine paradigm to study how the social ideologies often emerge at the margins and how they become dominant.

The example of Bhakti movements creates a counter-argument which defies the accepted notion that reality is hegemonic. Most Bhakti movements arose from the periphery and were absorbed into the mainstream with a fervour that did not spare even the kings and the brāhmaṇas who generally comprised the hegemonic classes.

The reason for discussing semiotics and its use in studying a text or a social phenomenon is to understand the *bhakti* phenomenon in medieval India in all its richness with particular reference to our saint-poetesses. At the same time, idea is to take the *bhakti* phenomenon out of religious discourse and to put it in a framework which is accessible to the modern student of cultural studies.

As this study proposes to bring out the intersemiotic transformations in the poetry of Akkā Mahādevī and Āṇḍāḷ, it is important to see how these two medieval saints created poetry in which their *bhakti*, their mysticism and their desire for *mokṣa* found meaning in the socio-cultural context of their times and our own. It is important to see how they make use of the classical *bhakti* discourse and mould it to suit their own individual experience thereby creating new social and even religious realities. Again to connect, we can say that if classical *bhakti* discourse as found in the Śāstras and ancient *bhakti* texts is the *langue* providing the model for exercise of *bhakti*, *bhakti* poetry itself is the *parole* which reveals the individual usage of the system.

The term "intersemiotic transformations" appears to be apt and is chosen consciously to explore and understand the creative processes in the poetry of Akkā and Āṇḍāḷ. It is interesting how they draw upon various semiotic systems like classical *bhakti* literature, mythology, contemporary secular traditions, rituals and folklore. We shall also take a look at how their poetic compositions became a source of inspiration for creative expression across genres in later periods.

We can say that this intersemiotic transformation is happening at two levels. First, where poets themselves are using images, metaphors, symbols and signs from varied discursive fields to give vent to their creativity — this constitutes intersemiotic transformations within the works of the poetesses in question. And the second type of transformation is happening when the poetry/life of these poetesses is re-written and re-interpreted by later generations to express their creative energy in different genres.

If we talk about signs, signifiers and signified as word, written sign and meaning, respectively, then we will see that these poets draw their signifiers from various sign systems mentioned above but they use them in such innovative ways that they constantly lead to creative formations of unique signifieds. However, as soon as we refer to the process of signification, we have to keep in mind that all structuralist and many post-structuralist theories of signification tend to arrive at the same idea, that all meaning is ideological and is predetermined by hegemony. In other words, meanings assumed to be natural are in fact arbitrary and enforced. However, the *bhakti* phenomenon is a unique historical process which presents a different example altogether to the *sahṛdayī*s (partakers of the experience) as well as to the students of this literature.

Bhakti poets defy the ideological meaning while using the signs from dominant discursive fields. For instance, ideology of the heroic age invested divine powers in the king. The king was held to be next to God and an agent of God on the earth, executing the Divine Will. Patronized by the king, even the greatest of our poets used God as a metaphor to signify the greatness of the king in their writings. In other words, in this age the poets and writers used God as a signifier, where actually the signified was always the king. Similarly, gender relations across all major cultures presupposed dominance of man over woman. This was reflected in all art forms where the woman was generally conceived as an object of desire or a threat to the integrity of a man.

Bhakti poets effect an inversion in this signification while using the signs from the same discursive fields. They use all the royal imagery but make the king the signifier and God becomes the signified. They invoke the God with all the royal virtues and embellishments. Similarly in gender relations the dominant position of the man-husband is substituted by the ever desirable God-lover. In fact, most *bhakti* poets, regardless of their gender, take upon the persona of a woman and call out to their chosen God as their lover.

In the period of Tamil Saṅgam, a poet named Kumatturkknnanār sings in praise of Cera king Imayavarampan Netunceralatan:

> *. . . having destroyed the enemy's forts*
> *and flushed with the glory of increasing might*
> *you are filled with loftier aspiration.*
> *This feat is like that*
> *of the glorious,*
> *ferocious*
> *and victorious Lord Muruka*
> *who, riding on his elephant,*
> *cut into the vast space*
> *of the dense dark sea . . .*
> — *Ancient Indian Literature*, vol. III, p. 133

Here the poet is using God Murugan as a metaphor to sing the glories of his king. Every image, every sign derived from God Murugan's attributes is tending to highlight the king's godly qualities.

In *bhakti* poetry, however, there is a reversal of these metaphors. While the signs are same, the signifiers and signifieds change places. For instance:

> *Glory be to your feet that spanned*
> *The earth as Vāmana. Glory be to*
> *Your strength that destroyed Laṅkā as*

Kodaṇḍa Rāma. Glory be to your fame
That smote the bedeviled cart as Kṛṣṇa
In the cradle. Glory be to your feet that
Threw and killed the demon-calf
Vatsāsura. Glory be to your merit that
Held that mountain Govardhana as an
Umbrella. Glory be to your spear that
Overcomes all evil. Praising you always
humbly we have come to you for boons.
Bestow your compassion on us.

— Srirama Bharti 2000: 100

All the endearments used for the king are being used here for the God. Extraordinary strength, the weapons, the glory, the ability to protect his subjects were the virtues ascribed to a great king. The *bhakti* poets used these adjectives to narrate the glories of their chosen God. Another example can be a poem by Nammāḷvār which is quoted by A.K. Ramanujan:

First the discus
rose to view,
then the conch,
the long bow,
the mace,
and the sword;
with blessings
from the eight quarters,
he broke through
the egg-shell of heaven,
making the waters bubble;
giant head and giant feet
growing away from each other,
time itself rose to view:
how the lord
paced and measured

all three worlds!
— Ramanujan 1981: 108

In the same context, Ramanujan says that "the (early *bhakti*) poems blend the erotic, the heroic and the sacred as later *bhakti* poems do". Here again the idea is that all the signifiers drawn from these discursive fields which earlier helped to innumerate the qualities of the kings now were turned towards service to God through *bhakti* poetry.

To say the least, *bhakti* works, in fact, draw upon the collective unconscious of a whole race and contain innumerable frames of references belonging to innumerable semiotic fields thereby generating innumerable layers of meanings, which are then conveyed across to different time and space zones.

More on Intersemiotic Transformations

Translation across languages and forms constitutes an important part of medieval art and literature in India. The attainment of literary status on the part of different literary languages, it has been observed, resulted from the translations from Sanskrit/Prākr̥t into various regional languages. However, the translation endeavour of the medieval period was much more than merely translations of influential texts like the *Rāmāyaṇa*, the *Mahābhārata* and other Jaina and Buddhist texts from Sanskrit and Prākr̥t. The exchange through translation during this period involves the exchange of forms and styles not only between languages but also across genres. We have to contend here with a great deal of translations across languages (interlingual translations) and within the languages (intralingual translations). Beyond this, we enter the domain of what Roman Jacobson designated by the term Inersemiotic Translation. The Sanskrit *Rāmāyaṇa* was not only translated into regional languages like Tamil and Braj, for instance, but such literary texts were transformed into the genres of theatre as in the case of *Rāmalīlā* of the north and

Kathakali of the south, which was originally called Rāmanaṭṭam (the Rāma Play). These theatrical translations of sacred stories were again subjected to re-enactment through non-human forms of theatre-like string and shadow puppet plays.

The *bhakti* traditions of the medieval period were, except in Bengal, for the most part inspired by either Śaivism or Vaiṣṇavism. The literary and aesthetic expressions of these movements bear a special relation to the sacred narratives of these traditions. The *Bhāgavata Purāṇa* and the *Rāmāyaṇa* became the storehouses of episodes, characters, symbols and metaphors in the aesthetic expressions of Vaiṣṇava schools of *bhakti*. Similarly, symbols and metaphors of the sacred stories of Śiva are re-enacted in Śaivite *bhakti* expressions. The compositions of Āḻvārs of Tamil Nadu retell the key episodes of Kṛṣṇa/Viṣṇu/Rāma stories from the *Viṣṇu Purāṇa* and *Rāmāyaṇa*. This in itself can be seen as an act of intersemiotic translation, as the sacred narratives are translated into compositions of devotional lyricism. The Tamil Śaivite compositions of *Tevaram* time and again allude to the central episodes of *Śiva Purāṇa*.

The translation exchange in pre-modern India was of a different nature than it is understood to be today. The genre of translation of the period was closer in meaning to what we now consider adaptation. The source text was only a spring board for a free and imaginative reconstruction in a new language or form. Fidelity to the original was not at all necessary, at least not in terms of textual fidelity.

To get a glimpse into a pre-modern translation which always coalesces into creative expression, we can consider briefly Āṇḍāḷ's *Tirupāvvai*. Here translation also happens between two cultures and landscapes. In stanza IV, which is a hymn to Lord Viṣṇu, who is extolled as the source and symbol of fertility, one finds the Vedic concept of the rain-bearing

God Indra and the fertility God of the Tamil land coalescing into each other:

> O Dark-rain-cloud! Dear as Kṛṣṇa!
> pray reveal yourself in full measure. Enter the deep ocean, gorge yourself, roar and ascend high: darken like the hue of the primaeval Lord Padmanābha, Strike like the resplendent discus on his mighty shoulder, roar with thunder like the great conch in his hand, come pouring down on us like arrows cast from his Śārṅga bow, that we too may live, and enjoy the bath festival of Mārgaḷi.
>
> — Srirama Bharti 2000: 94

Also the whole poem rivets on the interesting transformation of a pre-Vaiṣṇavite fertility ritual, *Pavai* into an expression of Vaiṣṇavite devotional rite.

In the Vaiṣṇavite tradition, the stanza quoted above is further translated into a ritualistic act because this is the stanza recited in Śrīvaiṣṇava temples when the sacred idol is given *abhiṣekam*. This clearly shows that *bhakti* texts inhabit spaces of transformations across languages, cultures and genres.

The indebtedness of *bhakti* expressions to the heritage of the sacred lore is no doubt vital for *bhakti* movements where the *saguṇa* (form with attributes) element is dominant. But to say that this is true of all *bhakti* movements is an oversimplification. "Does the Śiva temple made of ice have a cupola of sunlight?" asks Allama, the twelfth-century Kannada saint-poet. The two processes of imagination involved in *saguṇa* and *nirguṇa* types of *bhakti* are concisely expressed in a paradox oft-quoted in Vīraśaiva texts of Karnataka: "The *bhakta* makes a temple out of void whereas the *jñānī* makes void out of the temple". In other words, *saguṇa bhakti* emphasizing the dualistic nature of the devotee and the deity and in a way "imagines" the deity whereas *nirguṇa bhakti* "de-imagines" the same phenomenon. This paradox is most gnomically expressed in a couplet of saint Kabīr:

> *jala meiṅ kumbha kumbha meiṅ jala hai, bāhara bhītara pānī*
> *phūṭā kumbha jala jala hi samānā, yeh tath kaho jñānī* ||

> Earthenpot is in the water, water is in the earthenpot
> Water is inside as well as outside
> Pot breaks and water merges with water
> The wise have said this truth.
>
> — Mukund Dwivedi 1981: 237

Though the conflicts between form and formlessness are recognized in *bhakti* traditions, the embodied and the imagined is not considered despicable as in Judaic traditions. Again as Allama says in one of his *vacana*s:

> *Both Form and Formless*
> *Are abstractions*
> *One is invocation and the other dissolution*
> *One is involvement, the other non-involvement*
> *Beyond both these means*
> *"Is Goggeśvara"*
>
> — tr. H.S. Shivaprakash

Allama recognizes that *saguṇa* and *nirguṇa*, the concrete and the abstract, the embodied and the un-embodied are both imperfect translations of the ultimate formless reality to which he too paradoxically gives a local appellation, "Goggeśvara".

Elsewhere he also talks about how one has to transcend the "symbol" (*kuruhu*) with "awareness" (*aruhu*). Viewed in this light, the *bhakti* imagination involves a translation between "image" (*prati*) and non-image (*aprati*). "They are making Images for the non-Image which has no image" (*pratiyilladapratige pratiya maduvarayya*).

In this sense, the *bhakti* traditions are keenly aware of the playful and tentative nature of the verbal and the non-verbal expression situated in a web of translations. The recognition, the translation and creativity, the concrete and the abstract, form and formless, the speakable and the unspeakable are interdependent and interfluent, is the very basis of the poetics and aesthetics built into the work of *bhakti* poets. Even when concepts, images and the materials are taken from an earlier source, they are translated into the individual context of *bhakti* experience and expression. Even deities are translated. Thus the primal God Śiva is translated in *Tevaram* into the heart enchanting locales of temples of the Tamil country. However the same Śiva is translated into diverse manifestations of this principle in the *aṅkita*s, i.e. the signature lines of Vīraśaiva poets of Karnataka. For the cowherd saint Ramanna, Śiva is the cosmic cowherd. For Akkā Mahādevī, He is sometimes paramour, sometimes husband, sometimes father, sometimes *guru* and sometimes God. Both the inevitability and the futility of the endless chain of translations is inscribed into *vacana* texts. In Āṇḍāḷ's poems also many roles that Viṣṇu as Kṛṣṇa takes up in the mythology are translated into a personal understanding of Kṛṣṇa's love for His *bhakta*s. In a way, Āṇḍāḷ explores not only her own relationship with Kṛṣṇa but also how Kṛṣṇa relates to her in all His dynamism. When she becomes the simple *gopikā*, she belongs to the entire community and seeks Kṛṣṇa's compassion; but as a bride, she would not be contented with anything less than her sole right over Him as her husband.

6

Āṇḍāḷ
Śrīvaiṣṇavite Woman Āḻvār Saint

ĀṆḌĀḶ was born in Srivelliputtur in Tirunelveli district of Tamil Nadu in mid-eighth century CE. According to the legend associated with her life, Viṣṇucitta Āḻvār, the head priest in the Srivelliputtur Temple, found this baby girl in his *tulasī* grove (basil-garden). He brought up the girl with enormous affection and care, thinking of her to be a gift of God.

Āṇḍāḷ grew up in Viṣṇucitta's household in a very pious and devotional atmosphere. In Āṇḍāḷ's time *bhakti* (devotion) had already captured the imagination of the people as senior Nāyaṉmār and Āḻvār saints had already been singing in rapture the songs of love for God. According to Prema Nandkumar:

> Āṇḍāḷ grew up at a time when the Bhakti movement was in its noon-day glory. The first group of Āḻvārs had sung of the Lord in manifold ways, and the general public fondly repeated these songs as though they were the Tamil versions of Vedas, for the songs were musical, literary and above all, embedded with the wisdom of the ages. To Āṇḍāḷ and her companions singing the *pāsurams* must have been a favourite pastime.
>
> — *Devotional Poets and Mystics*, 1978, repr. 1991: 47

Āṇḍāḷ's foster father Viṣṇucitta was a great poet and saint (one of the Āḻvārs himself) and under his tutelage Āṇḍāḷ must have received knowledge about the legends of Viṣṇu and his *avatāras*. Myths about her say that her consciousness was so infused with the *saṁskāras* of *bhakti* and devotion from a very tender age, that when she precociously fell in love with Kṛṣṇa *avatāra* of Viṣṇu, she adored herself with the garland that her father kept for the temple deity. She must have felt that she had all the right to wear it. This act, which according to the sacred injunctions would be considered as an act of grievous sin, was given a legitimate sanction by the Lord himself who appeared in Viṣṇucitta's dream and commanded him that henceforth only the garlands worn by Goda (Āṇḍāḷ) would be acceptable to Him. After this sign of confirmation of reciprocation of her love from the Lord, Āṇḍāḷ now was immersed in emotion of intense love for Him and craved for a union with her *iṣṭa*. In her life Āṇḍāḷ achieved this goal of union with her chosen Lord at Śrīraṅgam. Viṣṇucitta Āḻvār is directed in a dream to prepare for Āṇḍāḷ's marriage with the Lord. Accordingly, Āṇḍāḷ decked up as a bride, is taken to Śrīraṅgam in a procession in a palanquin. When she reaches Śrīraṅgam, she goes into the sanctum and sees her Lord Nārāyaṇa lying on Ananta, she goes forward and merges into the figure of her *iṣṭa*.

This is the story of her life as it comes down to us through various myths and legends. She attained the status of an Āḻvār saint and was the only woman among eleven Āḻvār saints. She is considered to be a reincarnation of Viṣṇu's consort Bhūdevī. Hence her statue finds place next to that of Viṣṇu in the *sanctum sanctorum* of many of the Śrīvaiṣṇava temples. All the other Āḻvār saints are generally placed together in a much peripheral place in the *prākāra* of a temple.

Āṇḍāḷ's Mādhurya Bhakti

Āṇḍāḷ had composed two poems *Tiruppāvai* and *Nachiar Tirumoḻi* and both of them display the *mādhurya bhāva* which means that she addresses the God as her Lover in these poems and describes her feelings as a beloved of her Lord. These poems are like two beautiful garlands of thirty *pāsurams* and 143 *pāsurams*, respectively. These two poems reveal that a very evolved consciousness is at work here. *Tiruppāvai* is a single narrative poem with thirty song stanzas (*pāsurams*) and *Nachiar Tirumoḻi* is a song-sequence of fourteen poems with ten *pāsurams* (stanzas) each. In *Tiruppāvai,* the theme is a journey to the house of Lord for a meeting with Him (union with the Chosen One). In *Nachiar Tirumoḻi* the theme is more openly *viraha-bhāva* (sentiment of love in separation) for the chosen one (Kṛṣṇa). In *Tiruppāvai* songs can be conventionally categorized as *mādhurya bhakti* because here the poetic personae are none else but *gopikās* and Kṛṣṇa (the classical source and reference point of *mādhurya bhakti* begin with Kṛṣṇa and the *gopikās*). However, the songs in *Nachiar Tirumoḻi* sequence are a standard example of "bridal mysticism" or *viraha bhakti* (which is often not distinguished from *mādhurya bhakti*) because these songs describe the anguish of a beloved/*bhakta*/bride from her *iṣṭa*. *Viraha bhakti* is the chief sentiment that runs through most of the *bhakti* poetry. Here, the *bhakta* (devotee) in the role of God's beloved/bride expresses her deep anguish due to the separation from her Lover/God.

In *Nachiar Tirumoḻi,* the *bhakta* Āṇḍāḷ is madly seeking her Husband/Lover who is none other than Kṛṣṇa Himself. In this poem she exercises her exclusive rights as a wife/beloved on Him. She chides Him, abuses Him, pleads to Him and wants Him intensely. But in *Tiruppāvai,* compassion for the community is privileged over individual passion and the *bhakta* Āṇḍāḷ feels the bond with her friends and wants all of them as well as the rest of the community to partake of the grace that flows after the ritual (*pavai*) is undertaken.

It is evident that while *Nachiar Tirumoḻi* celebrates intense personal emotion for the God, *Tiruppāvai* celebrates the common human bond within the community and then that of the community with the God. *Nachiar Tirumoḻi* is exclusive in approach, *Tiruppāvai* is inclusive in approach. *Tiruppāvai* is generally treated as an earlier composition and *Nachiar Tirumoḻi* follows thereafter. However, a close reading indicates that since *Tiruppāvai* is a poem about a rendezvous with Kṛṣṇa and *Nachiar Tirumoḻi* is one about the desire to have a meeting with Him, *Nachiar Tirumoḻi* could easily be sequenced as a composition written prior to *Tiruppāvai*. Also song compositions of *Tiruppāvai* are more intricate and esoteric in nature. The later part of this study discusses in detail various elements that go into making *Tiruppāvai* a highly complex yet a very refined act of creative poetic expression.

To say it differently, songs in *Tiruppāvai* and *Nachiar Tirumoḻi* are about an intense desire to merge with God physically as well as metaphysically. In *Nachiar Tirumoḻi* she depicts various episodes of her love affair with God Himself. In the fourteen decads of *Nachiar Tirumoḻi*, the sixth one is extremely popular where Āṇḍāḷ is depicting the dream of her marriage to the God:

> *I had a dream O Sister! The town was decked*
> *with festoons and golden urns.*
> *Sorrounded by a thousand caparisoned elephants*
> *our Lord Nārāyaṇa came walking towards me.*
> — Srirama Bharti 2000: 112

The sequence called *varṇamayiram* is considered very auspicious in Tamil Nadu and is sung at the time of wedding by the priest. This particular sequence is significant, as Āṇḍāḷ describes every rite and ritual of marriage in minutest detail revealing the divine bridegroom in all His Glory. In this song, she is actually describing the vision of the Lord as seen by her in the dream. She is sharing her revelation with us through her song. Thus, the entire poem becomes a medium for expression of an experience of *bhakti* which is not accessible to a non-*bhakta*.

The poem *Tiruppāvai* is also about the significance of living in higher realms of awareness. The entire poem is a very complex work of art which enjoins in itself a highly symbolic design of a theological base. *Bhakti,* as it has been conceived in Vaiṣṇavism, is expounded in the scheme of the poem in all its subtlety. Apparently the poem is a simple song of celebration, among the *sakhīs*, *gopikās* (friends), of a ritual which is a portent of prosperity and fulfilment for all of them. However, just a closer look at the structure and one can see the subtle message of the poem which is to dissolve lower forms of desires into the highest desire, i.e. to become one with the God.

Eric J. Lott in his essay "The Divine Drum: Interpreting a Primal Symbol" describes how the girls in *Tiruppāvai* initially ask for *parai* (the drum) along with other material graces from Kṛṣṇa as a consequence to successful realization of their Margali bath ritual. The "drum" signifies the meaner desires. It is understood as "what we desire" or as a "paltry thing". The etymological meaning of *parai* (= lowly, mean) thus being brought out (*Sri Āṇḍāḷ* 1985: 35). In stanza 26 of *Tiruppāvai,* Āṇḍāḷ says:

> We have performed the Margali rites as our elders decreed. Now hear what we want: conches like your milk-white *pāñcajanya* which reverberates through all creation with its booming sound, a big wide drum and singers, who sing *pallaṇḍu,* a bright lamp, festoons and flags, — O Lord, grant us these.

But as the poem progresses further, this desire is taken over by a single overriding desire which is to be with Kṛṣṇa and be with Him in all the births.

> Know that these goods are not what we came for. Through seven lives and forever we would be close to you and serve you alone. And if our desires be different, you must change them.
>
> — Stanza 29

There are two important suggestions here — one that the *bhakta* values the *sānidhya* (togetherness) of God above everything else and two that once the revelation of God has been experienced, all lowly desires are automatically shed off. This is the purifying effect of God's company.

Lott comments in this respect:

> The more usual Vaiṣṇava position is (that) the lesser life-goals (e.g. the pastoral concerns of verses 3 and 4) are not in themselves evils; they are rather good and valuable. Yet what is needed above all is the vision of everything in life utterly dependent upon the grace of the Lord . . . God's gracious aid is essential, therefore (we are) to move from one level of life-goal to this highest level in which all the lesser goals eventually become included. To use more traditional language, *sādhanā* (means of worship) *bhakti* needs to be transposed into *sādhya* (that which is the goal of worship) *bhakti*; God as *upāya* (means) is to be experienced as final *upeya* (goal). — *Śrī Āṇḍāḷ* 1985: 39

As said earlier, in Āṇḍāḷ's *bhakti* scheme *mādhurya bhāva* was predominant as it fell into place naturally due to her gender. To experience this *bhāva* (sentiment) might have been primarily an act of pure imagination for other Āḻvārs as all of them were males. For *bhakta*s like Āṇḍāḷ, it was extremely important to ascribe a specific form to God, as without conceiving the form they could not relate to Him.

What transformations Āṇḍāḷ effects in inherited conventions and beliefs through her *mādhurya*-centred compositions and how other genres of art and culture integrate Āṇḍāḷ's life and works will be dealt with in the next chapter.

7

Transformations in Āṇḍāḷ's Life and Work

Āṇḍāḷ's Nachiar Tirumoḷi Celebrating Desire through Transformation of Classical Love Elements into Sentiment of Bhakti

THE fourteen ***pāsurams*** of *Nachiar Tirumoḷi* offer a glimpse of various possibilities of *bhakta*'s love for God in *mādhurya bhāva,* specifically "bridal mysticism". If removed from their context, these poems can be read as intense love poems complete with carnal passion. However, as soon as they are put in their original composition context, they become ecstatic songs of extreme longing for the God. These songs are a celebration of human desire, which becomes sacred when directed towards the Chosen One. The passion for God presupposes *vairāgya* (detachment), which is absent in common man–woman relationship. In *bhakti* dynamics *vairāgya* and sense of desire and passion go hand in hand. While *vairāgya* manifests itself for the objects of the material world, passionate desire manifests for the Chosen God. In *bhakti,* the equation between *vairāgya* and the "passion for God" is directly proportional, more *vairāgya* means more intimate desire for the God. Less *vairāgya* means less intimacy with the God. That is why, in *bhakti,* passion is a sacred sentiment, as the object of passion is the Creator Himself.

Āṇḍāḷ frankly sings about her desires as a young woman craving for the union with her lover. But she places these desires in a higher context, where the object of the desire is transcendental and therefore the desire also loses its limiting carnal aspiration. Āṇḍāḷ creates this intense *bhakti* sentiment in *Nachiar Tirumo̤ḻi* by drawing her images from Viṣṇu mythology and her form from the classical *aham* (love) poetry in Tamil. Besides frank expression of passion, two other significant features of the classical Tamil love poetry that Āṇḍāḷ makes use of are: making the nature an important character in the poems and using the dialogic form (every poem in *Nachiar Tirumo̤ḻi* is an address to someone or something). Consider, for instance, the following poem from *aham* tradition:

> *What She Said*
> *Like milk*
> *not drunk by the calf,*
> *not held in a pail,*
> *a good cow's sweet milk*
> *spilled on the ground,*
> *it is of no use to me,*
> *unused by my man:*
> *my mound of love,*
> *my beauty*
> *dark as mango leaf,*
> *just waiting*
> *to be devoured*
> *by pallor.*
> — Kuruntokai 27 (Ramanujan 1985: 69)

and the following one from the thirteenth *pāsuram* of *Nachiar Tirumo̤ḻi*:

> *I weep and pray; the fellow does not even show his face to say,*
> *"Fear not", nor ever comes to caress, embrace, roll and leave.*
> *Grazing cows in the dense forest, he plays his flute endlessly.*
> *Go bring the trickle from its hole and wipe the fever from my brow.*
> — "Last Wishes", *Nachiar Tirumo̤ḻi*, 13: 5, from *Nālāyira-Divya-Prabandham* (Srirama Bharti 2000: 125)

This passion gets heightened in the eighth verse of the same (13th) hymn where she says:

> The Lord of Govardhana my lover is a terrible highway bandit. While I pine away, he does not care to inquire if I am living or dead. If ever I see that rogue, I shall tear these worthless breasts of mine by their roots, and fling them on his beautiful chest, then settle my score with him.
>
> — "Last Wishes" *Nachiar Tirumoḻi*. 13.8 from *Nālāyira-Divya-Prabandham* (Srirama Bharti 2000: 126)

All the poems quoted above are similar in their expression of desire as well in making use of the dialogue as a poetic tool. However, in last two verses, which are by Āṇḍāḷ, the context is *bhakti*.

Nature is another intimate component in ancient Tamil poetic form, which is used by Āṇḍāḷ extensively in her compositions. Alexander M. Dubianski discusses the characteristics of all the five love *tinai*s (themes) in the Tamil love poetry in detail.[1] Each theme be it pre-marital clandestine love, separation in love or union in love is associated with plants or flowers characteristic of the respective landscapes. Therefore *kuriñci, mullai, palai, marutam* and *naytaḷa* are themes as well as landscapes in various geographical regions in the Tamil land. Āṇḍāḷ makes use of nature in a way very different but not entirely independent of Tamil classical resources.[2]

---

1 Alexander M. Dubianski, *Ritual and Mythological Sources of the Early Tamil Poetry*, The Netherlands: Egbert Forsten, 2000, pp. 79-171.

2 Vidya Dehejia in a small note on "Āṇḍāḷ and Tamil Caṅkam Poetry" confirms this point. She talks about *Nachiar Tirumoḻi* poems in this section and says that:

Āṇḍāḷ speaks of the *tenral* (southern breeze) and *tinkal* (Moon) adding to the sorrows of love (*Nachiar Tirumoḻi,* hymn 5, verse 10) — an age-old theme of Tamil love poetry. She refers to the concept of *peruntinai* or excessive love which breaks the rules of social →

Āṇḍāḷ, like other *bhakti* poets, does not express her love directly in the love conventions which use natural landscape as a stage where drama of love unfolds in the *aham* poetry but some of the conventions naturally sieve down into her expression, which are then transformed by her in her own way. For instance, the idea of addressing the female friend and sharing with her the agonies of love and betrayal by the beloved, can be traced back to the *kuriñci* theme which focuses on pre-marital love, which should be kept "hidden" (*kalavu*). In this theme, the love is not to be revealed. It is kept a secret and can be revealed only to lover's close friend or heroine's close friend or confidante. Āṇḍāḷ uses this convention in both her works but refines it according to her need. In *Tiruppāvai*, this convention comes only as a formal device but in *Nachiar Tirumoḻi* she makes a very expansive use of this device to express her feelings for her chosen Lord. She makes every perceived object in nature her confidante and addresses living or non-living beings with equal urgency and urges them to take her message to her beloved or find a way of union with Him.

In fact, the *Nachiar Tirumoḻi* song sequence uses aspects of nature and interweaves these images with the mythology and classical form of Tamil love poems. This leads to an excessively intense expression of bridal mysticism. Āṇḍāḷ sees the entire world with all its creatures in the light of her relation with the God. Kāmadeva, the God of Love, is worshipped, *koel* bird is chided; ocean, rainclouds, *kayā* flowers, white conch, peacock, friends, relatives all are invoked in a *bhakti* context,

→ decorum, when she speaks of word getting round that she left her home and family and went to her beloved (*Nachiar Tirumoḻi* hymn 12, verse 3). She displays an intensive awareness of nature, which is a hallmark of Caṅkam poetry as is evident from A.K. Ramanujan's very choice of title for his translations of those classical poems — "The Interior Landscape" (Dehejia 1990: 23).

where they all remind her of her beloved. The simplicity of the verses arises from the use of very common images from nature and from Kṛṣṇa myths. Āṇḍāḷ cleverly sings praises of her Kannan while expressing her deep desire to become one with Him and no one else.

> *The Lord took water from Bali's palms; in one stride,*
> *He took the earth as well. Living among good people*
> *in Araṅgam, he plans to plunder us poor folk now.*
> — "A Delirius State", *Nachiar Tirumoḻi, 11 Nālāyira-Divya-Prabandham* (Srirama Bharti 2000: 121)

And

> *Take a look at these breasts of mine,*
> *They are blindfolded by a red-corset. Seeking the*
> *conch-wielding lord alone, they shun the sight of*
> *petty mortals. Since they will not enter another household,*
> *end this life of mine here, and take me to the banks of Jamunā.*
> — "Entreaty to the World", *Nachiar Tirumoḻi, 12 Nālāyira-Divya-Prabandham* (Srirama Bharti 2000: 123)

In *Nachiar Tirumoḻi*, Āṇḍāḷ is making use of devices of Tamil *aham* poetry. At the same time these images create a fit framework for the bridal-mystic *bhakti* form.

Tiruppāvai: Bhakti Text as Many Layered Intersemiotic Transformations

As Āṇḍāḷ is a Viṣṇu *bhakta*, the frame of reference in her poetry is constructed from the whole gamut of Viṣṇu mythology as expounded in classical, folk, religious and literary sources.[3]

However, the most important frame of reference for Āṇḍāḷ's poetry, especially in songs of *Tiruppāvai*, is provided by the Kṛṣṇa and Gopikās episode in Gokula and Vṛndāvana.

---

[3] Upaniṣads, Purāṇas (*Harivaṁśa, Brahma* and *Viṣṇu*), *Sattasai*, Tamil epics *Cilappadikāram* and *Maṇimekalai.*

This episode occurs in all the three purāṇas that predate Āṇḍāḷ — *Harivaṁśa, Brahma* and *Viṣṇu*. With slight differences of tone, the intention appears to be the same in all the three narratives. Kṛṣṇa is the incarnation of the Supreme Being conceived as Viṣṇu and therefore *gopikās*' love for Him refers to a mystical union with Him.

Āṇḍāḷ was thoroughly familiar with the Purāṇic material. How she gained access to this material remains debatable. One important clue in this regard is given by her foster father Viṣṇucitta Āḻvār, who had been composing and singing songs of Kṛṣṇa based on stories found in these Purāṇas.[4] It is

---

[4] We are referring here to *Viṣṇu* and *Brahma Purāṇa* and *Harivaṁśa* as they are major Purāṇas which narrate "Kṛṣṇa-Carita" and Kṛṣṇa and *gopikā* episode also. The *Bhāgavata Purāṇa* which is the most celebrated text on Kṛṣṇa's life cannot be taken into account as it postdates Āṇḍāḷ. It is dated as a tenth century text, while other Purāṇas are placed before fifth century.

It should be noted here that Kṛṣṇa and *gopikā* episode is found in a very elementary form in *Harivaṁśa Purāṇa* and it appears to be an adaptation of some folk performance or regional narrative. It is an erotic tale of love and longing. A brief summary of the episode is as follows:

On an autumn night of full moon, Kṛṣṇa is inclined to participate in *gopikās*' sports; he plays mesmerizing tune on his flute; all the *gopikās* leave their household and are drawn to the *Vṛndāvana*; Kṛṣṇa welcomes these love-lorn cowherdesses but soon disappears leaving them pining for him; imitating his acts and calling out to him; seeing them in such distress he manifests himself again and then follows the famous *rāsa-nṛtya*. After this night of longing and consummation, Kṛṣṇa goes away with Balarāma to Mathurā leaving the *gopikās* back in Vṛndāvana.

In *Brahma Purāṇa*, it appears in some of the text variations as an interpolation. In *Viṣṇu Purāṇa* this episode is rendered more suitably as a part of a larger whole. In *Viṣṇu Purāṇa* theological elements are dispersed in the tale:

"One (*gopī*), as she sallied forth, be held some of the seniors of the →

interesting to note, that Viṣṇucitta's songs touch stories found in these Purāṇas. Viṣṇucitta's songs also touch upon all the aspects of *viraha-bhakti*. Many of Viṣṇucitta's songs refer to the effect of Kṛṣṇa's presence and His music on the *gopikās*:

→ family, and dared not venture, contenting herself with meditating on Kṛṣṇa with closed eyes and entire devotion, by which immediately all acts of merit were effaced by rapture, and sin was expiated by regret at not beholding him: and others, again reflecting upon the cause of the world, in the form of supreme Brahman, obtained by their singing final emancipation."

— *Viṣṇu Purāṇa*, chapter 13, p. 424

At the end of the chapter, it is further expained:

"Thus the illimitable being, the benevolent remover of all imperfections, assumed the character of a youth amongst the females of the herdsmen of Vraja, pervading their natures, and that of their lords, by his own essence, all diffusive like the wind: for even as in all creatures the elements of ether, fire, earth, water and air, are comprehended, so also is he everywhere present, and in all." — *Viṣṇu Purāṇa*, p. 426

However it is only later in the *Bhāgavata Purāṇa* that a complete theological symbolism is added to the whole episode of what in this text is called as *mahārāsa*. A critique of this episode is given by Friedhelm Hardy:

"The version of the *gopī* story which we find in *BrP* (*Brahma Purāṇa*) and in a slightly longer form in *ViP* (*Viṣṇu Purāṇa*) is the first example of a full narrative treatment of the episode, and at the same time, of a religious interpretation in terms of normative ideology. The myth itself has become enriched by two major themes, the *rasa* dance and final *viraha*. The author has remained faithful to his source, the *Hv* (*Harivaṁśa*) by ignoring the figure of Rādhikā and the *gopī*s' jealousy, but by emphasizing *viraha* theme and sublimating *gopī*s' love as a form of *bhakti-yoga* he has removed the earthiness of the original story and eliminated the primary importance of Kṛṣṇa's physical presence among the *gopī*s and of their sensual perception of him." — Hardy 1983: 104

> When Govinda played his flute, he threw his weight on his left shoulder; his two hands came together; his eyebrows knitted, his belly rose, his mouth closed in. Deer-like and peacock-like maidens, their flowered coiffure loosening, their dress slipping, their *sāṛīs* held with one hand, stood shyly apart, running their collyrium-lined eyes over him.
>
> — Viṣṇucitta Āḻvār "The Lord Plays His Flute", in Srirama Bharti 2000: 54

In another *pāsuram*:

> The cowherd lord who lifted the mount and protected the cows has played his flute all day long to graze his calves. He comes back with his fellows, down the street. O Sister, come and see! I have never seen such a one before! My dress has loosened, my bangles do not stay, my young risen breasts are not in my control.
>
> — Viṣṇucitta Āḻvār "Maidens on Seeing the Lord", in Srirama Bharti 2000: 49

Then there are songs in Viṣṇucitta Āḻvār's oeuvre which cover all the myths found in "Kṛṣṇa Carita" and also some about "Ram Carita".The following song is a typical example of how myths about Kṛṣṇa's life are integrated in Āḻvārs' songs:

> The lord who destroyed the sinister *arjuna* trees, the angry elephant, the asura Pralamba, the fierce horse Keśin, the cart that ran amuck, and mighty wrestlers — as simply as the pots he broke to enjoy the sounds they made — resides in Tiruaraṅgam. He lifts devotees into the realms of the radiant Sun with a tall ladder-of-no-return, reveals himself and takes them into his service in Vaikuṇṭha.
>
> — Viṣṇucitta Āḻvār "About the Temple in Sriraṅgam", in Srirama Bharti 2000: 80

It can be fairly assumed that since Āṇḍāḷ was brought up in this household where songs about God's life were routine, she had integrated these myths in her life and her philosophy of *bhakti*. Later she herself sung some of the sweetest symphonies ever composed in *bhakti* tradition, expressing her own desire to merge with the Divine.[5] Her evolution as a *bhakta* must have been influenced by the circumstances in which her life was spent. Āṇḍāḷ's childhood was spent in the house of Viṣṇucitta or Periāḷvār, who was a temple priest when he found Godai as an infant in his garden. He was a great *bhakta*. Therefore, the atmosphere, in which Āṇḍāḷ was brought up, had the local temple of Śrīvelliputtur at the centre of its activities. This same temple was also probably the location of Viṣṇucitta's house, which might have been situated in one corner of the premises. She grew up seeing her father lovingly weaving flower garlands for the deity in the temple and adoring the God in various ways including singing His glories through his songs. As her father loved the temple deity, it became very natural for the little girl to look up to the same

[5] In order to understand Āṇḍāḷ's experience and her expression in her poetry from *bhakti* perspective, one can make use of an analytical mode which can be applied to all endeavours that humans take up to achieve something. Let us first understand it through an analogy of feeling of hunger and its satiation. When one feels hungry, then this feeling becomes the stimulus for search for food involving perhaps gathering of raw food items. Then these food items would be subjected to the process of cooking or some other kind of processing. After the food has been cooked one eats it and experiences the fulfilment of having eaten.

Now if we translate this analogy to *bhakti* poetics, it can be said that the hungry person is the *bhakta* or *sādhaka* or more generally the seeker who is seeking fulfilment in life in order to satiate the deep-seated hunger in his/her soul. He/she takes help of some means (*sādhana*s or instruments), by adopting these means he/she undergoes some *saṁskāra* (processing) and finally he/she attains the goal or *sādhya* (which is realization of God or fulfilment in case of *bhakti*). This can be shown with the help of a figure as follows:

Sādhaka (seeker) — (takes up) → *sādhanā* (spiritual practice) — (through some) → *sādhana*s (means) — (undergoes) → *saṁskāra* (*rite de passage*) — (and attains) → *sādhya* (goal).

deity as someone very important in her life and later as a grown up girl she wanted to experience the presence of this same God in a more manifest form.

Hence, to look at Āṇḍāḷ's situation in the above perspective, Āṇḍāḷ is the seeker (the *sādhaka*) who wants to experience the reality of God as her personal God. She begins her search with the help of the means that were in ample in her living atmosphere — temple deity, myths about Him and songs sung in His praise.

These means were part of her cultural tradition as well as her parental heritage. These "means" (*sādhana*s) were none other than the path of *bhakti* and ecstatic singing in praise of the Lord.

The path of *bhakti* as related in the experience of *bhakta*s is the path, where the goal can be experienced while still being in the path itself and the seeker can enjoy the *anubhava* or God experience at any stage in his/her journey. The goal for the *bhakta* is to be eternally in the company of the loved One. Before this goal is finally achieved, there can be other desires which will shed off on their own in the path. *Bhakta*'s steadfast approach will finally immerse him/her in the experience of loving union.

In *Tiruppāvai*, Āṇḍāḷ is moving with her friends to the house of the Lord. On this journey they set out with desires which they wish that the Lord would fulfil. Until they reach the house and come face-to-face with the Lord inside the *garbhagṛha* (*sanctum sanctorum*), they keep their wishes intact. Therefore Āṇḍāḷ asks for the objects, which can be used to offer worship to the Lord and other-worldly blessings like prosperity and "measureless wealth".

In stanza 26, Āṇḍāḷ clearly states what her group of cowherd girls want:

> Now hear what we want: conches like your milk-white *pāñcajanya* which reverberates through all creation with its booming sound, a big wide drum, and singers who sing *pallaṇḍu*, a bright lamp, festoons and flags — O Lord — grant us these boons.

However, after seeing the Lord, all the extraneous desires just drop off and she appeals to him to grant them nothing else but the boon of loving service to Him, i.e. *bhakti* in all their lives:

> Know that these goods are not what we came for. Through seven lives and forever we would be close to you, and serve you alone. And if our desires be different, you must change them. — *Tiruppāvai,* 29; Srirama Bharti 2000: 102

Closeness to their God bestows such fulfilment on them that now they do not need anything from this world and so cannot ask for any other boon but to be with Him in all their births.[6] Union (*sākṣātkāra*) with God gives the *bhakta* such a sense of completeness and oneness with all creation that all desires disappear. It is this mystery about *bhakti,* which makes it such a fascinating ideal.

Nevertheless, Āṇḍāḷ's *Tiruppāvai* is not a simple song of *gopikās*' love (*bhakti*) for Kṛṣṇa. It is a very rich tapestry of woman's relationship to Unmanifest Supreme. This poem touches so many psychological aspects of human psyche and those of religion, myth and culture, that it is ever pregnant with more than can ever be comprehended from a particular

---

6 It is this state, which is referred to as *prema bhakti,* sage Nārada says in his *sūtra*:

yajjñātvamatto bhavati stabdho bhavatyātmarāmo bhavati ।

"By knowing which [wo]man becomes intoxicated (or overjoyed) peaceful and completely immersed in the enjoyment of the Bliss of *Ātman*".

— *Nārada Bhakti-Sūtras*
Swami Sivananda

time/space zone. It moves in many time/space zones and many cultural/discursive fields.

Āṇḍāḷ's Tiruppāvai (Transformations of Various Cultural and Folk Elements into Bhakti)

At a more visible and grosser level, *bhakti* involves some basic paraphernalia like a temple, its deity (*sādhya*), *bhakta* (*sādhaka*) and means of *bhakti* (*sādhanas*). This paraphernalia is connected to and originates from a larger structure of community and its culture. Variants in this paraphernalia are provided by the community and its historical past and present. Sometimes *bhaktas* like Akkā Mahādevī shed off all these props and create their own path to their Chosen One while *bhaktas* like Āṇḍāḷ use the same paraphernalia to transcend all paraphernalia.

Āṇḍāḷ in her *Tiruppāvai* uses this basic *bhakti* paraphernalia and colours them with elements drawn from her community consciousness. Most of the traditional rituals are transformed into a unique kind of referent for the ideal of *bhakti*.

Mārgaḷi Bathing Ritual: Metaphor of Purification for Bhakti

The *Tiruppāvai* begins with invitation to all the girls of Ayarpadi (a street like a street from classic Gokula) to join each other for "Mārgaḷi" bath festival in the first stanza:

> In the month of Mārgaḷi of auspicious bright moon day, bejewelled girls who would join us for the bath! — come along. Graceful-girls-of-Ayarpadi cowherd clan, Sweet little ones! Nārāyaṇa is son of Nandagopa renowned for his sharp spear and fierce deeds; he is the darling child, lion cub of beautiful-eyed Yaśodā. Our dark-hued, lotus-eyed, radiant moon-faced lord alone will grant us our boons. Girls come, assemble, and win the world's praise.
>
> — *Tiruppāvai*, 1; Srirama Bharti 2000: 93

However, it is the fourth stanza, which explains the real nature of the bath Āṇḍāḷ intends to take with the other girls of her community. Water is a symbol of purification and cleansing. However, water of the river or a pond, which traditionally serves bathing purposes, seems to fall short of the purpose that Āṇḍāḷ wants to accomplish, i.e. to prepare herself and her mates for Kṛṣṇa's *bhakti*. Waters needed for His *bhakti* should have a semblance of His Form. Hence, in the fourth stanza, dark rain cloud, that is associated with Kṛṣṇa, is invoked. Being of the same colour as Kṛṣṇa, it is dear as Him. Different aspects of the journey of the cloud in its cycle on the earth are identified with some aspect of Kṛṣṇa's personality. Then the cloud is lovingly asked to come pouring down on them to soak them fully.[7] The waters of the cloud rain down on them as Kṛṣṇa's grace and all of them are immersed in it:

> O dark-rain cloud! Dear as Kṛṣṇa! Pray reveal yourself in full measure. Enter the deep ocean, gorge yourself, roar and ascend high; darken like the hue of primeval Lord Padmanābha, strike like the resplendent discus on his mighty shoulder, roar with thunder like the great conch in his hand, come pouring down on us like arrows cast from his Sārṅga bow that we too may live, and enjoy the bath festival of Mārgaḷi. — *Tiruppāvai* 4; Srirama Bharti 2000: 94

Āṇḍāḷ transforms above-mentioned ritual of bathing, which originates in the pre-*bhakti* milieu in ancient Tamil culture, purely into a symbol of *bhakti*. In fact, after the first stanza,

---

[7] It is clear that Āṇḍāḷ's bathing (*nīratal*) has a wealth of significance beyond the simple literal bathing suggested by the *pavai* vow. Kṛṣṇa (the Divine) is envisaged as a *tīrtha* (sacred purifying waters), and the "diving deep" is somewhat akin to that envisaged by the term "Āḻvār" as "one who dives deep (into the Divine)".

Only in this context does the absence, in the *Tiruppāvai*, of any description of bathing in physical waters, be it pond, tank, or river, make logical sense. Only then may we understand Āṇḍāḷ's request that Kṛṣṇa should "bathe us now in the waters", to be understood as the divine waters of Kṛṣṇa's grace.

actual bathing is nowhere mentioned in the whole poem. Āṇḍāḷ is certainly speaking of metaphorical bathing in which the *bhakta* dives deep into higher consciousness of God. Incidentally the name Āḻvār, given to this group of Tamil Vaiṣṇava saints including Āṇḍāḷ, has the same meaning — "one who dives deep (into the Divine)".

In fact, some religious readings of the poem suggest that Āṇḍāḷ is actually calling out to other ten Āḻvārs, waking them up into Kṛṣṇa consciousness. This however can be refuted, as many of the Āḻvārs were born after Āṇḍāḷ. Also all of them were great *bhaktas*, inherently so drunk with Viṣṇu *bhakti*, that there was apparently no need to wake them up into an awareness of *bhakti*.

Concept of Pavai Nonbu (Vrata or Vow)

Pavai is the Tamil word for a young girl, a woman, an image, a doll and also for the vow of young woman or vow of *pavai*. Hence, *Tiruppāvai* may mean "sacred woman"and also "sacred vow of woman". As a vow or *vrata*, *pavai* has been an ancient Tamil ritual, the popularity of which is established in literary works of Tamil Saṅgam period and also later Jaina and Śaiva poetry.[8] Ancient Tamil anthology *Paripatal*, belonging to

---

[8] Vidya Dehejia relates that:

"One assumes that it was from a variety of such sources belonging to the early Caṅkam (Saṅgam) anthologies, all of which reflect the popularity of the *pavai* ritual, generally in a secular context, that Āṇḍāḷ found material for her *Tiruppāvai* poems which she adapted to the worship of Kṛṣṇa. Śaiva saint Manikkavacakar probably drew on the same sources for his *Tiruvempavai* in which the god addressed is Śiva. A Jaina *pavai* song of early date, belonging perhaps to the eighth century and addressing the deity as Arivan, has survived as a single verse only, but it contains the essential components of the *pavai* theme. It provides a glimpse into the adaptation of the theme to a religion that stresses world renunciation, →

Saṅgam period, refers to a verse on river "Vaikai", where young maidens gather early in the morning and take bath in cold January waters and then pray for the gift of fine lovers and a number of children. Taking bath in a river or pond is the most significant part of this ritual, fasting, etc. are variants. For instance keeping fast and worshipping the Goddess for a fine husband is a popular ancient Indian custom with women. There are references in *Rāmāyaṇa* and *Mahābhārata* about Sītā and Rukmiṇī, who perform this ritual of fast and worship the Goddess to get in boon their desired husbands, Rāma and Kṛṣṇa, respectively.

In her *Tiruppāvai*, Āṇḍāḷ adapts this ancient Tamil ritual as one of the *sādhana*s (means) to attain her goal of Kṛṣṇa *bhakti*. As other instruments for attaining the same, she does nothing less than re-creating mythical "Gokula" itself as a pastoral idyll, where simple cowherd folk live without vice in complete harmony with each other. Their's is a well-knit community in which everyone shares the same fate. If nature is benevolent, all of them prosper, but if nature turns harsh, they suffer together. Āṇḍāḷ superimposes the image of this mythical "Gokula" (Ayarpadi) on her own town of Śrīvelliputtur, where the local Viṣṇu Temple "Vadaperumkoil" becomes the palace of Kṛṣṇa's foster father Nandagopa and the young girls of the community become the *gopikā*s. Thus the space zone in Śrīvelliputtur is translated into the mythical space of "Gokula". Āṇḍāḷ is aware of the interconnectedness of all human fate

→ and it also highlights the great popularity of the *pavai* tradition in Tamil-speaking region of south India".

— Dehejia 1990: 17

Later in *Bhāgavata Purāṇa* there is a reference to this kind of ritual. Once when the rains fail in Gokula, cowherds ask their young wives and daughters (*gopikā*s) to take up the *vrata* and worship so that the country gets rains in abundance. In the process of worshipping God they attain Kṛṣṇa Himself.

and hence calls out to all her friends (*sakhī*s) to take up the "Nonbu" (*vrata*). Āṇḍāḷ here changes the deity, who is the River Goddess or the Supreme Goddess to her own *iṣṭa* Kṛṣṇa. This *vrata* in her poem is transformed from a ritual for worldly achievement into a symbolic ritual for achievement of Kṛṣṇa *bhakti*. After the symbolic purification of Mārgaḷi bath, which is represented by soaking in the rain cloud and in a way affecting some kind of bodily cleansing, Āṇḍāḷ calls out the girls of Ayarpadi to take more *vrata*s to keep their minds from any kind of distractions:

> O people of the world, pray hear about the vows we undertake. Singing the praise of the Lord who sleeps in the Ocean of Milk, we shall abstain from milk, and *ghee*, and bathe before dawn. We shall not line our eyes with collyrium, nor adorn our hair with flowers. Refraining from forbidden acts, avoiding evil tales we shall give alms and charity in full measure, and pray for the elevation of spirit. Let's rejoice.
>
> — *Tiruppāvai*, 2; Srirama Bharti 2000: 93

Here we witness, what we have defined as *saṁskāra* — a process of adding all that is desirable and removing all that is undesirable. Initially they take these vows in order to prepare themselves for *bhakti* to bring prosperity and wealth to everyone in the community and to redeem it of any ill fate whatsoever, be it a natural calamity or an individual spiritual crisis. However, as the poem progresses these *saṁskara*s become a means to attain Kṛṣṇa.

Rituals of Classical Navadhā Bhakti Transformed into Modes of Poetic Narration

Amongst the nine aspects of *navadhā bhakti* (ninefold *bhakti*) — *śravaṇa, kīrtana, smaraṇa, pādasevana, arcana, vandana, dāsya, sakhya, ātmanivedana* — the first three aspects (*śravaṇa, kīrtana, smaraṇa*) relate to the "Name" of the God; the second three (*pādasevana, arcana, vandana*) relate to the "Form" of the God and the last three (*dāsya, sakhya, ātmanivedana*) are associated with the "Relation" to the God. Āṇḍāḷ makes use of these dimensions of traditional *bhakti* by weaving them into the narrative of her poem *Tiruppāvai*. In the earlier section, we discussed how Āṇḍāḷ transforms a state of mind into a ritual, i.e. the idea to become purified before meeting the God is transformed into a bathing ritual and taking up of some vows. However, in this context one can see how Āṇḍāḷ effects a reversal and how a traditional *bhakti* ritual is transformed into a linguistic mode to become a part of the song, which gives a different lease of life to the ritual itself.

Āṇḍāḷ draws her *sakhi*s attention to the miracle of Kr̥ṣṇa's name, form and relation to them. In fact, singing and chanting the names of Kr̥ṣṇa is one of the main themes of the poem:

> If we come pure and strew fresh flowers, with songs on our lips and feelings in our hearts, and offer praise with joined hands to our Lord Dāmodara — then he will forgive our past misdeeds, and even what remains will disappear like cotton unto fire. So come let us praise him.
>
> — *Tiruppāvai*, 5; Srirama Bharti 2000: 94

The phrase "If we come pure and strew fresh flowers, with songs on our lips and feelings in our hearts and offer praise with joined hands . . . " involves all the characteristics of *arcana* and *vandana*.

The first fifteen stanzas of *Tiruppāvai* are a celebration of Kr̥ṣṇa's names and also of his various forms in different *avatāra*s especially Rāma and Kr̥ṣṇa *avatāra*. Actually all the names of Kr̥ṣṇa originate from the miraculous deeds that he performed during his human stay on the earth. Āṇḍāḷ sings of many names and forms of her multifaceted Lord and by describing various facets of His magnificent being to her *sakhīs*, draws everyone's attention to His Supreme Godhead:

> Nārāyaṇa is the son of Nandagopa renowned for his sharp spear and fierce deeds; he is the darling child, lion cub of beautiful-eyed Yaśodā. Our dark-hued, lotus-eyed, radiant moon-faced Lord alone will grant us our boons. Girls come, assemble, and win the world's praise.
>
> — *Tiruppāvai*, 1; Srirama Bharti 2000: 93

She is in a way describing Kr̥ṣṇa's names, which are associated closely with his Divine actions:

> All the little ones have reached the place of worship singing the praises of the Lord who killed the demon Rāvaṇa and ripped the beaks of the demon-bird Bakāsura.
>
> — *Tiruppāvai*, 13; Srirama Bharti 2000: 97

These ways of *śravaṇa, manana* and *kīrtana* are entirely different from traditional chanting of God's names. Āṇḍāḷ in her own way sings the glories of the Lord's deeds, which is in semblance of traditional modes of *bhakti*. These modes of *śravaṇa, manana* and *kīrtana,* and also those of *pādasevana, arcana* and *vandana,* are transformed by Āṇḍāḷ in her invocations. All these are happening indirectly while calling out and preparing the *sakhī*s for an experience of Kr̥ṣṇa's *bhakti* which leads to liberation.

Just as she transforms the way of talking about the "names" and "forms" of her *iṣṭa*, Kr̥ṣṇa, Āṇḍāḷ also transforms the usual relationship of *gopikā*s to Kr̥ṣṇa as it is given in the Purāṇas and in myths about "Kr̥ṣṇa Carita". Purāṇas and myths talk about the relation of divine love between *gopikā*s and Kr̥ṣṇa, which is described under the rubric of *mādhurya bhāva* in classical *bhakti* poetics. Though Āṇḍāḷ uses the same frame of reference — Kr̥ṣṇa and *gopikā* episode in Gokula — she brings a different kind of bearing to this relation. She changes this relation from one of Lover and beloved to that of Lord and vassal. She addresses Kr̥ṣṇa in one of the songs as follows:

> Like the great kings of the wide world, who came in hordes and stood humbly at your bedstead, we have come to you.
>
> — *Tiruppāvai*, 22; Srirama Bharti 2000: 100

> And you who upset the despot king Kaṁsa's plans and kindled fire in his bowels — you are our master. We have come to pay respects to you. Grant us your favour of measureless wealth and blessed service, that we may end our sorrow and rejoice.
>
> — *Tiruppāvai*, 25; Srirama Bharti 2000: 101

*Gopikā*s in Āṇḍāḷ's *Tiruppāvai* stand in an aspect of humble self-surrender just as a vassal or a subject stands in front of his Lord and King. This change, effected by Āṇḍāḷ in the usual frame of *gopikā*s' *bhakti* attitude to Kṛṣṇa, is very much in keeping with her design and goal in the context of this particular poem. As in *Tiruppāvai*, it is not the individual salvation that is being sought but a kind of liberation for whole of the community. It is a search for bliss and harmony for all those who are related to each other through community living. Āṇḍāḷ makes sure in *Tiruppāvai* that not a single friend of hers is left behind. Using various means of calling out — gentle chiding, making fun, inspiring through example, she wakes up all the *gopikā*s. So the metaphor for waking up of the *gopikā*s, which is traditionally interpreted by some as a waking up of the Āḻvārs saints by Āṇḍāḷ, can be further interpreted as a waking up of the entire community and extendedly the entire human race by her.

Keeping the interests of the community over those of the self was voluntarily taken up as a mission by all saints in the history of *bhakti*. All the saint-poets, who became a part of all-pervading Bhakti movement, communicated the message of equality and fraternity of all human beings regardless of their caste, class, gender and religion. To bind people in love and harmony, and to show them a higher path of love for God through love for fellow beings were taken up and accomplished by all saint-poets.

Time and Space in Tiruppāvai

Āṇḍāḷ's infusion of mythical Gokula onto her own landscape and her use of subtle associations lend *Tiruppāvai*, a deep symbolic meaning. She constantly moves back and forth in time and space to allow for an experience of the three aspects of the Divine: Omnipresence, Omniscience and Omnipotence. Let us consider the following stanza:

> Look, the birds have begun their morning song. Child arise! do you not hear the great booming sound of the snow-white conch in the temple of Viṣṇu, king of the birds? He who drained the ogress Pūtanā's poisoned breasts, and kicked the cart that ran amuck, lies reclining in the Milk Ocean, sages and *yogīs* hold him in their hearts and gently rise, uttering "Hari", deep sound that enters our hearts and makes us rejoice! — *Tiruppāvai*, 6; Srirama Bharti 2000: 95

It becomes clear, how Āṇḍāḷ smoothly passes over to primeval time of creation from the present moment of being. She touches upon the myths about Viṣṇu and connects His various *avatāras* to her own *iṣṭa* Mādhava, Kṛṣṇa. Hence, though Kṛṣṇa has taken birth in a cowherd clan and fortunately lives in Āṇḍāḷ's community, Āṇḍāḷ never loses the awareness of His Omnipresence. Āṇḍāḷ here refers to "Ksheer Sāgara" (Milk Ocean), where Viṣṇu lies in reclining pose ever since and even before the creation happened. In the same sentence, she refers to child Kṛṣṇa's killing of ogress Pūtanā. Now, this time zone is Kṛṣṇa's childhood. Then in the next sentence, she refers to sages and *yogīs*, who generally live away from human habitations but Āṇḍāḷ listens to their chanting of Hari's (another name of God Viṣṇu) name. In the same moment is also audible the morning song of birds and the sound of "snow-white conch in the temple of Viṣṇu". Therefore, Milk Ocean of primeval times, "Gokula" at the time of Kṛṣṇa's infancy, India of the time of sages and *yogīs* (probably times of Upaniṣads), "Ayarpadi" street of "Gokula" of Kṛṣṇa's youth to which the maidens belong and this day in the life of Āṇḍāḷ when birds are singing in the morning and conch is resounding in the Viṣṇu Temple, all these come alive in one space of her awareness. And with these spaces come alive the respective times which belong to these spaces.

This is a general pattern which is present in all stanzas of *Tiruppāvai*. In effect, this pattern is followed in the poetry of all the eleven Āḻvārs. For example, following stanza from Tirumangai Āḻvār's *Periya Tirumoḻi* picked up randomly from *Nālāyira-Divya-Prabandham* also merges different times and spaces into a single space and moment:

> The golden-walled-city-of-Lanka's king Rāvaṇa's five-times-two heads were scattered by the hot *brahmā astra* arrows of our lord the bow-wielder. He resides in the Alundur where bumble bees into golden *punnai* flowers, then go to arrow-sharp-eyed dames to enjoy the five qualities of their coiffured hair.
>
> — *Periya Tirumoli*; Srirama Bharti 2000: 335

All the Āḻvārs maintain this awareness of immanence as well as transcendence of God. He is present in all spaces and times.

Sojourn to a Sacred Space: House or Temple

Another structural pattern that is seen in Āṇḍāḷ's poem *Tiruppāvai* is that of a journey taken up together by a group of girls of a cowherd community. The first five stanzas state the goal of the journey and the preparation necessary to achieve that goal. These stanzas talk about the nature of the ritual practice and the glory of the personal God whose *sākṣātkāra* (lit. appearing before the eye) is sought. Āṇḍāḷ's motto is to see Kṛṣṇa face-to-face. This rendezvous, however, can happen if Āṇḍāḷ and her friends are able to please Him by purifying themselves bodily as well as mentally. Purification of the body is primary and various *vrata*s and rituals are taken up to achieve that purpose. Purification of the mind comes next and this can be done by focusing all attention on Kṛṣṇa and by removing all the unnecessary thoughts from the mindscapes. Hence, Āṇḍāḷ insists that all of them hear and sing praises of Kṛṣṇa. This is not just to please Him but also to fill one's mind with Him and Him only.

This is the course of *bhakti-yoga*. Āṇḍāḷ creates this course, which can be taken up by any individual to have a *sākṣātkāra* with Kṛṣṇa, who is a manifestation of the Divine and is at the same time a symbol for higher awareness. *Tiruppāvai* in this way is also about expansion of the awareness.

If *bhakti* is considered as a kind of expression of a more expansive awareness, an awareness that has penetrated subtler levels of consciousness, then we can read Āṇḍāḷ's *Tiruppāvai*, an intense *bhakti* song. It is a symbolic representation of a journey of individual awareness from grosser levels to subtler and psychic levels where divine light (enlightenment) is experienced.

We have talked about the content of the first five stanzas of the poem. After these five stanzas, the next ten stanzas are sharply dialogic in nature. They dramatize the gathering together of the girls as all of them wish to undertake the journey to meet Kṛṣṇa with each other (as it truly becomes the *gopikās*) and not alone. So hereafter they go to each house and call out all their friends as they seemed to have planned in advance. Just as in mythical "Gokula" each *gopikā* had to overcome some or the other hurdle in order to join Kṛṣṇa in "*rāsa* dance" at the bank of Yamunā, these maidens from "Ayarpadi" also have to overcome many physical and mental barriers which generally appear in the form of laziness, sleep, illusions, etc.

However, these stanzas, though dialogic and conversational in nature, symbolically appear to be a call to reach out to deeper layers of one's own consciousness. As the self begins to recognize these layers, it becomes aware of the possibility of seeing all-linking, underlying Universal Consciousness, which is very close to what has been explained as *turīya* state of consciousness in the chapter on *bhakti* experience. Thus, though *Tiruppāvai* appears to be a simple undertaking to see and meet the chosen deity, Kṛṣṇa, who fortunately happens to be one of their own kins, it can also be understood as a journey of the individual self to the Cosmic Self, which can further be equated with full expansion of the individual consciousness.

Transformations of Āṇḍāḷ's Life and Works into other Genres of Art

The legends and myths associated with Āṇḍāḷ's life as well as the songs that she composed have become a source of creative expression for the generations of poets, dramatists, sculptors and musicians. This section is an attempt to look at the transformations of Āṇḍāḷ's life and work into other genres of art and ritual performances over a time of more than 1,000 years.

DRAMA

Śrī Kṛṣṇadeva Rāya's Amuktamalyada

Kṛṣṇadevarāya was a famous sixteenth-century Vijayanagara ruler who ruled between CE 1509 and 1530. He was a great connoisseur of arts and was a writer in his own strength. He wrote in Sanskrit and Telugu.

His *Amuktamalyada* is a famous verse-drama based on the story of Śrī Āṇḍāḷ. *Amuktamalyada* is characterized as a *prabandham*. *Prabandham* is the specific name given to a kind of writing in Telugu where the theme is focused on the main character; the main *rasa* is *Śṛṅgāra*; composed in ornamental style and is an original work.

Kṛṣṇadeva Rāya did include major features of *prabandham* in his writing but there are some clear deviations. One can see that the name of the story is "My Giver of the Worn Garland", *Amuktamalyada*, mentioned at the end of all seven chapters within the body of the text. The principal character, according to the title, is Āṇḍāḷ who wore and gave the garland to the Lord. However, it is strange, that Āṇḍāḷ comes into picture only in the fifth and the seventh chapter. The rest of the work is a beautiful delineation of the character of the city of Śrīvelliputtur; of the story of Viṣṇucitta; of the decadence of Śaivism and that of the philosophy of Vaiṣṇavism as the supreme religion.

This verse-play opens with Kṛṣṇadevarāya's dream, where he sees Lord of Veṅkaṭa (Viṣṇu) imploring him to write about the damsel who gave Him a worn garland and said to Him, "The marriage will be in *raṅgam*" and the play ends with the marriage itself.

This play does not in anyway deviate as far as the facts about Āṇḍāḷ's life are concerned. It is the same mythical story about Āṇḍāḷ, that had been available through the myths and legends, that evolved around the lives of Āḻvār saints including herself. The play appears remarkable for its flowery language and elaborate imagery. For instance, thirty-eight verse-stanzas are dedicated to describe the beauty of Āṇḍāḷ as a young maiden. To quote:

Her body, splendourous as gold
Her face, bright as moon
The redness of her lips
By their wealth and their colour,
Gave her not her name
But the clear black shade of her hair
With the arrogance of Beetles
Gave her the name "Śyāma"

. . . .

> Like a challenge to the Lord of Yadu, who posesses only one wheel in his strong shoulders, in the rabble with Manmatha, many curled hair locks befitted that young lady.
>
> — tr. from Telugu by Sujata Reddy

In the seventh and last chapter the marriage between the Lord of Śrīraṅgam and Śrī Āṇḍāḷ is described in fine detail with the divine bridegroom playfully participating in all the human rituals of marriage:

> Going to Velliputtur, they stayed in the groom's home that Viśvakarmā built. There the groom had the turmeric smearing ceremony and unction, bathed in perfumed waters to the flow of melodious music by great musicians and Nārada, with the flow of nectar. The *kaustubha* shined in his conch-like neck. [He] wore fine bracelets above the burly jewels, smeared perfumes, wore gold-threaded silk clothes and *tulasī* and a variety of flowers. Lovely garlands dangled on his bosom.
>
> And then, [he] formally entered happy Viṣṇucitta's house.
>
> In the ceremony, Sarvāṇī, Vāṇī and other Gods, sang the best songs of the history of Jānakī's marriage with Raghu.
>
> — tr. from Telugu by Sujata Reddy

This play is significant not for what it says about the life of Āṇḍāḷ but for how it says it.

Masti Venkatesh's Bhaṭṭara Magaḷu

Written in 1969, *Bhaṭṭara Magaḷu* is a verse-play written by the Jnanapeeth award winning writer Masti Venkatesh Iyengar. This was published by Jeevana Karyalaya, Bangalore.

Though it is not directly based on Āṇḍāḷ's story, it is inspired by it, says Masti in the introduction:

> Those aware of Vaiṣṇava tradition believe that Viṣṇucitta is the mother of baby Āṇḍāḷ.
>
> History says that Bhaṭṭa got a child. It also says, it was like

> Janaka finding Sītā. When I was brooding on this ten years ago, the story of Attuḷai crystallized in my mind. As time went by, it became clear and took shape of the play.
>
> It was born in my imagination and has no basis in the tradition.
>
> If traditionalists feel that accepting this story is a crime, let them not take the child of the story to be Āṇḍāḷ. Even that great *bhakta* should forgive my audacity that made up this story inspired by history.

The play tries to understand and depict the episode of Āṇḍāḷ's miraculous birth in human terms.

A young man called Mannār comes to the Sage Bhaṭṭa to tell his story of woe. His dear wife Attuḷai, whom he married after many years of love, is reported dead. This false rumour is spread by those jealous of their love when Mannār is away travelling. He is at a loss and wants to take *saṁnyāsa.* Bhaṭṭa asks him to wait and sends him on a pilgrimage. *Saṁnyāsa* can wait, he says.

The next day Attuḷai and her mother come to Bhaṭṭa with their story of woe. The same mischievous rumour-mongers have told them that Mannār had died during his travel. Bhaṭṭa connects the two stories and asks them to tarry in his *āśrama* till Mannār returns from his pilgrimage.

Mannār returns as a *saṁnyāsī.* He had defied Bhaṭṭa by taking *saṁnyāsa* in his anguish. He is shocked to find his wife alive. Now it is too late and he cannot go back to married life. Attuḷai's pleadings, that his decision was based on misinformation, have no effect on him. Distraught, Attuḷai attempts suicide by drowning. But Mannār rescues her. Seized by passion, she forces him into love making. Mannār feels he has violated the code of *saṁnyāsa* and goes away for penance. Attuḷai becomes pregnant soon. She is in a dilemma. If she goes back home with the child, she has to face calumny from wicked villagers. At this point Bhaṭṭa finds a way out. He suggests that after the child birth Attuḷai should abandon the child in his garden and go home. He assures them that he will take care of the child telling people that she is the gift of God.

In the last scene, the baby daughter is seen at the root of the banyan tree covered in a *sāṛī*. Says Bhaṭṭa:

> You are rolled in a *sāṛī*. Mother Raṅganāyakī has come to dwell on earth. Come into my hands O great mother.

He then goes on to compare her with Sītā. He also feels his dead mother has come back to be his daughter. He adds:

> The father left you. The mother was afraid to call you her own. Still, I will not ask what you have come into the world for. From now on you are my child. . . . Let your life be pure for ever. (Let your parents merits) walk you on path of virtue as if you are the *avatāra* of Raṅganāyakī and place you in the front row of devotees. Come child, come. In world's eyes, you are of immaculate birth, Lakṣmī, Sītā and Bhaṭṭa's daughter.
> — Iyengar 1969: 54-55

Without disrespecting the tradition, this play humanizes saint Āṇḍāḷ's story.

CINEMA

Tirumal Perumai by A.P. Nagarajan

The genre of *bhakti* films is a very important stream in modern Indian cinema, particularly in the south. Films like *Sant Tukaram, Sant Jnaneshwar* (Marathi), *Avvaiyar, Haridas* (Tamil), *Vemana, Potana* (Telugu), *Jagatjyothi Basaveshwara, Bedara Kannappa, Bhakta Kanakadasa* (Kannada) have been some of the biggest box office hits in twentieth-century Indian cinema. Apart from testifying to the hold of *bhakti* world-view in contemporary India, these movies have produced great character singers/actors like K.P. Sundarambal, M.S. Subbalakshmi, Tyagaraj Bhagawatar, V. Nagiah, Dr Rajkumar, who specialized in the roles of devotional saints. Although full feature films have not been made on Āṇḍāḷ or on Akkā but Āṇḍāḷ is the subject of a part of a film in Tamil and Akkā features in a very good documentary film in English.

We will now take a look at a very well-known Tamil film by a renowned director of the 1960s and 1970s, A.P. Nagarajan. The title of the film is *Tirumal Perumai,* a sequence of four episodes centring on the lives of four Āḻvārs. The first episode centres on the story of Viṣṇucitta and Āṇḍāḷ. These roles are played by Shivaji Ganeshan, who ruled Tamil cinema for nearly three decades, and K.R. Vijaya, a very famous heroine of the 1960s and 1970s, respectively.

This film was part of the revival of *bhakti* themes in cinema spearheaded by A.P. Nagarajan. He made a series of devotional films known for their spectacle and grandeur. The first of the series was *Tiruvilaiyadal,* retelling the stories from Tamil *Śiva Purāṇa, Tiruviliyadalpurāṇam.* Following the phenomenal success of this motion picture, he followed it up with another Shivaji Ganeshan starrer, *Tiruvarutselvar,* a sequence of episodes about three Nāyaṉmārs saints. *Tirumal Perumai* about four Āḻvār saints was the next in this series.

The episode on Āṇḍāḷ retells the legend about Āṇḍāḷ's appearance in Viṣṇucitta's "*tulasī* grove" (basil garden), her growing up into a great devotee of Viṣṇu and her final merger into deity of Śrīraṅgam. Apart from remarkable portrayals by the lead actors, the excellent music by K.V. Mahadevan is the chief source of the film's strength. The songs used in the film include, apart from Āṇḍāḷ's own compositions, a devotional poem on Kṛṣṇa by the famous twentieth-century Tamil poet Subrahmanya Bharathiyar.

One of the scenes depicts with a song addressed to Kṛṣṇa being sung by Viṣṇucitta while collecting flowers for *pūjā.* At this point he discovers a baby-girl in the garden, which he accepts as Lord Viṣṇu's gift. The next important scene is the one in which Āṇḍāḷ is discovered wearing the garland which is to be offered to Lord. To Viṣṇucitta, this is sacrilege. After knowing that Āṇḍāḷ had "desecrated" the garland before offering it to Lord, he throws it away only to discover it goes on its own around the neck of Lord's idol. This is a vindication that *bhakti* is superior to ritualism. Viṣṇucitta's learned piety is thus humbled. Upon her coming of age, Viṣṇucitta wants to fulfil his fatherly duties by marrying her. He sets about looking for a bridegroom in spite of Āṇḍāḷ's protests that she belongs only to Lord Viṣṇu. Her absorption in the Lord is depicted through the picturization of the famous Kr̥ṣṇa song by Bharathiyar, which opens with the line:

> *parkum idaiyalellam nandalāla* ı
> *un kariya niram tonrudada nandalāla* ıı
>
> — Wherever I turn my eyes O Nandalāla, I see your dark colour O Nandalāla!

The next song picturization is that of the famous first stanza of *Tiruppāvai*. Āṇḍāḷ is depicted as performing the Mārgaḷi rite singing the stanza with a group of young girls (*gopikās*). This is after Viṣṇucitta becomes reconciled to Āṇḍāḷ's resolve to wed none other than the Lord.

The climax of the episode is the dramatization of the legend of Āṇḍāḷ's merger with Lord Raṅganātha in Śrīraṅgam. The episode emphasizes Āṇḍāḷ's unorthodox devotion and marriage as opposed to traditional religion and marriage. The spiritual power of Āṇḍāḷ is shown to be superior to that of her foster father and senior saint Viṣṇucitta. In spite of having the superstar Shivaji in the lead role, it is K.R. Vijaya playing Āṇḍāḷ who gets foregrounded in the episode.

A.P. Nagarajan's treatment of the story emphasizes the feminine and the devotional as opposed to the masculine and the rational-one of the *leitmotiv* of *bhakti* expressions. The film projects the mythical framework that sets Āṇḍāḷ's life and at no point does it question this framework. This is in complete contrast to Madhushree Datta's film on Akkā Mahādevī which is included in this study.

RITUAL PERFORMANCE

Araiyar Sevai: Ten-Day Annual Performance of Āḻvār's Songs in Tamil Śrīvaiṣṇava Temples

Śrī Nāthamuni's compilation of Āḻvār's poetry is famous as *Nālāyira-Divya-Prabandham*, which literally means "Sacred Book of Four Thousand". *Divya-Prabandham* is divided into four books, each of which contains one thousand hymns. These four books are: *Mudalayiram, Periya Tirumoḻi, Iyarpa* and *Tiruvāimoḷi*. *Iyarpa*, which is the third book, contains stanzas that are meant to be recited and while other books, that are collectively known as *Isaippa*, are musical stanzas that are meant to be sung on music.

In the beginning, it was Śrī Nāthamuni who first created the tradition of performance by performing Āḻvār songs before the *arcā* (image of the deity, set for the purpose of worshipping) form of the deity at Śrīraṅgam. He used simple song-based tunes and *tāla*s which made them popular among the common people who could all sing according to their own capacity and talent. Later this art performance became a part of the *Ṣoḍaśa upacāra* worship of the Lord.

This tradition developed into a highly specialized theatrical performance called as "Araiyar Sevai" which is now an annual event in all major Śrīvaiṣṇava temples in Tamil region. It is a ten-day festival that takes place in the month of Tai (January–February). The festival is preceded by a celebration of the marriage between Śrī Selva Nārāyaṇa and Śrī Āṇḍāḷ, who is established as Tayar or Śrī Selva Nāyakī. After this, Kalyāṇa Utsava works of all the Āḻvārs are presented in a sequence as a part of the performance during the next ten days. Āṇḍāḷ's poetry generally is presented on the fifth or sixth day of the festival. To quote the famous Araiyar, Srirama Bharti:

> Throughtout the festival the Lord graces the northern *maṇḍapam*, and the *ācārya* graces the southern *maṇḍapam* directly opposite. The Araiyar stands by the *ācārya*, to his left members of the audience who also participate in various ways, are spread all around. The programme takes the listener through the various stages of artistic creativity beginning with simple songs, through dance and mime to total theatre and finally into the deeply spiritual experience of soul realization. The festival ends with the auspicious *tirumañjanam* (ritual bath for the deities) followed by distribution of food offerings.
>
> — Srirama Bharti 1999: 5

Āṇḍāḷ's works that fall right in the middle of the ten-day festival offer a great scope for a complete theatrical show with basic paraphernalia of music and accompaniments supplied by the Araiyar perfomers at the peak of Araiyar Sevai.

Āṇḍāḷ's *Nachiar Tirumoḻi* is a poem of 143 verses or 14 decads which centre on the theme of erotic love and longing. These decads are full of dramatic images drawn from nature which involve the wilderness and its habitants as the addressees of Āṇḍāḷ's dialogic rendering. During the Araiyar Sevai performance, the entire *Tiruppāvai* scenario ("Āṇḍāḷ Goṣṭhī of *Tiruppāvai*) is interwoven with the various decads of the *Nachiar Tirumoḻi* which are then presented with dance, music and commentary. All the decads of *Tirumoḻi* have a dramatic situation, for instance, in decads 4 and 5, Āṇḍāḷ is sad and lonely and in her loneliness draws circles in the sand and also sends birds as messengers to Kṛṣṇa. This allows for involvement of the audience, who take turns to draw circles with coloured sand with a blindfold on their eyes (Srirama Bharti 1999: 34). Decad 6 where Āṇḍāḷ tells her friend about her auspicious dream about marriage with the Lord Himself is performed as *kummi,* i.e. as clap-and-step dance in a circle by six to eight members of the Araiyar group. During the performance various sets like the procession of the deity on a *kuruṇḍu* tree with clothes hanging on the branches, pots of butter spread about, a parrot made up of betel leaf, etc. are also used to create a dramatic touch.

In spite of all the dramatic appeal, *Divya Prabandham* texts and their performances actually move only in a sacred space and even if they move out of the temple space they remain associated with things that are considered sacred and auspicious in the Śrīvaiṣṇava community. Hence, occasions like birth and marriage, which are part of the major *saṁskāra*s (*rites de passage*) in the journey of an individual on the earth call for rememberance, recitation and sometimes even performance of these sacred Āḻvār outpourings to invoke God for blessings and grace.

The Araiyar Sevai performance in itself is an act of worship and *bhakti*. It requires complete surrender of the self to the love of God. Describing this idea of *bhakti* and surrender, Srirama Bharti says:

> The performance of *Araiyar Sevai* requires immense concentration and inner control; perfect co-ordination of feeling, music and bodily movement is required and a total switching off of the rational mind to allow the creative mood to come into effect. The *Araiyar* tradition prescribes fasting for a day and evacuation of the bowels with castor oil before a scheduled temple performance. The performer must observe a vow of silence and contemplate on the devotion of Lakṣmaṇa (who would carry out Rāma's command in spirit) and of Bharata (who would carry out Rāma's command in letter), to be true to the letter and the spirit of the Āḻvār's works. There is no room for the capricious or personal interpretation of the Āḻvār by the performer. He must empty himself and allow the Āḻvār to occupy his being, as part of the *yoga* or the total process, the artist must practise

> cheerfulness of mind through contemplation of Viṣṇu, firmness of mind through devotion to the *guru*, alertness of memory through *japa*, *tapa*, *dhyāna* and *prāṇāyāma* and contemplation of Hayagriva, and disinterestedness in the fruits of his labours through contemplation of *Gītā* — Kṛṣṇa. He must control his diet to maintain lightness of body and freedom from all bodily demands during performance.
>
> — 1999: 4

Āṇḍāḷ's Life and Works into Modern Poetry

A very appropriate example of intersemiotic transformations of Āṇḍāḷ's life and work into modern poetry is a fairly long poetic piece written by K. Satchidanandan, the famous Malyālam poet. This poem has been translated into English by A.J. Thomas. Thomas's sensitive translation has successfully captured the complex images employed by K. Satchidanandan. "Āṇḍāḷ Talks About Love" is a long poem based on life and legend of Āṇḍāḷ and her love for Śrī Raṅganātha.

According to the legend, Āṇḍāḷ was just fifteen years old when she was carried as a bride in a palanquin in a wedding procession to the temple of Śrīraṅgam. After having the *darśana* of the Lord, Āṇḍāḷ is supposed to have merged into the deity lying on the serpent. Her love had been precocious. In her childhood she fell in love with the God and took a vow that none other than the Lord of Śrīraṅgam will be her husband.

Out of Āṇḍāḷ's two poems, her *Nachiar Tirumoḻi* is about personal human love. *Nachiar Tirumoḻi* reveals a young woman who is deeply in love and is pining with desire for union with her lover. As the object of desire is God, all the pining receives a touch of divine sanctity where the base emotion is transformed into a divine desire for the union with the God Himself. Though the discourse takes on the usual vocabulary of human desire, it is understood to be a transcendental desire.

K. Satchidanandan's poem is also a depiction of love, but here the poet is exercising the benefit of being an outsider who can enter into the persona and at the same time can see more objectively. Here, the poet is able to hint at the distinctions between what is purely human desire and what was the desire of this Āḻvār saint who had transcended human desire.

In the beginning of the poem Āṇḍāḷ is depicted as if she is talking about the possibilities which could have opened to her different kinds of love in her evolution as a woman. Innocent and immature love of an adolescent, then a more mature beloved who is open to her lover, a bride who has to undergo the pain of separation as her husband goes to war, then again clandestine love of a woman well versed in the art of love-making. In spite of these possibilities that were open to Āṇḍāḷ as an embodied human being, she choses a different kind of love which very few who tread this earth are capable of.

The poem clearly depicts various kinds of love and how Āṇḍāḷ makes her own choice which is different from common choices. The first and the last stanzas are quoted here to hint at the contrast between what is possible and what is chosen. In the first stanza Āṇḍāḷ could have been a young girl just entering into adolescence, slowly becoming aware of her desires, yet still shy of expressing herself openly. She could have been one, who is not fully mature and is ignorant of what goes into a rendezvous:

Thinking that if she so much as utters a word,
With the soft warmth of that word it may dissolve
Like snow — without speaking to him, and
Containing it within herself, stifled, like
The goblin that lives under water on the riverbed;
With the discomfiture of an ant whose tiny legs
Got stuck in honey; to see in the sea-eye,
Him sprouting a golden feather on the fourteenth-day moon,
Leaning the dark-rosewood-body on the blossomed cassia
tree

And sniffing it and caressing it softly, hiding it from her mother;
Deeming the bed as soft as the body of a hare, as a thorny murikku *tree*
And feeling her body smarting; and turning into a karavīra *plant*
That strains its ears for a little breeze to throw down a flower on him;
And, disentangling her hair at dawn, confused that it is a bunch of tender leaves,
Heaving a deep sigh and like a mad woman whose mind does not settle down,
The long eyes smarting with pain, sitting with her chin on her palm —
This is one kind of love.

Āṇḍāḷ doesn't own this kind of love. She seems to understand this as a natural development of a woman's life. The last stanza depicts Āṇḍāḷ's kind of love which is intense desire for the God and where there is a movement through the body to a state where she goes beyond the body:

Turning body into an infinitely sacred temple
With nine doors, having sculpted Him with the chisel of meditation
On the soft stone of dream, washing Him with my tears
And installing Him in the sanctum of my heart with
Eight kisses, and daily waving the āratī *of my flaming eyes*
And offering the soft petals of my lips
And adorning Him with the deep-blue silk cloth
Of my tresses washed in the breeze from Kāverī
And smearing the sandal paste of marrow from my bosom
Where only love blossoms; like the anklet
That strains its ears for the tunes of the flute
Like the hoods that rise in the Yamunā, yearning
For the flowery-feet dancing on them,

Turning the entire body into ears, with palms folded,
Holding my breath, thinking that each fish is He,
He, the turtles, tigers, boars, the dwarfs that pass
Through the street, He the hill-tribes wearing bows and arrows,
Labourers who go with hoes and axes slung across their shoulders,
He, the cowherd blowing on his reed-pipe,
He, the soldier wearing the sword —
Seeing the puruṣa who took ten incarnations in
Each being thus, and paying Him obeisance,
And untouched by thirst, hunger, lust,
Unaware of rain or shine or mist
Unmindful of hairs turning gray, and
Body ageing, sitting at the base of
The ancient kadamba *tree and*
Doing penance —
This is my kind of love.
— tr. from Malyalam by A.J. Thomas

What connects the poem to Āṇḍāḷ and her *bhakti* in these stanzas is the imagery that is drawn from nature and the green landscape which we witness in Āṇḍāḷ's own poetry more particularly in *Nachiar Tirumoḻi*. This poem as a dialogue with Āṇḍāḷ's life and her poetry reflects on the persona of the saint as it is revealed in *Nachiar Tirumoḻi*, where the desire for the Chosen One takes form in the images that form the repertoire of human expressions in love.

Āṇḍāḷ in Classical Dance and karnatic Classical Music

DANCE

Many Bharatnāṭyam classical dancers these days take up Āṇḍāḷ's songs into their performances. In fact, just as Kabīr and Mīrā are popular with Indian classical singers, verses from

Āṇḍāḷ's *Tiruppāvai* and *Nachiar Tirumoḻi* have become a part of dancers' choice compositions. In Chennai, many famous dancer's like Rukmini Devi Arundale, Padma Subramaniam and Anita Ratnam have choreographed performances that focused entirely on Āṇḍāḷ.

Famous theatre and dance critic, Sunil Kothari in his essay on "Impact of Vaishnavism on the Indian Art with Particular Reference to the Classical Indian Dance and Dance Drama Traditions" reports:

> In recent times Rukmini Devi has choreographed a dance-drama on the life of Āṇḍāḷ in Bharat Nāṭyam with the help of the musician Papanasam Sivan and her troupe of kalākṣetra artists. It also forms a part of the repertoire in a solo presentation where brief sequences with a few songs are presented. These songs underline the desire of the devotee to merge with the Lord. — Parimoo 1987: 431

Famous film actress, Bharatnāṭyam dancer and politician Vyjayanthi Mala Bali reported in a leading Indian daily, *The Hindu,* that being a Vaiṣṇavite she liked to perform dance-dramas on Āṇḍāḷ's works and that she was one of the first dancers to perform Āṇḍāḷ's *Tiruppāvai.*

Another Bharat Nāṭyam stalwart Padma Subramaniam did a complete dance ballet, "Pavai Nonbu" at Vani Mahal, Chennai, on 31 December 2005.

In July 2006, Malathi Iyengar choreographed "Kodhai's Dream" under the aegis of Rangoli Dance Company which was presented at Barnsdall Gallery Theatre in Hollywood.

Anita Ratnam who is the guiding force behind Arangam Dance Theatre in Chennai has released a DVD on Bharat Nāṭyam which has compositions like "Āṇḍāḷ Kauthuvam" based on Āṇḍāḷ's life and compositions.

Many other dancers like Rama Vaidyanathan from Delhi have used song compositions of Āṇḍāḷ in their dance.

MUSIC

Singing of Lord's name and His glory in delight is one of the chief characteristics of *bhakti* and therefore Āṇḍāḷ was not only the composer of the hymns but probably was also the first singer of her own verses. Though the singing of *Tiruppāvai* and *Nachiar Tirumoḻi* is as old as Āṇḍāḷ herself, in present times Āṇḍāḷ's songs have become a regular part of classical singing in the south. Contemporary singers of Carnatic classical music in south India, especially in Tamil Nadu and Karnataka, have been fascinated by Āṇḍāḷ as much as by the other Āḻvār and Nāyaṉmār saints. All the major Śrīvaiṣṇava singers like M.L. Vasanta Kumari and R. Vedavalli have been singing Āṇḍāḷ's songs in their concerts. These days, it is very common to find singers who begin their concerts with *pāsurams* from *Tiruppāvai* or *Nachiar Tirumoḻi* as a mark of auspiciousness. To quote V.S. Sampathkumaracharya in this context:

> It may be noted that one of the greatest Karnatic musicians Ariyakudi Ramanuja Iyengar set to music the thirty songs of *Tiruppāvai* and used to sing one or two in every one of his concerts and popularized them. Another famous musician T.K. Rangacharya set to music several *pāsurams* and popularized them. The *Tiruppāvai* songs are being sung by the late M.L. Vasanta Kumari and other famous vocalists. Another well-known musician R. Vedavalli has also set several *pāsurams* to music and has been popularizing them.
>
> — V.S. Sampathkumaracharya 2006: 29

Besides, Śrīvaiṣṇavites like M.A. Jayashree, a Sanskrit scholar and musician from Mysore, has been working on *Tiruppāvai* songs for a long time to make them accessible to the younger generation.[9] She takes up the form of singing that involves "Śruti" tradition of olden times. Śrīvaiṣṇavas maintain a strong connection with what they call "tradition" and learning and singing Āṇḍāḷ's verses is one of the means to that effect.

---

9 See Appendix A.

Āṇḍāḷ as a Part of Contemporary Tamil Culture

Āṇḍāḷ literally means "one who rules". Āṇḍāḷ's real name was "Godai". She ruled the heart of Kṛṣṇa, so she is given the name of "Āṇḍāḷ". Now she rules the heart of people and has become a part of everyday living culture in south India especially in Tamil land. Āṇḍāḷ touches people's lives in many ways. Verses from her songs have been indoctrinated by Śrī Rāmānujācārya in the *ṣoḍaśopacāra pūjā* course. They form a part of everyday ritual worship in Śrīvaiṣṇava families. In the month of Mārgaḷi (December–January) the whole of *Tiruppāvai* is sung everyday in the morning at homes as well as in the temples. Special religious congregations are held during this month all over Tamil Nadu, Karnataka and parts of Andhra Pradesh, where besides singing, chanting and recitation of Āṇḍāḷ's works, commentaries by scholars and priests on these works are also organized.

Āṇḍāḷ's Temple in Śrīvelliputtur is supposed to be the second biggest *gopuram* in Tamil Nadu. Its structure and carving are so clear and symmetrical that Tamil Nadu government has adopted this structure as its emblem.

Āṇḍāḷ serves as a model of beauty and purity for young girls and women. When a girl attains puberty in Vaiṣṇava brāhmaṇa families, she is dressed up as Āṇḍāḷ and is taken to the temple on one of the days during her first menstrual cycle. It is common to see little girls dressed up as Āṇḍāḷ in fancy dress competitions. It is Āṇḍāḷ's typical hairdo that is put up as a big bun to the left side and her garland that mark her distinction.

One can see cosmetics named after Āṇḍāḷ in and around Śrīvelliputtur region. *Sindūram*, turmeric powder, etc. are named after her. People keep the names of their daughters after the names of Āṇḍāḷ. Common among them are: Paavai, Āṇḍāḷ, Soodikkoduthal, Nachiar, Soodikodutha Nachiar,

Kothai and Poongothai. It is common to see lines from Āṇḍāḷ's songs printed on marriage invitation cards. The famous decad "Varṇamayiram"of *Nachiar Tirumoḻi*, about the auspicious dream of Āṇḍāḷ, is sung in all Śrīvaiṣṇava weddings. According to Srirama Bharti:

> Decad 6, in which Āṇḍāḷ tells her friend of her auspicious dream is recited in sing-song by priests shortly after weddings; it is called "Seerpadi", and is intended to invoke Āṇḍāḷ's blessings over the couple for prosperity and for progeny. — Srirama Bharti 1999: 34

Thus, we see that while on one hand, this saint-poetess has attained the status of a Goddess in Śrīvaiṣṇava religion; she has made great forays into the everyday living culture of all layers of society in south India. However, now limiting her to southern region will be like stating a half truth, as scholars, dancers, performers, musicians and artists all over the world are engaging themselves with Āṇḍāḷ and her life more and more with every passing day.

8

Akkā Mahādevī
Vīraśaivite Woman Saint

AKKĀ Mahādevī's life coincided with the upsurge of Vīraśaivism in Karnataka. Basavanna, who was the leader of śaraṇa movement, set up a common ground of interaction for the Śivaśaraṇas in Kalyāṇa. This was called *anubhava mantapa* (lit. Hall of Experience). *Śaraṇa*s frequented this place to hold discussions on social, spiritual and political concerns.

Most often these dialogues were in the form of *vacana*s. It is believed that Akkā Mahādevī, during her journey as an ascetic-wanderer, visited Kalyāṇa to meet Allama Prabhu, Basavanna and other *śaraṇa*s at *anubhava mantapa*. The sixteenth chapter, "Ṣoḍaśopdeśa" of the famous fifteenth-century compilation of *vacanas* called *Śūnya Sampādane*, narrates the interaction between Akkā and Allama Prabhu.

Besides the supposition, made in *Śūnya Sampādane* that Akkā Mahādevī visited Kalyāṇa and interacted with *śaraṇa*s, there is enough evidence in her own *vacana*s indicating that she subscribed to the tenets of Vīraśaivism and considered herself as one among the *śaraṇa*s. She sees *śaraṇa*s in high regard. The *vacana* quoted above is an example where she clearly praises *śaraṇa* Cennabasavanna. In another *vacanas*, she says:

> *To see, to talk and to converse*
> *With your śaraṇa*s *is a pleasure.*
> *What is there that your śaraṇa'*s *experience cannot do?*
> *What is there that your śaraṇa*s*' discourse cannot do,*
> *O Cennamallikārjuna?*
>
> — Yaravintelimath 2006: 167

Yet in another *vacana*:

> *The ground Thy* śaraṇas *have trod*
> *Is holy, Lord!*
> *The city where Thy* śaraṇas *live*
> *Is city of Kailāsa!*
> *The spot where Thy* śaraṇas *stand*
> *Is thine own abode!*
> *O Cennamallikārjuna Lord, . . .*
> — Bhoosnurmath and Menezes 1970: 287-88

Akkā Mahādevī's life and her work are inseparable from each other. In fact, her poetry is the most dependable source of information about her life, her ideas and the way of living she chose. No historical details support the hagiographies that evolved later as a part of development of Vīraśaiva religion. Harihara (*c.* CE 1190–1250) was the first biographer and was closest to Akkā in time and locale. In his poetic *Mahādeviyakkana Rāgāḷe*, he delineates the major events in Akkā Mahādevī's life. Following is a brief sketch of Akkā'a life based on his *Rāgāḷe*. Akkā Mahādevī was born to pious parents Nirmala and Sumati Shetty in the village of Udutadi, near Balligavi in Shimoga district. Her name was Mahādevī and the epithet Akkā got associated with her only later. Her parents, it seems, were already on *śaraṇa* path. This family must have been well educated and cultured as she seems to have lived in the company of the wise from the beginning. Her *vacana*s reveal a very fine sense of the scriptural and religious tradition. She was also initiated into the *śaraṇa* tradition early in life. One of her *vacana*s confirms this:

> *I got liṅga by guru's grace*
> *And jaṅgama by guru's grace*
> *I got pādodaka by guru's grace*
> *And prasāda by guru's grace*
> *I conversed with gentle devotees by guru's grace.*
> *Because, no sooner was I born*

Then the holy guru smeared
The sacred ash on my brow,
And put liṅga on my body
— Yaravintelimath 2006: 146

At the age of sixteen, she seems to have caught the attention of a feudal Lord often mentioned as a Jaina king named Kauśika. Kauśika wanted to marry this beautiful girl by all means. Akkā however was not keen on marrying anyone. She believed, like sixteenth-century Rājasthānī woman-saint Mīrā, that her marriage had already taken place and that her husband is Śiva (Cennamallikārjuna). But probably King Kauśika threatened her parents into giving Mahādevī's hand in marriage to him. Marriage did take place but didn't last as Kauśika could not keep the promises he had made to Mahādevī before tying the knot with her. Consequently Mahādevī simply walked out of the marriage leaving behind all modesty and shame. Harihara's account finishes at this point where Mahādevī, now Akkā Mahādevī (sister Mahādevī) goes on her spiritual journey worshipping Śiva in every form of creation. To quote from Harihara:

The flower bearing plants were meant for Mahādevī's pūjā
As if their faces had flowered in love and joy
In the streams
Among bamboos
In ponds, lakes, tanks and rivers
In hills and valleys
Among hoards of tigers and deers
Among bears, wild elephants and bulls
She came walking
Remembering Mallinātha everywhere.
— tr. H.S. Shivaprakash, Harihara, p. 77

Akkā Mahādevī was a great devotee of Śiva and chose the form of Cennamallikārjuna as her personal god (*iṣṭa devatā*).

Cennamallikārjuna is also her *aṅkita* (the signature) used by her in all her poetic expression. Her relationship with Śiva, her Chosen God, cannot be defined merely in terms that are commonly used by critics and scholars like "bridal-mysticism" or even by other conventional forms of reading *bhakti* poetry. It is simply beyond all conceivable definitions of love. This mystical relationship feeds on the indefinable, occultist religion of Śiva. Her *vacana*s reflect an enormous range of emotions which inform of her relation to her *iṣṭa* Cennamallikārjuna.

Akkā's Vacanas

Akkā Mahādevī is considered to be one of the finest *vacanakāra*s among the *śaraṇa*s. Her name is taken in same breath as the names of the *śaraṇa* stalwarts like Allama, Basavanna, Siddharamayya, Ajaganna (Ajaganna's compositions are not available but his *vacana*s were regarded by other *vacanakāra*s especially his sister Muktayakkā in high esteem) and Cennabasavanna. Akkā's *vacana*s have played a very significant role in expositing Vīraśaiva philosophy. Furthermore a large number of them seem to have been written exclusively with this purpose in mind. Some 360 of her *vacana*s are extant. Besides *vacana*s, she wrote four other works: *Yogāṅga Trividhi, Sṛṣṭīya Vacana, Padagaḷu,* and *Akkagaḷa Pīṭhike.*

The compilation of her *vacana*s by various anthologists throws up an interesting fact. Almost all the anthologies arranged her *vacana*s according to *ṣaṭsthala* (six stage/phase system) philosophy and all the anthological compilations happened after *Śūnya Sampādane.*

Śūnya Sampādane was compiled in the beginning of the fifteenth century which was 300 years after the *śaraṇa* movement took place in Kalyāṇa. This sudden focus on bringing together *śaraṇa* compositions was not without a reason. Vijayanagara emperors, in the process of strengthening their empire, started patronizing Vīraśaiva faith which during the twelfth-century *śaraṇa* movement had brought together all sections of society in its fold and now could be conveniently upheld as state ideology that supported all social groups. In addition, due to its affiliations with "Śaiva Siddhānta" philosophy, it helped to appropriate the Śaiva *maṭhas* which had become very powerful in Karnataka by this time. Hence, it has to be kept in mind, while studying the *vacanas*, that *Śūnya Sampādane* is a text constructed with a definite political purpose. There is no way of knowing the actual sequence of the *vacanas* in the oeuvres of śaraṇas included in *Śūnya Sampādane*. The *ṣaṭsthala* scheme could have been imposed on the available compositions of the *vacanakāras* by *Śūnya Sampādane* editors. Therefore, it is difficult to determine the sequence of Akkā Mahādevī's *vacanas* also.

Another feature associated with Akkā's *vacanas* and her life is her journey to *anubhava mantapa* in Kalyāṇa, which, in fact, is the point of focus in *Śūnya Sampādane*.

However, this journey is not mentioned at all by her first biographer Harihara's in his text *Mahādeviyakkana Rāgaḷe*. In fact, Harihara does not mention "Kalyāṇa" at all, not even in his accounts of Prabhudeva's and Basavanna's lives. It is a fact that though historically, geographically and even in terms of time or public memory, Harihara was closest to the centre of *śaraṇa* rising,[1] he strangely did not care to write about "Kalyāṇa" and *anubhava mantapa*.[2] In his essay "Journeying to Kalyāṇa", H.S. Shivaprakash says:

---

[1] Birthplace of Harihara is Hampī, which is only sixteen hours journey on horseback to present-day Kalyāṇa.

[2] Present-day *anubhava mantapa* is a place where there are many caves and the tourist guides generally point out at different caves saying that they belonged to the *śaraṇas* like Akkā and Allama. Also *anubhava mantapa*, which appears to be a small place, is supposed to have brought together some 196,000 śaraṇas under its roof at one point of time!

> Surrounding a lake on the outskirts of the city, are the caves where the leading saints are said to have performed their *sādhanā* over 800 years ago. These and a few ancient structures nearby are the only signs that history sought to remake itself in this very place.
>
> — Sen and Kaushal 2004: 215

Also the Vīraśaiva proposition, that Akkā's spiritual progress happened exactly in the six phases as expounded by Vīraśaiva philosophy, is a conjecture which might have been imposed by the fifteenth-century *vacana* compilers who were working with a set framework for consolidation of Liṅgāyata religion under the regime of Vijayanagara emperors. Another objection for this kind of sequencing is that it presupposes an evolutionary model for human consciousness. Though a common mind seems to attain maturity in gradual stages of development, there have been examples throughout history where humans have shown themselves capable of extraordinary creative powers at a very young age. Ādi Śaṅkarācārya stands out as an example. A creative mind need not necessarily show higher levels of creativity or evolution in successive stages of an increasing time-frame. Saint-poets including Akkā Mahādevī were highly evolved and creative human beings.

Akkā Mahādevī was only sixteen-year old, when she defied the social norms by walking out of her marriage and shedding all signs of civil modesty including her clothes. The works that she has left behind in the short span of her life indicate her spiritual and mystical achievement. This, for a woman in the twelfth century, is extraordinary!

Therefore, all the available frames of studying poetry fall short of understanding her poetry and her life.

Only after granting that she was an extraordinary woman, one can proceed to look at her creative expression. It is quite probable that her strength as a poetess and her creative genius were clearly perceived by the pioneers of the *śaraṇa* movement. And when she was received at *anubhava mantapa* after a tough and thorough examination of her spiritual attainments by chief *śaraṇa*s like Allama Prabhu, she was assigned this work of expounding Vīraśaiva concepts and beliefs in her compositions. In other words, it is quite possible that she was used by these leader saints as one of their women spokespersons.

At the same time a substantial number of her *vacana* compositions seem to be bursting out of this idiom of propaganda into finest expression of her mystical experiences. In such *vacana*s, one does not find any theological exposition or religious propaganda, rather a simple statement of immediate urgency of the experience of a different state of consciousness.

A new frame for her journey on the spiritual path in the light of above-mentioned suggestions must be conceived, where, though the physical and geographical journey to Kalyāṇa and then to "Kadaḷīvana" is given significance, the progress towards the final goal is considered more as mental process than as a physical progress.

Akkā Mahādevī's *vacana*s are like a magical text that opens itself only on the page which suits the seeker at the moment of choice. They reveal an extensive range of her engagements with esoteric ways of *sādhanā*. Her *vacana*s explore a simple pathway to the chosen deity, expound major tenets of Vīraśaivism and reveal the sufferings and ecstasies of a woman in love. Above all, her *vacana*s hold a key to the esoteric techniques of Yoga and Tantra. This subject is dealt at length by her in a less popular work called *Yogāṅga Trividhi*. What is special about Akkā's quest is that she enjoins *bhakti,* i.e. loving devotion with yogic and tantric *sādhanā*. For her, as in fact for all *bhakta*s, liberation (*mokṣa*) is secondary to *bhakti*, loving union with the chosen one. Akkā Mahādevī becomes more and more established in her oneness with Śiva, "Cennamallikārjuna" as she crosses all other hurdles on the path of *bhakti* — the body, the mind, the intellect and the ego through *bhakti* and through other yogic techniques that she mentions in her *vacana*s in a highly symbolic language wrapped up in deceptively simple vocabulary. For example:

Associating with the ignorant
Is like to light a fire
By rubbing stones;
Associating with the wise
Is like taking butter
After churning curd.
O Cennamallikārjuna, jasmine tender,
Associating with your devotees
Is like a hill of camphor
Catching fire.
— Vinaya Chaitanya 2005: 84

And:

Can a dry bamboo sprout again?
Can a burnt pot become clay again?
Can a fruit dropped from its stalk
Return to it again?
If the toiling and moiling men
Utter a word unknowingly,
Do the steadfast devotees
Return to earth again,
O Cennamallikārjuna!
— Yaravintelimath 2006: 128

As has been stated earlier, the path of *bhakti* is the path of complete surrender. Anything that comes in the way of *bhakti* — internal or external, of the world or of the mind, has to be surrendered. Major hurdles are posed by the senses (the body), the mind, the intellect and the ego. There are ways and means to overcome these hurdles. Besides Yoga and Tantra, three other paths of liberation expounded in the classical Hindu scripture, *Bhagavad-Gītā* are: *karma-yoga, jñāna-yoga* and *bhakti-yoga*. *Karma-yoga* begins with the body and purifies the being through detached action; *jñāna-yoga* takes up the instrument of mind and conquers it by understanding the transitory nature of the world; *bhakti-yoga* is the only path that works simultaneously on the body (engaging the senses through worship and ritual), mind and intellect (focusing it on one object-God in exclusion to all other objects) and ego (surrendering it at the service of the God and fellow devotees) and leads the *bhakta* to ecstatic bliss of union with the ever expansive Cosmic Consciousness which is considered to be higher than the liberation (*mokṣa*). It is for this reason that all the scriptures and classical texts acknowledge the supremacy of the path of *bhakti* over that of *jñāna* and *karma*. In addition esoteric practices of Tantra and Yoga sometimes go hand-in-hand with other chosen paths. Akkā Mahādevī's work *Yogāṅga Trividhi* reveals that she had been practising extreme austerities and other tāntric *sādhanā*s at certain stages in her life.

We can thus see that Akkā's life and works are a confluence of two distinct strains of Indian spirituality: the path of Yoga/Tantra emphasizing discipline and austerity, and the path of *bhakti* underscoring surrender and spontaneity. The former is expressed in her *Yogāṅga Trividhi* and the latter in her *vacanas*. At the same time we can say that elements of *bhakti,* and Yoga and Tantra intermingle in her works and all her works are inclusive of these elements in various degrees. It is interesting to note that in most of the later transformations of her works, Akkā's yogic/tāntric facet is more or less neglected.

9

Transformations in Akkā's Life and Work

Transforming a Social Reality: The Gender

AKKĀ Mahādevī, the saint from Karnataka, took the Vīraśaiva path that was very different from the path of Āṇḍāḷ. Āṇḍāḷ lived a kind of protected life in the household of her foster parents. Akkā was exposed to the harsh realities of the male dominant society when she chose to walk out of the marital house.

Being a woman ascetic and wanderer, that too naked and young in the eyes of the world, Akkā had to face immense problems in the external world, while the internal problems that anyone on the spiritual path faces also remained equally strong for her. First and biggest problem was that of the physical body. She fought the battles for the body at external as well as internal levels.

She walked out of the protected walls of her earthly husband, King Kauśika's palace to follow her own way of being. Did she chose to be naked or was she stripped off her clothes when she showed her determination to leave the householder's life? Probably she had no choice in the beginning when she walked out of king's palace and then she chose to be as she was.

Clothes are/were the first symbols of feminine modesty.

nūla mariyalihūda kaṇḍu
nācuvuḍu lokavella vū

While looking at what is hidden behind the yarn, though (the) whole world shies away from it.

But what could be the value of outward modesty if the mind is full of vile desire? Akkā believed in the purity of mind and not in mere signs of external modesty. Walking naked, which might have been forced on her initially by the circumstances, could later be integrated into herself by Akkā through her spiritual understanding of the body:

The hand that earned wealth can be taxed.
But can the beauty of the body be taxed?
You can snatch my dress and ornaments.
But can you snatch away
the Peace that wraps me round?
Does one who, being clad in
The light of Cennamallikārjuna,
Has shed all shame,
Need clothes and ornaments,
O fool?

— Yaravintelimath 2006: 141

Body and gender are important issues raised often in her *vacanas*:

If the cloth that covers them slips,
Men and women become shy,
If you, lord of life,
Envelope the whole world,
What is there to be shy of?
If Cennamallikārjuna, jasmin tender
Sees the whole world as Eyes,
What shall you cover and hide, O man?

— Chaitanya 2005: 93

Men see her as a woman and in spite of her ascetic bearings they do not spare her easily. She had to confront them and deal with them to keep them away by using various means like persuasion, dialogue or even rebuke:

Don't hold me. Don't
Stop me. Let go
Of my hand, the hem
Of my sāṛī. Don't
You know of the worst hell
For those that break
The promise made in black and white?
You shall be doomed
If you touch the woman
Married to Cennamallikārjuna.
— tr. H.S. Shivaprakash

Men do not let her alone as one would leave alone a naked male *sādhu* passing by to some unknown destination in his own glory. Halegeyadeva, second compiler of the *vacana*s in the *Śūnya Sampādane*, narrates that Akkā had to pass a virginity test by Kinnarī Bommayyā. The encounter is mystified but for a modern reader it appears to be nothing short of a rape. Kinnarī Bommayyā, according to the text, puts a staff into Akkā's vagina, from where only the *bhasma* (sacred ashes associated with Śiva) fall off. Akkā had immense courage:

Seeing bare round breasts
And the beauty of full youth
You came, O brother.
Brother, I am no female,
I am not a prostitute;
Then seeing me again and again,
Who did you think I was?
Men other than Cennamallikārjuna, jasmine-tender
Will not suit us (me), O Brother.
— Chaitanya 2005: 34

These dangers of physical rape along with other kinds of struggles that Akkā had to face in the society were purely due to her womanhood. For the men heading towards the spiritual or ascetic goals, the journey begins from a different mark lined much ahead of the point where a woman starts. H.S. Shivaprakash in his essay, "*Vacana*s of Akkā Mahādevī" says:

> A lonely woman, beautiful and walking nude, she encountered many obstacles. . . . Time and again she had to fight, plead and argue herself out of male traps.
>
> — Sen and Kaushal 2004: 33

Akkā had to fight with men at least at three levels. She had to struggle to be free first from the man-husband and the shackles of a patriarchal household. She never wanted to associate with Kauśika but was forced into a marriage with him. Then she had to struggle against the men in the outside world who seemed ready to devour her like wolves. When she escapes one kind of rape in the household, she undergoes another kind of rape in the external world. This was the price a woman must pay if she wants to be herself. Her struggle did not end here, she had to prove the purity of her intent in front of men saints also. It is said that like Basavanna, Allama Prabhu also knew Akkā's spiritual status but still he put her to a very crude and harsh investigation. He directs her in no uncertain terms to either prove her chastity or be gone! But Akkā Mahādevī showed Herculean valour in all her fights and came out victorious.

Allama Prabhu puts his conditions in front of Akkā Mahādevī before he allows her entry into *anubhava mantapa*:

> *Why come you hither, pray,*
> *O woman in the lusty bloom of youth?*
> *At the word woman our śaraṇas*
> *See red! If you can tell*
> *Your husband's identity, come sit;*
> *Else pray, be gone!*
> *If you desire the joy of fellowship*

With our Guheśvara's śaraṇas,
Tell who your husband be,
O Mother!
— Bhoosnurmath and Menezes 1970, vol. IV: 293

Allama again questions her as to why, if she has shed off all modesty, does she cover herself with her long tresses:

What does it mean:
That God loves you, and you love God?
Shedding your garment when your spirit is pure,
Why do you cloak yourself in hair?
This shame that lurks within your heart
Thus shows outside: it will not please
Guheśvaraliṅga! — Ibid.: 298

Akkā gives an answer that makes the *śaraṇa*s including Allama Prabhu understand that here is no ordinary woman they are dealing with. In one of her *vacana*s quoted as an answer to Allama Prabhu in *Śūnya Sampādane*, Akkā says:

Unless the fruit is ripe within,
The outer peel will never lose
Its gloss. . . . I covered myself
With this intent:
Lest sight of seals of love
Should do you hurt (your sensibilities)
Is any harm in this?
Pray do not tease me who am
In Cennamallikārjuna, God of Gods.

— Ibid.: 299

One important point in her journey is that her rejection of men is not negative. She rejects only those men who come in her way of *bhakti*. She seeks and celebrates the company of those men whom she deems special due to their *śaraṇa* status. She fondly remembers her *guru* in her *vacana*s. In one of her *vacana*s, she talks about being initiated by the *guru* early in her life:

I got liṅga by guru's grace
And jaṅgama by guru's grace.
I got pādodaka by guru's grace.
And prasāda by guru's grace.
I conversed with gentle devotees by guru's grace.
Because no sooner was I born
Then the holy guru smeared
The sacred ash on my brow,
And put liṅga on my body,
I was blessed,
O Cennamallikārjuna!

— Yaravintelimath 2006: 146

As pointed out earlier, she seeks and loves the company of other *śaraṇa*s and seekers. "Thanks to the companionship of your *śaraṇa*s/I am filled with the joy of *anubhava* spiritual experience" she says and more:

Playing, singing, telling, hearing,
Walking and speaking with devotees
Has been a happy conference.
As long as I live by your grace
I will spend my days with those
Who are happy in the company of Linga,
O Cennamallikārjunayya!

— Ibid.: 105

There are innumerable *vacana*s where Akkā celebrates the virtues of her *śaraṇa* brothers like Basavanna, Allama Prabhu and Siddharamayya:

Because I was Basavanna's household daughter,
He gave me piety as his grace.
Because I was Caenna Basavanna's handmaid's daughter,
What was left as his grace.

Because I was the daughter
of Prabhudeva's handmaid's maid,
he gave me knowledge as his grace.
Because I was the infant daughter
of Siddharamayya,
He gave me soul as his achieved grace.
Because I was Madivala's own daughter
He gave me a spotless grace with conviction.
Because all these innumerable ones
Stroked my head, regarding me as their favoured child,
I became fit for the holy feet of Cennamallikārjuna!

— Ibid.: 175

Her journey to Kalyāṇa also actually is taken up purely to live in the company of other spiritual seekers with whom she could share her experiences and ideas. Only when she establishes herself as a respectable *śaraṇe* is she left alone to pursue her own path.

Transforming Personal Reality: The Consciousness

After confronting the body question as a social reality at external level with the outside world, Akkā now had to confront this body at yet another level — level of gross senses which pull the body and mind towards the material plane. Her movement through and beyond the senses is very authentically portrayed in her *vacanas*.

My mind always thinks of belly.
I cannot see you.
I cannot penetrate you.
I am entangled in this world of illusion (māyā).
Pray, make me unite with you,
O my Lord Cennamallikārjuna!

— Ibid.: 110

In another *vacana*, Akkā talks about the need to become free from fruits of *karma* (action) in order to go beyond limitations of the consciousness created by desire, anger, greed, pride, jealousy, etc. and to achieve true knowledge about the absolute reality or her Cennamallikārjuna:

> *So long as one is engaged*
> *In reaping the harvest of virtue and vice,*
> *One is a body of desire,*
> *An abode of anger,*
> *A den of greed,*
> *A temple of infatuation,*
> *A cover of pride,*
> *And a cloak of jealousy,*
> *Unless this sense ceases,*
> *There is no scope for knowing*
> *Cennamallikārjuna,*
> *Mark, O brothers.*
>
> — Ibid.: 144

Through various yogic practices, most basic bodily desires are made silent. She conquers the senses through control over the mind. The distractions caused by the senses are described as the *māyā*, and the cause and effect of these distractions are the external world (*saṁsāra*). Akkā describes the difficulty of withdrawing the senses away from the external world. She holds constant dialogue with her Cennamallikārjuna to save her from the *māyā* which is laid down by Him to keep his *līlā* (cosmic-play) going:

> *Māye haunts the body like shadow*
> *Māye haunts the life force as mind*
> *Māye haunts the mind as memory*
> *Māye haunts memory as perception*
> *Māye haunts perception as forgetfulness*
> *Māye haunts the hoards of worldlings*

With its shepherd's stick lifted up
O Cennamallikārjuna
Nobody can conquer "Maye"[1]
Spread out by you.
— tr. H.S. Shivaprakash

In another *vacana*, she prays that Śiva by his own grace should make her go beyond His *māyā*:

Māye swallowed up Hari
Māye swallowed up Aja (Brahmā)
Māye swallowed up Indra
Māye swallowed up the moon
Māye swallowed up the big ones,
Who claimed to know
Māye swallowed up the ignorant
Who claimed not to know
Māye has pervaded all the fourteen worlds[2]
O Cennamallikārjuna, O Master,
O Compassionate one
Rid me of my māyā.
— tr. H.S. Shivaprakash

Hence, for Akkā *māye* poses its own challenges to her personal self. She is not talking about the concept of *māyā* in general as a means of all human bondage but of *māye* in particular where the limitations posited by external as well as internal attachments come to hinder the path of evolution for the seeker.

---

1 *Māyā* which is a feminine principal in Vedānta, is called as *māye* by her and is neuter gender in Akkā Mahādevī's *vacanas*. Sometimes she even uses male gender to represent *māyā*.

2 Fourteen worlds are depicted in *Caṇḍīkadalam Mantra*. Below: *atala, vitala, sutala, talātala, rasātala, mahātala, pātāla*. And above: *bhū, bhuvaḥ, svaḥ, mahaḥ, janaḥ, tapaḥ, satya*.

Akkā's Yogāṅga Trividhi: A Site of Transformation of Tantra into Bhakti-Yoga

Apart from *vacana*s Vīraśaiva saints also composed *svara-vacana*s (*vacana*s for singing) and esoteric texts like Allama Prabhu's *Mantragopya* and Akkā's *Yogāṅga Trividhi.* Most studies of Akkā have depended mostly on *vacana*s than on other texts. Scholars' preference for *vacana*s is quite understandable. They speak directly to the modern reader without the mediation of obscure esoteric symbolism which *svara-vacana*s and esoteric texts are replete with. However, the absence of any attention to texts other than *vacana*s has rendered the existing texts, including the most perspicacious of them, lopsided. *Vacana*s have been viewed as expressions of freedom ("I sing as I please", as Basavanna said). However, after examining texts other than *vacana*s, one discovers that *śaraṇa*s' freedom is based on "the secret discipline" that informs both *svara-vacana*s as well as esoteric texts. In fact, some of these esoteric symbols spill over into *vacana*s, particularly the species called *beḍagina vacana*s. Like texts of tāntric tradition called *sandhābhāsā* (twilight language) and *ulaṭīyabhāsā* (inverted language) of *nirguṇa pantha*s of the north, these texts employ a transluscent language distinct from *sarala* (direct) *vacana*s. Allama Prabhu has composed the maximum number of *beḍagina vacana*s. Akkā has hardly written such transluscent *vacana*s. However her *Yogāṅga Trividhi* employs many conventions of *beḍagu.* The examination of this esoteric text is complimentary to our understanding of *vacana*s particularly because of its intertextual and intersemiotic dimensions. Unlike other such works, Akkā's work is characterized by great lucidity of diction and clarity of images that is present in her *vacana*s also.

Yogāṅga Trividhi is a remarkable text as it shows a convergence of *bhakti* and tāntric *sādhanā*. In Tantra and Yoga the goal of *sādhanā* is enlightenment. In *bhakti,* the goal is not merely enlightenment but *bhakti* itself, which is sheer joy of union with the *iṣṭa*, the Chosen One. Complete self-surrender and surrender of the ego at the feet of the *iṣṭa* is true *bhakti*. Here in *Yogāṅga Trividhi*, Akkā Mahādevī considers *sevā* (selfless service) of the *guru*, God and other *bhakta*s as her supreme delight even after she has become completely liberated from the dualities in her consciousness. Even in Āṇḍāḷ's *Tiruppāvai*, which is purely a *bhakti* text, the goal finally is not partaking of boons and gifts from God but to be able to live in His *sānidhya* (close vicinity with Him).

However, *Yogāṅga Trividhi* can also be reasonably described as a short poetic treatise on experiences of awakening of *kuṇḍalinī śaktī* (power). Akkā Mahādevī describes this song as *tattva-pada* (song of essences). She writes about her experiences using a symbolic language which is an inherent part of tāntric discourse. *Kuṇḍalinī-yoga* is a part of Tantra and in common parlance it might be described as a yogic discipline to complete awakening of the inner potential which leads to self-realization. With respect to consciousness, *kuṇḍalinī* awakening leads to attainment of *turīya* state of consciousness, where all the limitations of the gross, subtle and causal body are lifted. The awareness reaches an expansion, where all the states of consciousness become enlightened simultaneously.

Bhakti Elements in Yogāṅga Trividhi

All the elements of *bhakti* can be seen in *Yogāṅga Trividhi*:

1. This work ends with a "Phalaśruti" (statement of the boons that get conferred on the individual who reads or copies or sings the text of this work):

   > Whoever copies or sings with love *Yogāṅga Trividhi* will be rid of disease, rebirth and suffering — One with liṅga they prosper in happiness.
   >
   > — *Yogāṅga Trividhi*, stanza 66

2. There is desire in *bhakta-sādhaka* for complete surrender of the self and ego:

Slave of your slaves servant of your servants

I took refuge in your feet — O great *guru* (*ghana guru*) Nurture me with your compassion.

— Ibid., stanza 57

Make me a slave in the house of *bhakta*s
Give me the eternal joy — of partaking
The leftovers of *bhakta*s.

— Ibid., stanza 63

3. There is no other desire left in *bhakta* except for the desire to be in His *sānidhya:*

While walking, speaking, dressing and eating
I will not let go of your feet — this resolve
Be established in me.

— Ibid., stanza 50

4. Joy is found in union with the supreme:

Being rid of the support of aṅga and taking refuge in liṅga;
My heart has completely merged in liṅga — therefore I have no quality of aṅga anymore.

— Ibid., stanza 48

However in spite of features of *bhakti* in it, *Yogāṅga Trividhi,* is primarily a tāntric text.

Tāntric Aspects of Yogāṅga Trividhi

All tāntric and yogic texts ascribe enormous importance to the *guru*. In *Yogāṅga Trividhi,* Akkā Mahādevī begins by offering worship first to the *guru* and next to the God. In Tantra, *guru* and God are considered as One. *Guru* literally means one who dispels the darkness. Human *guru* is a realized soul who has already achieved the state of *jīvan-mukti* (liberation). Symbolically the *guru* is a principle that leads to removal of all obstacles on the path of *sādhanā* by showing the correct path to the seeker.

In Tantra besides other rites and rituals, *guru* is worshipped as equivalent to God. Sir John Woodroffe quotes from *Guru Tantra*:

> If the *guru* is pleased, Śiva is pleased; if he is displeased; Śiva is displeased. If the *guru* is pleased, Śivāṇī is pleased; if the *guru* is displeased, Śivāṇī is displeased. Hence O Maheśāni! the *guru* is the Lord, the sustainer and the annihilator. It is he who can give *mokṣa*.
>
> — Woodroffe 1978: 72

Following the same lines of tāntric tradition, Akkā Mahādevī begins with the desire to place the *guru* at the centre of her being:

> *O Somaśekhara O guru*
> *Grant us the desired fruits-shine*
> *In the space of my heart.*
> *I begin depending on*
> *The wisdom of guru, the pure one — with great delight*
> *I will sing the song of essences.*
>
> — *Yogāṅga Trividhi,* stanzas 1 and 2

After offering worship to the *guru* and the God, Akkā sings about the state of a *yogī* in an extremely mystical light and it is for this reason that the stanzas 7 to 38 are highly symbolic in nature. Akkā Mahādevī is using very subjective metaphors in these stanzas. For instance, in the following stanza she talks about mind as a wild Goddess that needs to be shackled:

> *Capturing Māri (destructive Goddess) wandering in the town and shackling her heavily — that town*
> *I sold to a wise man.*
>
> — Ibid., stanza 16

Yet there are some explicable references to tāntric-yogic symbols describing the path and the state of enlightenment:

> *Listening to resounding music watching the burning flame drinking the shower of amṛta — in effect*
> *I gave up births and deaths.* — Ibid., stanza 19

The music referred to here is *nāda*, the primal sound, flame is the eternal light and *amr̥ta* is the nectar that drips from the *bindu cakra*. These are some of the common effects that a tāntric practitioner experiences during the course of his/her *sādhanā*.

In stanza 21, she refers to *suṣumṇā nāḍī*, the psychic channel which is the path taken by rising *kuṇḍalinī*:

> *Closing the gaps of nine doors*
> *I filled my mind into suṣumṇā — look*
> *Amr̥ta's pitcher is overflowing.*
> — Ibid., stanza 21

Akkā Mahādevī repeatedly refers to the physical body as a "pot with nine holes", "house with nine doors", etc. *Suṣumṇā* is a psychic channel situated in the middle of the spinal column. According to Sir John Woodroffe:

> It is said that there are 3½ crore of *nāḍīs* in the human body, of which some are gross and some are subtle. *Nāḍī* means a nerve or artery in the ordinary sense; but all the *nāḍīs* of which the books on *yoga* speak are not of this physical character, but are subtle channels of energy. Of these *nāḍīs*, the principal are fourteen; and of these fourteen, *iḍā, piṅgalā* and *suṣumṇa* are the chief; and again, of these three, *suṣumṇā* is the greatest, and to it all others are subordinate. *Suṣumṇā* is in the hollow of the *meru* in the cerebro-spinal axis. It extends from *mūlādhāra* lotus, the *tāttvika* earth centre, to the cerebral region. — Woodroffe 1956: 47

Stanza 31 is a direct reference to the rising of *kuṇḍalinī śakti* in the form of a serpent at least up to three *cakras*:

> *The snake in the pit lifted up her tail*
> *Litting up three regions — when I*
> *Expanded into undivided light (?)*
> — *Yogāṅga Trividhi*, stanza 31

"Snake in the pit" is nothing but the *kuṇḍalinī* which is visualized in yogic and tāntric discourse as a serpent sitting in three and a half coils in the *mūlādhāra cakra* (the root centre) situated below the edge of the spine. Akkā Mahādevī is talking about the rising of *kuṇḍalinī* from *mūlādhāra* to *anāhata cakra*, i.e. heart centre and the consequent experience of light. Regarding the ascent of *kuṇḍalinī*, a renowned Kāśmīr Śaivite scholar Lilian Silburn writes:

> The awakening and the ascension of the most vibrant *kuṇḍalinī* is therefore a gradual process of reintegration of the various levels, withdrawing into one. One another somewhat like rods sliding one within another or Russian dolls, one fitting into the other. At every stage of the withdrawal, everything is reduced to a point (*bindu*), from which radiate ever greater realities as *kuṇḍalinī* rises from centre to centre through the median channel (*suṣumṇā*). The *Parātriṁśikā* sings of it in a beautiful passage (pp. 270-71): "The heart within which everything shines gloriously and which is shining everywhere, is the one lasting light, the Supreme Heart. . . . O awakened ones, adore this Heart — the universal emission — vibrating within the heart of the *suṣumṇā* in the great bliss of union." — Silburn 1988: 10

Tantra and Vīraśaiva Philosophy in Yogāṅga Trividhi

The most important example of intersemiotic transformations in *Yogāṅga Trividhi* is found in how Akkā Mahādevī relates the entire tāntric vocabulary of *cakra*s to the *ṣaṭsthala* scheme of the Vīraśaiva philosophy. From stanza 41 to stanza 46 in *Yogāṅga Trividhi*, Akkā Mahādevī takes up every *cakra* beginning from the base (*mūlādhāra cakra*) and talks about the state of evolution related to that centre not only in classical tāntric discourse but also relating it to the state of evolution in *ṣaṭsthala* scheme. As discussed earlier *ṣaṭsthala* scheme in Vīraśaivism is conceived as an evolutionary ladder for the seeker's (*bhakta*'s) state of consciousness.

Bhakta, maheśeśvara, prasādī, praṇaliṅgī, śaraṇa and *eikya* are the stages through which the consciousness passes before it enjoys complete union with the Supreme or as she calls it *liṅga-aṅga saṁyoga*. Akkā Mahādevī relates these stages of evolution in Vīraśaiva philosophy to the ascent of *kuṇḍalinī* rising in the *cakra*s and opening of corresponding centres of the (en)light(enment). For instance:

> *To the primal liṅga in the base cakra (ādhāra [mūla])*
> *Whoever offers the fragrance joyfully —*
> *By turning the earth to the nose*
> *Is a real bhakta.* — *Yogāṅga Trividhi*, stanza 42

In the above stanza, Akkā Mahādevī is talking very succinctly about *mūlādhāra cakra* (the root centre). This *cakra* in tāntric philosophy is associated with the element earth and with the sense of smell through the nose. What Akkā Mahādevī accomplishes in this three-line stanza is remarkable as she first of all links the *mūlādhāra* to the *liṅga* (to the primal *liṅga* in the *ādhāra cakra*) thereby liberating the *cakra* from the usual sexual associations. Next, she describes the utter surrender and focus of the sense of smell to the gross element earth. In the next stanzas all the senses are being surrendered to the respective elements. This is an indication of how the surrender which is the essence of *bhakti* begins in the very beginning of Tantra *sādhanā* also. Here again, she conjoins Vīraśaiva philosophy with *bhakti* and Tantra philosophy by naming this stage as the stage of a *bhakta*.

In this manner she goes along in the next five stanzas to describe the ascent of *kuṇḍalinī* and the preliminary requirements that go along at respective stages. At *svādhiṣṭhāna cakra*, for instance, the sense of taste is surrendered and this is ascribed as the *sthala* of Māheśvarī as referred to in the Vīraśaiva philosophy.

After the *kuṇḍalinī*, which is recognized as *śakti* (energy, power), pierces through the six *cakra*s situated in *suṣumṇā nāḍī* in the spinal column and rises up to *ājñā* (eye-brow centre), there is no coming back, it then goes up to *sahasrāra* (crown centre) in the middle of the head and joins the Supreme Consciousness represented as Śiva.

In the last twenty stanzas of *Yogāṅga Trividhi*, Akkā Mahādevī describes this state of union attained by a *bhakta* when the surrender is complete. Like in tāntric philosophy, it is said in Vīraśaivism also that *kuṇḍalinī* awakening leads to the elimination of the limits of the physical body and those created by dualism in the mind. Akkā Mahādevī says:

> *Being rid of the support of aṅga and taking refuge in liṅga*
> *My heart has completely merged in liṅga — therefore*
> *I have no quality of aṅga anymore.*
>
> — *Yogāṅga Trividhi*, stanza 48

Further:

> *My body is guru, my breath liṅga*
> *My soul the moving linga "cara" liṅga, (jaṅgama) — thus*
> *How can I have body and mind anymore.*
>
> — Ibid., stanza 58

It is evident that the metaphors that Akkā chose to describe the state of union or self-realization come from Vīraśaiva philosophy. In classic tāntric terms, *liṅga* is Śiva, the Supreme and *aṅga* is *jīva* (the Individual). However, these terms of reference come from Vīraśaivism, where the words *aṅga*, *liṅga* and *jaṅgama* (*guru*) are very frequently used to relate the experiences of a *śaraṇa*.

This interconnectivity of various aspects of *bhakti*, Tantra and Yoga, that are exposited in *Yogāṅga Trividhi*, clearly reveals Akkā Mahādevī's spiritual achievements. She was an evolved *yoginī*, *bhakta* and a tāntric *sādhanā* practitioner. She had experienced the awakening of *kuṇḍalinī* which is a rare phenomenon. The scope of her knowledge and experience was much ahead of the ken of a common poetic talent. This is why the range of her experiences encompasses many areas which are generally seen as exclusive of each other but they seem to find an interconnectivity in her awareness. One witnesses a kind of convergence of Vīraśaivism, Yoga, *bhakti*, Tantra and poetry in this work.

Tiruppāvai and Yogāṅga Trividhi: Two Similar but Different Journeys

A contrastive study of *Tiruppāvai* and *Yogāṅga Trividhi* would reveal to us not only the difference between *saguṇa* and *nirguṇa bhakti* of the two poets in question but also the difference between the two ways of structuring spiritual practice and experiences in poetry.

The common point is that both works have been conceived like journeys. Further, both of them are *bhakti*-centred.

Āṇḍāḷ's poem is a journey from home to temple (i.e. Kṛṣṇa's house). Each stanza is a step in that direction. It concludes, on reaching the goal, with a fervent prayer for no blessing other than devotion. Her deity inhabits a human space: He has a name, form, family and a myth. He is constituted of several narratives. Also, the journey is collective — Āṇḍāḷ keeps on gathering more and more girls on the way. Her intense personal devotion is a social phenomenon as well.

Akkā's poem does not have such clear spatio-temporal co-ordinates of the journey. Her journey takes on a more expressly symbolic colouring. It is a journey from without to within. The stages of this journey are expressed in terms of incredible imagery of the *beḍagu* mode.

Āṇḍāḷ's journey is undertaken with a single-minded devotion unmediated by any human agency. This is not the case with Akkā. Her poem begins and ends with salutations to *guru*, not to God. Her *bhakti* is mediated by *guru–śiṣya* relationship which is characteristic of the paths of Tantra and Yoga. The key images, as has already been pointed out, hark back tāntric psychic physiology involving *nāḍī*s, *cakra*s, etc.

Even at the climactic moment, Āṇḍāḷ's devotion is dualistic in the sense that it emphasizes otherness of the Lord, her intense love and longing notwithstanding. Akkā's poem is about the conquest of this otherness pertaining to an abstract deity, who has a name but no existence outside the personal experience. He is often identified with Cennamallikārjuna, Śiva Himself.

As we move from Āṇḍāḷ to Akkā, we move from *saguṇa* to *nirguṇa*, the exoteric to the esoteric, the dualistic to the monistic, from the mythical to the mystical, from sanctification of space to that of the self.

Āṇḍāḷ's world is temple-centred whereas Akkā's is self-centred. Between these two modals lies the infinite variety of *bhakti* experiences and expressions.

Vacanas of Akkā Mahādevī Reflecting Contemporary Performances

The mode of existence of *vacana*s in the twelfth century is a matter of considerable debate. Were they composed orally or written down? The fact that the verbal texture of *vacana*s is constructed on principles of repetition, parallelism and contrast, which according to Roman Jacobson are characteristics of oral poetics. A.K. Ramanujan also emphasizes upon the orality and spontaneity of the *vacana* literature. Under the sub-heading "The Vacana Form and the Oral Poetics" in his Introduction to *Speaking of Siva*, he says:

> The Sanskrit religious tests are described as Śruti and Śmr̥ti. Śmr̥ti is what is remembered, what is memorable; Śruti is what is heard, what is received. Vīraśaiva saints called their compositions *vacana* (what is said). *Vacana*, as an active mode, stands in opposition to both Śruti and Śmr̥ti: not what is heard, but what is said; not what is remembered or received, but what is uttered here and now.
>
> — Ramanujan 1973: 37

He further relates:

> A *vacana* is a religious lyric in Kannada free verse; *vacana* means literally "saying, thing said". In these Vīraśaiva saint-poets' experience spoke in a mother tongue. Pan-Indian Sanskrit, the second language of cultured Indians for centuries, gave way to colloquial Kannada. The strictness of traditional metres, the formality of literary genres, divisions of prose and verse, gave way to the innovations and spontaneity of free verse, a poetry that was not recognizably in verse. The poets were not bards or *paṇḍits* in a court but men and women speaking to men and women. They were of every class, caste and trade; some were outcastes, some illiterate. — Ibid.: 12

The hypothesis that they were composed orally appears more probable for many more reasons. *Vacanas*, like most compositions of *bhakti* tradition, were meant for performance that involved singing, dancing and acting. Allama Prabhu speaks of having "sung" his *vacanas*. Basavanna also refers to singing performance when he says: I sing as I please (*Ānu olidante hāduvennu*). The *vacanas* expressing devotional love by Basavanna, Akkā and several others have references to singing and dancing in devotional abandon.

The presence of a handful of *vacana* poets, who were professional performers of theatrical and semi-theatrical forms, points to yet another dimension of the relationship between *vacanas* and performances. The *vacana* poets, belonging to nomadic performing tribes, have composed *vacanas* which can be considered free translations of their performances into the *vacana* form. Some examples follow.

The following *vacanas* of Akkā Mahādevī can also be seen as intersemiotic translations of contemporary performances:

> *Like the monkey at the tip of the stick*
> *Like the puppet at the point of the string*
> *I have acted O Father as you made me act*

I have spoken O Father as you made me speak
I have lived O Father as you made me live
O Cennamallikārjuna, O world's driving force.
— tr. H.S. Shivaprakash

These lines refer to a street masquerade, to acrobats, to puppeteers and to actors, respectively. Akkā Mahādevī might have witnessed these shows during her wanderings through the land. In another *vacana* she refers to this world as putting up an empty show:

Ugh! This empty show of the world!
First of all comes the masked one.
Saying "O father! O Pa!"
In the middle comes, a moustache-masked,
As if daubed with ghee.
At the end comes a mask of old, old age.
The moment your eyesight ceases
The play of the world ends.
O Cennamallikārjuna.
— tr. H.S. Shivaprakash

Above *vacana* is a more metaphorical consideration of the world itself as a big performance. Many of Akkā's *vacana*s reflect contemporary rituals like those of marriage and worship. In the following *vacana*, which is very famous and which immediately reminds one of the sixth decad of Āṇḍāḷ's *Nachiar Tirumoḻi*, Akkā, like Āṇḍāḷ, relates her dream to her friend:

O Sister, listen sister dear,
I dreamt a dream, I saw
Rice, betel and coconut
I saw, O dear,
A gorava boy
With short-matted locks of hair
And shining teeth

Coming home for Alms,
. . . .
Seeing Cennamallikārjuna
I opened
My eyes. — tr. H.S. Shivaprakash

Yet in another *vacana*, she describes a marriage, her own:

Erecting a pavilion with an emerald floor,
A golden festoon, a Diamond
Pillar, and a canopy of
Brimstone, decorated with pearls and rubies,
They celebrated my marriage
With a wrist band, with water
Poured from hands and with
Everlasting rice,
My own people married me
To a groom called Cennamallikārjuna.
— Yaravintelimath 2006: 169

These *vacana*s are a glimpse into just one aspect out of an extensive range of subjects that Akkā takes up in her ouvre. These *vacana*s hint at the drama that the world puts up and also our participation in the show through the rites and rituals that we create to lead us into various stages of life on earth.

Poetry of Akkā Mahādevī as a Source of Intersemiotic Transformations into Other Genres of Art

Just like Āṇḍāḷ, Akkā Mahādevī has become a part of collective unconscious of people in Karnataka and other parts of south India. Akkā Mahādevī's life and her poetry have been a constant source of inspiration for not only the Liṅgāyata community in the state of Karnataka but for all Śiva *bhakta*s around the world. Following is a description of some important works in other genres of arts which have been influenced by Akkā's persona as a woman, as a rebel, as a saint and as a Śiva devotee.

Śūnya Sampādane

Śūnya Sampādane is the first organized collection of *vacanas*. It was two centuries after the heyday of *vacanas*, these oral texts were committed to writing on palm-leaf manuscripts which were collected, classified and commented upon in Vijayanagara. It was around this time that the first version of *Śūnya Sampādane* was compiled.

One of the achievements of Vīraśaiva tradition is that it developed anthologization as a creative genre. *Śūnya Sampādane* is an unusual anthology. The *vacanas* are arranged not by author, period or subject-wise but are interlaced as dialogues of an imagined drama centring around how the protagonist Allama, in different episodes enters into a verbal contest with the greatest living saints of those times and emerges the champion.

Śūnya Sampādane belongs to a very unusual genre. (It is referred to as *Sukathā Prasaṅga*.) It can be considered a dramatic anthology. The *vacanas* of Vīraśaiva saints are arranged here in the form of dialogues situated in an imagined context. The purpose of the work seems to uphold the greatness of Allama Prabhu, who turns out to be the fulcrum of the work. The sequence of episodes provides the context for dialogues forms the background of Allama's debates with other *śaraṇas*, out of which he turns out to be the victor. Alternatively the work can be considered the dramatic biography foregrounding Allama's interaction with the contemporary *śaraṇas*. This anthology was first compiled by Śivagaṇa Prasādī Mahādevayya in the fourteenth century. According to S.C. Nandimath:

> The four versions of the *Śūnya Sampādane* have so far been traced. The idea of making such a compilation seems to

> have occurred for the first time to Śivagaṇa Prasādī Mahādevayya. His originality lies in arranging the *vacanas* in such order as to convey an impression of an actual dialogue or discussion between two or more *śaraṇas* on a set theme and to show how such discussion was a means to the furtherance of a seeker's progress. That is how, he assumed, discussions must have been carried on both at *anubhava mantapa* and elsewhere, where *śaraṇas* met. The first compilation comprises 1,012 *vacanas*. The next version, containing 1,599 *vacanas*, was the work of Haḷegeyadeva, while the third was prepared by Gummalapura Siddhaliṅgeśa Śivayogī, disciple of Tontada Siddhaliṅgeśvara and contains 1,439 *vacanas*. The fourth compilation, with 1,543 *vacanas*, was made by Gulura Siddhavīranārya which while preserving the core and essence of the previous versions, almost constitutes an independent version. — Bhoosnurmath and Menezes 1970, vol. I: XI

One of the most fascinating episodes of *Śūnya Sampādane* is concerned with Akkā Mahādevī's advent in "Kalyāṇa" and her debates with leading *śaraṇas* of *anubhava mantapa* including Allama. Apart from Akkā and Allama, Basavanna, Cennabasavanna and Siddharamayya also participate in the debate.

Śūnya Sampādane, which in itself was an intersemiotic translation of original *vacanas*, became a source for further intersemiotic transformations. For instance, Gulura Siddhavīranārya's text was versified with some modifications by the poet Chamarasa in his *Prabhuliṅgaḷīḷe.*

Though the central episodes remain nearly the same in all the four versions, some of the differences, which appear to be minor, are significant. The treatment of the episode concerning Akkā Mahādevī is a point in case. Haḷegeyadeva, who is known for putting in a lot of mythological trappings to brace up the story of Mahādevī, has included a detailed encounter between Akkā Mahādevī and Kinnarī Bommayyā. The other versions give only a hint of this encounter. The minute and open description of the physicality of the virginity test by Kinnarī Bommayyā is described by Haḷegeyadeva in a way which is very disturbing to the pious. This interpolation made by the second anthologist was cut down to the bare minimum by the third and fourth anthologists to see that the saint's image is not tarnished. Perhaps it was not Haḷegeyadeva's intention to tarnish the saint's image but this must have become embarrassing later as Akkā's life story became more popular. Her encounter with Kinnarī Bommayyā is the first test Akkā has to pass before entry into Kalyāṇa. The second test takes place in Mahāmane when Akkā's purity is interrogated by leading *śaraṇa*s like Basavanna and Allama. Haḷegeyadeva's version of the first encounter is worth a detailed summary.

The first compiler Mahādevayya himself divinizes Akkā Mahādevī's birth by describing her as a *rudrakaṇikā* (one of the female attendants of the Rudra) who descended to the earthly plane at the behest of the great Lord. Haḷegeyadeva elaborates it further:

> On being sent to find out about the court of Śiva and Devī, the disguised attendant, while on his way, touched the woman of unblemished body and an embodiment of Devī's sāttvic aspect, she unaware that he was a hidden attendant of Śiva mistook him for a heretic and became irritated. Having read her thoughts he said to her: "Go down to the human world. Become the bride of the heretic". At this the *rudrakaṇikā* lost her pride and filled with terror prostrated before Bhavānī. The great Goddess took compassion, lifted up her head and said, "Do not fear. Overcome the curse and gain the grace of Śivagaṇas like Allama Prabhu and come back". After having been sent so the pure bodied *rudrakaṇikā* was born out of the womb of Jñānī, the pious wife of Śiva's devotee Nirmalaṅga in Udutadi.
>
> — Basavaraju 2004: 159, tr. H.S. Shivaprakash

The passage shows how Haḷegeyadeva is keen to make the story more elaborate through the mythopoeic imagination of the anthologist-narrator. In accordance with Devī's command Akkā is wedded to King Kauśika. Having severed her bond with him, she is on her way to "Kalyāṇa" to receive the blessings of great saints as a prelude to the final destination, "Śrīśailam". This is the time when she is espied in the outskirts of Kalyāṇa by Kinnarī Bommayyā who is impressed by her nakedness and divine beauty. He thinks to himself:

> If she is proved to be united with *liṅga* I will bow down to her as a *guru* mother or else if she has the false attachment to the body I will make her my woman.

He then accosts Akkā. Akkā tries to put him off and then reminds him that he is like her brother as Śiva alone is her husband. But Kinnarī Bommayyā considers this empty talk and takes hold of her by force. Akkā tells him to take her body if he can be so senseless and do what he likes. Kinnarī Bommayyā touches all parts of her body, but when his fingers reach her vagina he finds the sacred ash there. Frightened, comforting himself, he speaks a *vacana*, suggesting that every part of Akkā's body is filled with Śiva.

He is now penitent. However Akkā comforts him saying, "Kāma's bow which consumes fourteen worlds is beyond you and me." Kinnarī Bommayyā is thankful to her and admits that he is reborn through this encounter.

The third anthologist, Siddhaliṅgeśa Śivayogī, more or less follows the same storyline. Though he avoids the elaborate account of the second anthology, he gives it an interesting twist. Allama himself sends Kinnarī Bommayyā to prove to all the devotees how Akkā has conquered lust. The last anthologist, Gulura Siddhavīranārya, also keeps the same storyline and retains the bit saying that the test happens at Allama's suggestion.

It is interesting that though the non-realistic nature of the episode is underlined in the anthologies, the later anthologists attempted to cut down the embarrassing near-rape scene and give it Allama's sanction.

After this "physical test" on the outskirts of Kalyāṇa, which, in the anthologies, is depicted as a symbolic holy city, Akkā goes through a spiritual test set by Allama Prabhu in *anubhava mantapa*. *Sūnya Sampādane* depicts the tale of her strict reception at the hands of Allama Prabhu.

Basavanna introduces her to Prabhudeva and to the assembly of the *śaraṇa*s. Basavanna's *vacana*s 8 and 9 indicate that he knew her to be an advanced *śaraṇa*. All the same Prabhudeva puts her to a severe test, possibly with a view to revealing her great worth to the assembly and clear any doubts that might be lurking in their minds. His first question is about her husband. No woman, especially a young one, could, according to Prabhudeva, be admitted to the spiritual academy unless she was duly married. Akkā Mahādevī replies that she has given herself away to Lord Cennamallikārjuna. She sings:

> *O sir, I love the beautiful One.*
> *The Formless One, who is beyond*
> *Death or dissolution;*
> *Cennamallikārjuna is my groom:*
> *All other husbands in the world*
> *Are naught to me.*
> — Bhoosnurmath and Menezes 1970: 265

HARIHARA'S MAHĀDEVIYAKKANA RĀGAḶE

Harihara (*c*. CE 1190–1250) is the earliest poetic biographer of Śaivite and Vīraśaiva saints. The Nāyaṉmārs of Tamil Nadu were known in Karnataka by the twelfth century as *purātana*s (the ancient ones). There are a large number of references to *purātana*s in Vīraśaiva poetry in Karnataka. At the same time, Vīraśaivas were aware of the difference between the path of the ancient ones and their own. Harihara's works, based on the life of Tamil saints, are called *Purātanara Rāgaḷegaḷu*.

Harihara also composed poetic biographies of the leading Vīraśaiva saints — Basavanna, Akkā Mahādevī and Allama Prabhu. This group of works is called *Nūtana Purātanara Rāgaḷegaḷu*, i.e. poems about the "New Ancient Ones". "*Rāgaḷe*" is a new type of poetic narrative that Harihara shaped. "*Rāgaḷe*s" are story poems mostly written in blank verse but sometimes employing prose. In addition to his "*rāgaḷe*s", Harihara has composed a work in *campū* metre based on Kālidāsa's *Kumārasambhavam*. He is also the author of a devotional work called *Pampa Śātaka*, 100 verses in praise of Lord Virūpākṣa in Hampī.

Though the leading Vīraśaiva saints were to become the protagonists of many poetic biographies in successive centuries, Harihara was closest to them chronologically. Harihara's works are spontaneous overflow of devotion. At the same time, in his depiction of the lives of Vīraśaiva saints, Harihara shows greater realism than his successors. Harihara's life was spent in "Hampi", which was to become the site of not only the Vijayanagara empire but also of the Vīraśaiva renaissance which led to compilation, anthologization and exegesis of the compositions of twelfth-century saints. Harihara's works antedated the Vīraśaiva resurgence proper in Vijayanagara particularly during the rein of Prauḍhadevarāya I (1419-46). The process of mythologization of the lives of saints begins with Harihara, for instance, all Vīraśaiva saints according to the depiction come into the human world because of having attracted a curse in Kailāsa (Śiva's abode).

Despite this, Harihara is not insensitive to the human dimensions of saintly figures on the earthly plain. This is clear from all his works on Vīraśaiva saints.

According to later biographers, Akkā Mahādevī was never married. The reason is that the canonization of Vīraśaiva saints had gone on by then to the extent that the biographers had begun to see them as superhuman by birth. The possibility, that Akkā could have got married before her enlightenment, was just out of the question for them. In Harihara's work, Akkā was married to King Kauśika.

Here follows a brief account of Akkā's life as told by Harihara.

King Kauśika happens to see the young beauty Mahādevī while once passing through the streets of his city. He becomes completely possessed by her:

> *Mahādevī in the heart, Mahādevī in the eye*
> *Mahādevī in the forest,*
> *Mahādevī in every touch*
> — Nagabhushanswamy 1996: 71; tr. H.S. Shivaprakash

He then commands his ministers: "You fools why you are not doing anything. Can't you see I can't live without Mahādevī". They rush to Mahādevī's house and tell her parents of the king's desire to marry their daughter. The parents are all too happy but Mahādevī is infuriated. She wonders: "How can light be united with darkness, you fool? What does wisdom have to do with ignorance?" She bluntly refuses to marry the king because he is a *bhavi* (a non-believer in Śiva). The king hears about this. His passions transform into rage. He orders that if Mahādevī refuses his offer of marriage, her parents should be instantaneously put to death.

To rescue her parents from impending death Mahādevī agrees to marry the king on the condition that:

> *I will worship Śiva as I wish*
> *I will be in saints' company as I wish*
> *I will be absorbed in the service of guru as I wish*
> *I will unite with the king as I wish.*

On these conditions and only on these conditions does her marriage with the king take place. However this contract could not hold for long. The partaking of marital sex, a source of unending joy for Kauśika is a source of abysmal anguish for Mahādevī. Harihara describes it in his inimitable prose:

Mahādevī's indifference became King Kauśika's empire of lust
As that great devotee was longing for dawn, Kauśika was longing for the
dawn not to break. To the king, the sexual intercourse punctuated by
Mahādevī's protest appeared like a dream and an illusion. Thus when
Mahādevī was still going through the sexual intercourse, the sun dawned as
If it was the sun of Mahādevī's Śivajñāna (spiritual wisdom).

— Ibid.: 75-76

On another occasion when she is being forced into sex, a Śaivite mendicant arrives at the palace. In keeping with one of the conditions agreed upon, i.e. to be in the company of saints as she likes, she jumps out of Kauśika's bed and rushes to give hospitality to Śiva's devotee. Unable to contain his anger, Kauśika stops and threatens her. Taking this as a breach of contract, Mahādevī walks out of the palace and the town of Udutadi as if:

The town's virtue was leaving in a woman's form
As if the town's "Śiva bhakta" (devotion to Śiva) was leaving for the hills . . .
Covered by the thick cloth of her hair
Like a parasol of deep devotion
Wearing the Āṇḍāḷs of faith,
Her body filled with great vairāgya' (detachment)
Led on by the wealth of mṛda-bhakti . . .

— Ibid.: 76

She ultimately reaches Śrīśaila, there to worship all pervading Mallinātha (one of the names of Śiva). However, Kauśika is not yet free from lust. Harihara depicts this in a highly dramatic episode. Kauśika disguises himself as a Śiva devotee and pretends to surrender to her in order to recover her. Mahādevī speaks to him in a *vacana*:

> *Why should I live with you for all to see*
> *What has darkness to do with light?*
> *Or flame with coolness? Or delusion with wisdom?*
> *Or sunlight with the moon or me with you?*
> *Get lost, you fool.*
>
> — Ibid.: 79

Kauśika does not stop even now. He tries to bribe some fake devotees and *gurus* into advising Mahādevī to return to him. But this also does not work. The saints, who wanted to advise her to return to the husband, are so overwhelmed by her unflinching devotion to Śiva that they ask Kauśika not to persist any more.

As stated earlier, it is interesting to note that Harihara's *Mahādeviyakkana Rāgaḷe* does not mention Akkā's journey to Kalyāṇa at all. It seems to be an addition made at the time of composition of *Śūnya Sampādane* in the fourteenth century. Later biographers follow *Śūnya Sampādane* and not Harihara. Also though Akkā Mahādevī's *vacana*s mention Kalyāṇa, this does not automatically follow that she referred to a geographically located city. It might be a completely metaphorical journey to Kalyāṇa on her part (Kalyāṇa is Kailāśa).

As far as her address to *śaraṇa*s like Bommaiah, Allama Prabhu, Basavanna and Cennabasavanna is concerned, it could in all probability be an interpolation made by the copiers and compilers later as the saint's reputation and her popularity increased.

Intersemiotic Transformations of Akkā's Vacanas into Modern Literatures

The medieval Kannada works like Harihara's *Mahādeviyakkana Rāgaḷe* and the different *Śūnya Sampādane* anthologies point to different ways of recreating Akkā's life and works. Harihara depicts Akkā Mahādevī as an embodiment of Śaivite devotion whereas *Śūnya Sampādane,* an allegorical dramatic anthology, narrates episodes not found in Harihara like the "Kalyāṇa" episode. This is to fit Akkā's life into the anthologists' scheme of constructing a narrative of the *vacana* movement with Allama Prabhu as its centre.

In the process, the anthologies mythify the life of Akkā. Later medieval hagiographic accounts of Akkā's life continued this mythification.

The twentieth-century recreations of Akkā's life are for the most part in the direction of de-mythification. It is not that mythification vanished altogether. An early twentieth-century play by B. Puttaswamayya, called *Akkā Mahādevī* which became quite popular in professional theatre, continues the process of mythification. Here also Akkā Mahādevī's life begins not in the human world but in "Kailāsa". However, some of the popular novels in the early twentieth century follow a different path. Here Akkā's life is narrated in human terms. One such well-known novel *Giriya Navilu* (*The Mountain Peacock*) (1960s) by Basavaraj Kattimani, though it takes names and events from Chamarasa, foregrounds the human dimension of Akkā. She emerges as a mortal woman who attains spiritual progress through suffering and struggle with society and milieu.

B. Puttaswamayya's series of historical novels centring around the twelfth century *śaraṇa* movement, the Kranti Kalyāṇa Series, is a novel, based on close study of historical research material accessible at that time. In the fifth volume of this series, *Mugiyada Kanasu* (*The Unending Dream*), there is a whole chapter on Akkā Mahādevī's visit to "Kalyāṇa" and her spiritual debates with *śaraṇa*s in *anubhava mantapa*. The depiction in this chapter is indebted to *Śūnya Sampādane*.

MATE MAHADEVI'S TARAṄGIṆĪ: A NOVEL

A voluminous novel by Mate Mahadevi is another ambitious attempt to recreate Akkā's life and mission. The author became the first woman Jagadguru of Liṅgāyata tradition. She set up an organization called Basava Dal, supposed to spread the message of Liṅgāyata religion and philosophy as interpreted by her. She claims to teach a religion based on reason and scientific temper.

Taraṅgiṇī derives its overall framework from Harihara's *Mahādeviyakkana Rāgaḷe*. However, it does not speak of Akkā's origins in Kailāsa. The name of Akkā's father, Oṁkār Shetty, and that of the king who was won over by her beauty, Kauśika, are also taken from Harihara. The episode of Akkā's marriage, found in Harihara, is deleted in this novel. When Kauśika asks for her hand in marriage, Akkā Mahādevī agrees to marry him only after completing a vow for five weeks. Kauśika, it is agreed, should not disturb her during the period of vow. Seized by lust, Kauśika breaks his promise with the result that Akkā Mahādevī refuses to marry him. The episode in Kalyāṇa, also not found in Harihara, occupies a great deal of space in this novel. Thus this novel roughly follows the pattern of *Śūnya Sampādane*. The story of Akkā's life concludes in *Kadaḷī* forest in Śrīśailam.

The author, in her preface, speaks of how she actually went to *Kadaḷī* in Śrīśailam along with her disciples to get the feel of the region. She also speaks of how dangerously close she was to a roaring tiger but remained unharmed. The description of *Kadaḷī* is woven into the last part of the novel. The concluding paragraphs of the novel give a clue to the overall tone of the work:

> Speech turned mute because of the experience beyond the body, mind and intellect. Logic came to a halt when breath forcibly entered *sahasrāra*, thousands of lightening bolts appeared to gleam opening the gate of *paścima cakra* in which *prāṇa-vāyu* merged. The eyelids were lowered and a wheel of light began to revolve. The light of consciousness was melting like camphor in the flames of the great light. The current of light began to flow in the cave in the womb of *Kadaḷī*, which is like the heart of Cennamallikārjuna and slowly became one with the vast cosmos.
>
> — Mahadevi 2005: 804; tr. H.S. Shivaprakash

This passage is characteristic of the exaggerated narrative style. Though the author appears to divest the story of mythology, the depiction of Akkā's character is excessively idealized. There are innumerable unending discourses that punctuate the narrative all too frequently. All this is a far cry from the intensely human and experiential tone of Akkā's own *vacana*s.

Though following the same path of idealization, the play written by Taralabalu Shivakumar Swamiji on Akkā's life is more appealing because it depends more on Akkā's own compositions to depict her life.

All these writings constitute the depiction by the faithfulness to the character of the saint already canonized by Liṅgāyata tradition. The treatment of the protagonist in these works entails an a priori kind of reverence deriving from the tradition.

This is where modern Kannada women writers after 1970s started looking at Akkā in a totally different way.

MODERN KANNADA POETESSES' RESPONSE TO AKKĀ

A large number of poems came to be written on Akkā in Kannada after the 1980s, a period which saw a sudden upsurge of women's poetry in Indian languages. A large number of women's poems written in Kannada since then are indebted to Akkā Mahādevī in a very interesting manner. Here is a poem by Kannada poetess Bhagya Jayasudarshana:

For Akkā

You cut all the knots that
Bound you and became
Free of the constraints
Imposed from within and without.
You were bold, firmly resolved
In your outbursts and sciences.
The clothes with which you draped your soul
Turned greener in your inner storms
Your thunders and your rains,
Your enemies surrendered to you
In the open fields of elemental
Movements, you were the empress
of the empire of Cennamallikārjuna.
In the battles which I fight, I hold
The weapons, weapons that
Cannot rust, weapons
That cannot be sharpened, weapons
of mud and plaster;
I roam in the circle of my defeats,
Oh I haven't gone naked, roaming
The streets of small desires.
But Akkā do you know
My nakedness within,
And that I've shivered
With the winter's cold.

— Zide 1993: 93; tr. Author

The poem is based on the contrast between Akkā Mahādevī, the ultimate symbol of woman's freedom, on the one hand and the self of a modern woman too human to wage Akkā's kind of elemental struggle. What is celebrated in such poems, addressed to Akkā directly or referring to her indirectly, is more her radical act of human daring than her spiritual transcendence.

We shall now consider another poem by Hema Pattanshetty in which the reference to Akkā is more oblique:

About Void
Without nakedness
You cannot get the void
Whatever you get
Because of nakedness
Will not stay with you
All relationships turned into void
Frightened by nakedness
Turning into a complete lie
The frank heart full of love and friendship
Everything beyond the truth is false
Is there any other truth
When truth has no basis in truth
How can you trust
The talk about uniting the earth and the sky.
The nakedness of the void
Came to me as void —
The darkness of the void
Because of becoming naked there
I have got now
The inexhaustible
Void of voids all around

— Pattanshetty, *Nimma Purushasuktadalli*;
tr. H.S. Shivaprakash

Hema Pattanshetty's poem is also built on the same contrast as the previous poem. Though Akkā is not directly invoked, she is represented by the concept of nakedness and of void, a synonym for Śiva in Vīraśaiva philosophy. The contrast between void as a principle of metaphysical transcendence and void as existentialist nothingness is taken for each other in this poem.

The following poems by Savita Nagabhushan are the humanized reworkings of Akkā's own *vacanas*. The first one is a rewriting of Akkā's "journey poems", whereas the second is a transformation of the series of Akkā's poems about warding off mortal male intruders.

Footpath alone is enough. . . .
Hungry,
I surrendered to trees
Thirsty,
I bowed down to rivers
My heart was won
By the lovely-teethed gorava
To hills
To parrots, koil birds
To soft breezes
I folded my hands
Why should a doer
Be shackled by the world?
I shrugged off the end
And moved on
When the time is ripe
Even a footpath is enough
To lead to Kadalī
Does not Cennamallikārjuna
Know this?
Don't
Don't frighten me
I will touch and feel the fire
Don't stop me
I will jump into the ocean
And swim
Don't laugh

I will ride a mirage-horse
Don't sniff
I build a sand castle
Don't wake me up
Let me brood over eggs
Don't be angry
I am lost in love-God
Don't pluck
I will flower
Don't call me
I want to be here
Don't . . . Don't . . . Don't . . .
Don't follow me in vain.
— tr. H.S. Shivaprakash

Though examples can be multiplied, the above poems sum up the response of a modern woman to Akkā Mahādevī, the fascinating symbol of rebellion against and freedom from male norms. However, there are significant differences between Akkā's times and our own. Akkā's path of transcendence was clearly laid out for her but this path is not clear in modern times of agnosticism and doubt. Another significant point is that the spiritual journey of Akkā is not directly mentioned or analysed by anyone of the poets. Her life is either mythologized or relegated as something which cannot be trodden by a common woman. Like in one of T.S. Eliot's poems, "The Love Song of J. Alfred Prufrock", in these poems one finds an invocation of inability due to human limitations and thereby a kind of refusal to take on the role one secretly aspires for. Even though Akkā's spiritual attainment is at times recognized and acknowledged, it is an ideal that the modern woman cannot emulate. Akkā's beloved was "without body, without birth . . .".

However, the beloved of modern poets is with the body and subject to birth and death. The discontent with the relationship embodied in traditional marriage is another link between Akkā and her twentieth-century counterparts. The solutions sought are totally different. Though there are other saint-poetesses who attained freedom and transcendence within the bounds of marriage, why did modern women poets turn to Akkā in such a big way? The reasons are to be sought in the changing sociology and psychology of the modern, educated and working woman trying to find her way out of patriarchal mores.

Besides these poetesses from modern Karnataka, who tried to hold dialogue with Akkā Mahādevī, each from her own station and perspective, there is a male poet from Kerala, K. Satchidanandan, who has registered his response to Akkā. His poem comes up with a more intimate glance at Akkā's mental bearings. Akkā is a poetess of great universal appeal, who had hitherto been confined to the linguistic and geographical boundaries of Karnataka. Translations of Akkā's works into English had been taken up on a large scale after A.K. Ramanujan took the initial steps. And these translations have helped to break the boundaries for Akkā Mahādevī. That Akkā's example was inspiring to poets outside the Kannada milieu is demonstrated by K. Satchidanandan, the renowned Indian poet writing in Malayalam.

His poem is a lyrical evocation of Akkā's journey towards Cennamallikārjuna, her destination. Unlike the poems by Kannada poetesses, Satchidanandan's poem is an intense and impassioned communion with Akkā's poetic journey:

Akkā Speaking
O Śiva O Cennamallikārjuna
Open the door
I have come, Word, all naked
Yours, all my hidden fire,
The coconut flower in my body
Yours, this offering, the crescent moon

Of my dreams. Yours,
The divine Gaṅgā of my words
Yours too, the kālakūṭa *venom*
That I drink everyday
So is the ḍamaru *of my* prāṇas
So too the dance of time that my feet,
Freed from anklets dance
Yours, too, this minute
Born in countless yonis,
Having seen countless worlds,
Having traversed hells
I have come
Like a shepherd grazing many
Magical worlds greeted by the unripe mango
Of joy, afraid, I began searching
For you in mountains and forests,
Unaware of your being in my womb-vessel
Without giving out even a little finger
Silent, like the fragrance of campaka,
Like the glow inside gold
Like pungent taste in the chilli,
Unaware that you pervaded me
I dressed myself in countless coral
Beads of Kailāsa,
I became all alone, yet not alone,
In the world
For me, kalpavr̥kṣas, *all trees*
Sañjīvnīes, *all plants*
Śivaliṅgams, all stones
Holy places, all my destinations,
Amr̥ta, all drinking water
Kalyāṇa saugandhikas, *all flowers*
So long as my Beloved is within me
You glow inside me without flames

Penetrating me without bleeding
You ecstasy of union without copulation
Taking me, without slightest movements,
Beyond planets
Sprouting without sowing
You, parrot's eye and nest,
The nest and the flowering tree,
Tree and the forest,
Forest and earth,
Earth and the (fivefold,)
world, the world and dream
The mind-stuff the dream inhabits
O Hara O Mallikārjuna
I have shut the door
I am coming step by step
Lightenings are bathing me
Floods are decking my hair with jasmines
I, standing, naked, clothed with morning sunlight
Come O blue-throated one
With your snake-garland
I hear the echoes of hooves of your ox
In the ghāṭs
I see your crescent glow
Turning into emerald the sandal leaves
Filling the breeze with Gaṅgā
No more the smoke of kitchen fire
Or the daggers of the wicked eyes
Embrace me with your blue arms
Put out my awareness
Suck my life out with just a kiss
From now on, just the two of us
In eternity's waves
My life-breath will sing blue

Against which the elephant has rubbed its body.

— tr. H.S. Shivaprakash

K. Satchidanandan in this poem is able to recreate the mystic union that is conceived in all *bhakti* experience. The images used here refer back to the idiom that Akkā has employed in her own *vacana*s though the form is different. Satchidanandan's poem also seems to transcend the gender as the persona of the poem speaks of "union without copulation" which again was the motto of the *bhakti* experience.

The above examples show how Akkā's life and works continue to haunt the imagination of our own age of secularist values in diverse ways.

Transformations into Drama, Dance and Music

In spite of the fact that Akkā's name is associated with the twelfth-century Vīraśaiva movement, which has become a recurrent thematic preoccupation in Kannada literature of succeeding epochs, particularly modern period, Akkā Mahādevī has not become the subject of any major work in drama and theatre. Basavanna's life is a popular subject with theatre people. Akkā Mahādevī is more popular with poets and fiction writers than with theatre people. However, there are some exceptions.

If we consider *Śūnya Sampādane* to be a theatre piece, different versions of this work give fascinating treatments of her entry into Kalyāṇa. This has already been discussed. Prior to this, Harihara had also depicted Akkā's life with a lot of dramatic force in his narrative poetry.

In the twentieth century, though many plays were written about Basavanna, there are only two plays worth mentioning about Akkā. The first is by the well-known novelist and playwright of Karnataka, B. Puttaswamayya. This play was written for Gubbi Theatre, one of the most influential professional troupes of Karnataka. As it was consciously written for the theatre of spectacles, the text draws heavily on myths and legends about Akkā and casts them in larger-than-life mould. Later he wrote a six-volume novel *Krānti Kaḷian* on twelfth-century movement, which won him Sahitya Akademi Award.

Yet another attempt to stage Akkā's life was undertaken by Sri Kumara Swamiji of Taralabalu in the late 1970s and early 1980s. He wrote the play *Sharan Sati Linga Pati* and produced it himself for Taralabalu Kalasangha in Sirigere. A fairly memorable production of this play was done by the National School of Drama graduate Ashok Badardinni for the same troupe. Swamiji's play, that follows Harihara, Chamarasa and *Śūnya Sampādane* editions for Akkā's life-story, is written in traditional manner and Badardinni used techniques of modern drama school theatre. The scene depicting Akkā's departure from Udutadi following the break-up with her husband was done with great sensitiveness. Apart from this, the text and production was lacking in the complexity so essential for depicting Akkā's life. Only the traditional devotional content was emphasized. Relevence of Akkā's life to present times was not even touched upon.

On the whole, plays on Akkā do not have the kind of complexity and contemporary relevance like those on Basavanna's life. One has to turn to modern Kannada women's poetry for that kind of exploration of contemporary significance of the great saint-poet.

Transformations into Cinema: Scribbles on Akkā

Scribbles on Akkā is a film made on Akkā Mahādevī by Madhusree Dutta. This film is a juxtaposition of a series of representations of Akkā's life and works through documentation, image, allegory, interviews and discussions.

The film can actually be seen as a cinematic version of intersemiotic transformations of Akkā Mahādevī's life and works into other genres of art. The theme of Akkā's life and poetry is translated into various forms of life and art. It shows and, in turn, represents how Akkā is represented in temple structures, in images and idols, in contemporary poetry, in theatre, in public announcements, in professional theatre, in painting, etc. Besides this, the film is also about how the message of Akkā's life translates into contemporary life especially into the lives of women.

The film opens up with taking out into the open the framed paintings of Akkā in a kind of procession and ends with putting these frames back together in some kind of careful order. This scene becomes a symbolic representation of what the film has to offer to the viewer. As these frames offer different portraits of Akkā Mahādevī, so does the film offer different readings of Akkā's life and works. Each time the film-maker shifts the frame of reference, Akkā's life and her poetry open up new signifieds for a single floating signifier — Akkā Mahādevī.

Though the film is on life and works of Akkā Mahādevī, the film-maker clearly conveys her message that all women share Akkā's spirit of independence and positive survival in spite of hurdles and obstacles. The film-maker accomplishes this by merging the roles played by the protagonist. These roles range from that of a contemporary Indian woman to Akkā herself. The film opens in a modern metropolis showing women engaged in earning their livelihood through various kinds of employments. These women appear to be taking on all the hardships posited by life in a very graceful manner. Even a fisherwoman, who is thronged by people at a seaside fish market, has a smile to offer. After showing this spirit of survival, the common thread that connects women in all times and places, the scene shifts directly to Udutadi, the birthplace of Akkā Mahādevī.

On the outskirts of the village there is a temple and the deity of the temple is none other than Akkā Mahādevī. Villagers regard her as their local deity, offer worship to her idol in the usual manners of ritual worship with incense, light, flowers, *prasādam,* etc. They take out long processions bringing out Akkā's idols, decking up young girls as Akkā, singing her glories, etc. In short, this episode depicts how mythologization of Akkā's life has been rendered complete by installing her image as a Goddess in the temple.

The film-maker however reconstructs Akkā in all her dimensions in such a way that women from all layers of society respond to her life and works in their own way, from their own station, from their own level of awareness, wisdom, education, class, caste, etc. In fact, we can divide women into two categories according to the relationship they form with Akkā Mahādevī. There are women from traditional conservative backgrounds who place a kind of blind faith in Akkā and her powers and then there are women with some kind of self-awareness who connect with Akkā on a completely different plane. Through the first category of women, the film-maker is able to project the dimensions of faith and spiritual achievement that is integral to Akkā's life (for instance, the old woman who has contributed towards the construction of the temple courtyard and all the women who are interviewed at the procession). This group of women, however, does not create a dynamic relation with Akkā, as they put her on a pedestal in the temple, worship her like a Goddess and recreate the established roles for getting about the struggles of Akkā, thereby relegating their own responsibility to bring about any change in the established orthodoxy. But the women in the second category are actually questioning and negotiating with the values and principles that Akkā's life represents and are trying to recreate their own identities on the basis of these negotiations. The film captures these women in their milieu as poets, translators, painters, etc.

The most interesting aspect of the film is that it orchestrates quotes from a host of intersemiotic translations within the film which in itself is an intersemiotic translation of Akkā's life history and poems. As mentioned above, the film opens and concludes with the framed popular paintings which reflect the image of Akkā also depicted in the "mythological play" which is both shown directly and through the documentation. In these versions, Akkā's nudity is mentioned, but it is made acceptable by draping it in her luxuriant tresses. By contrast, the representation of Akkā in the temple of Udutadi shows her completely dressed in a *sāṛī* with a *pallu* pulled over her head.

On the other hand, the modern representations of Akkā in present-day poems and paintings, and in narrative bits of Akkā's journey played by the Manipuri actress Savitri, these suggest a totally different way of looking at Akkā's persona. The difference between the representations that cover up nudity and those that open it up is that between traditional and modern ways of understanding the influential woman saint of the past. The first is based on faith and reverence. The women around Udutadi observe in their interviews that Akkā Mahādevī is their village deity. The modern artist Nilima Sheikh attempts to read Akkā's life, in her own words, "in the post-Colonial India". She also adds, "as we see her progress on her journey we understand our own journey". This perception is also echoed by the contemporary Kannada poetesses interviewed in the film.

Hema Pattanshetty describes her journey from attitude of awe and reverence to the one of questioning. She wonders why Akkā did not choose to live in this very world. Vaidehi speaks of Cennamallikārjuna being a lie in her poem quoted in the interview. Yet another representation is in terms of the extent to which Akkā's poetry is intercontextually translated, if only partially in the lives of present-day women both old and young. The idea of modern women trying to follow Akkā's journey is typified in the various roles that the actor Seema Biswas is made to play: The modern working woman, city girl visiting Udutadi, the Christian bride, the nun and at the end as a lonely young girl watching the procession of images. Overriding all these representations are the riddles of Akkā's poems sung and picturized in different ways. The solo acting by a male actor of the encounter between an infatuated Kinnarī Bommayyā and Akkā is a daring exploration of the irresistible fascination and repulsion of flesh. The same thing is echoed in the Savitri bits where she is shown, first walking, later crawling towards her goal. At one point she is shown as lying nude, tired and sweating. The last long shot of this bit shows Akkā played by Savitri walking nude towards the horizon.

The juxtaposition of different and even contrasting versions of Akkā's life and works in this film stays clear of reducing Akkā to anyone of those representations. Akkā comes out as text which is read "in contradictory and diametrically opposite ways". However, the meaning of her life is depicted as something eternally deferred.

The foregoing is not an exhaustive analysis of all the intersemiotic transformations in and of the lives and works of Āṇḍāḷ and Akkā. I have focused my understanding mostly on the texts or portions of them accessible in English translations. However brief my account, I hope it points to a variety of ways in which these two renowned saint-poetesses have been engaging the imagination during their own and later times.

Section Three

10

Living Bhakti Traditons

M.A. Lakshmithathacharya Swami on Śrī Āṇḍāḷ

M.A. LAKSHMITHATHACHARYA Swami was born in 1936 in Melkoṭe, Karnataka. He has served as the head of the Academy of Sanskrit Research, Melkoṭe, for twenty-five years. Swamiji has touched many fields of knowledge with his profound talent. As a Sanskrit scholar, he has raised this "language of gods" to a new level of awareness in India and abroad. As a "Master of Ubhaya Vedānta", "Bhagavad Viṣayam" and "Viśiṣṭādvaita", he has not only fulfilled the traditional role admirably but also opened new practical vistas in these three supremely rich spiritual fountains of knowledge and shown how the common man can benefit from them in this age. Following are the excerpts of a conversation held with him on 29 July 2007 in his house in Jainagar, Mysore:

Alka Tyagi: Swamiji what is the essence of Śrīvaiṣṇavism as a religion?

Swamiji: Śrīvaiṣṇavism emphasizes the importance of the Goddess "Śrī" or Lakṣmī. Association of "Śrī" is very much stressed. "Śrī" is playing the role of the mother in the universe. The God, conceived as father, is generally supposed to be strict and unforgiving. Therefore mother brings in compassion and forgiveness in the life of devotees. Another aspect of "Śrī" as a woman is that of "female principle" in general. Regarding this, I sometimes joke about how it is a religion of "Strī".

Once someone asked Rāmānuja, "Who is the right person to teach and learn *Tiruppāvai*?"

Rāmānuja answered:

> People who have moustache and rough cheeks are not the people to receive the teachings of *Tiruppāvai*. Such ruffians are not fit for this kind of learning. Only those people who have got "breasts" can receive it and enjoy it. That means only women can receive it. Even among women, only Āṇḍāḷ can teach it and only Āṇḍāḷ can receive it.

Here the word "breasts" is not merely a physical attribute but is a symbol of compassion, of the heart: a heart that swells with *bhakti*. Only a heart ever swelling with devotion can teach and understand *Tiruppāvai*. Hence richness of heart is required for *bhakti*. Men can make themselves fit for *bhakti* only if they develop a feminine swell of intense devotion in their heart. That might be the reason why all the saints before Āṇḍāḷ, assumed themselves to be women with respect to their Lord God.

Alka Tyagi: What is the significance of Āṇḍāḷ as an Āḻvār saint Goddess?

Swamiji: Woman as a form of Goddess assumes a position of great respect in this religion. Also Vaiṣṇavism was brought to the forefront of Hindu culture only after great Āḻvār saints came up from sixth century CE onwards. All the Āḻvār saints considered themselves to be the brides of the Lord regardless of their human gender. They wanted to become one with the Lord who is considered to be the husband *par excellence*. Most of the Āḻvār saints including Nammāḻvār superimposed on themselves a feminine consciousness in order to feel and express the love of a bride and beloved to the Lord. Hence "Bridal Mysticism" is at the centre of "Śrīvaiṣṇavism".

Since Āṇḍāḷ is actually a woman, probably that is the reason why she leaves behind all the other saints in expressing her passion towards the Lord. In *Nachiar Tirumoḷi*, she says, "Even at the mention of the idea that I should be given to someone in marriage, I will immediately collapse and die." This is the devotion she had for Lord Raṅganātha (stanza *Wanadai Wallum*). The clarity, the urgency and the depth of this kind of devotion are extraordinary. All the Āḷvār saints elevated the *bhāva* of human *śṛṅgāra* to *divine śṛṅgāra* where it becomes *bhakti* as the relationship with the Lord as husband.

Alka Tyagi: I think the attitude of *bhakti* serves as a tool to transcend all human desires which arise when human senses come in contact with their respective objects in the external material world. All these desires which have their objects in this world converge and become one single desire which has no object in this material world of senses but conceives of only one single transcendental object in the form of *iṣṭa devatā* which is what you call as *arcāmūrti*. It is this focus of the *citta* that leads to liberation or freedom from the attachments and bondages in the world. Do you agree?

Swamiji: Yes. However in order to engage the *citta* (mind) in the beginning it is important to have an object which is appealing to human mind. It is for this reason that *bhakti* rituals in all religions involve the image of the *iṣṭa devatā*. For all Śrīvaiṣṇava saints also *arcāvatāra* and *arcāmūrti* become a major point of focus. That is why icons are accorded great importance in this religion. "Iconic worship" is taken up with immaculate perfection in ritual techniques. Rituals are carried out exactly as they are laid down in the scriptures.

Through "iconic worship" we re-live history in our routine existence. Beauty of iconic worship is that we live ancient times in the present: we live *Rāmāyaṇa*, we live *Mahābhārata*. We relate to the roots of the culture and feel great strength through this urgency that we invest in icons. Recently, a novel in four volumes has come up about how the statue of Raṅganātha was protected by various communities during the Muslim invasions in fourteenth century. This Tamil novel by Renugopala is called *Tiruvaraṅganuḷa* (*Soujourn of Raṅganātha*). This is the kind of importance we attach to the icons. They are not merely statues for us, they represent a living form of the *arcadevatā*.

Alka Tyagi: Ācārya Rāmānuja lived in Melkoṭe for more than twelve years and transformed the temple, making it a famous Śrīvaiṣṇavite centre. Was it chosen for seclusion it offered, in order to be away from the political turmoil of the times?

Swamiji: In Melkoṭe, Rāmānuja came in twelfth century and renovated this much more ancient temple. This temple is unique in its conception. Generally temples are built after a community has settled in a certain region, in order to fulfil the religious needs of the people. Therefore most temples are actually called *grāmāśritālaya* (lit. the temple which has existence due to the village). But here the temple is at the centre of the community as the community came up only because the temple already existed here. Therefore, Melkoṭe is known as *ālayāśritagrāma* (lit. the village that depends on the temple for its existence). Here everybody is there for the God in the temple. Here people of each and every community are important and have their own role in the life of the temple. Melkoṭe temple is actually considered to be the house of the Lord Tirunārāyaṇa and the Goddess accompanying Him is "Yadugirināyikā". Since these are not merely icons for us, we treat them as our royal father and mother living a grand life in their grand house where there are innumerable servants in the form of devotees who would do the routine work for them like giving *abhiṣeka* (ritual bath). So a priest, a washerman, a cook, a barber, a trumpeter all serve the Lord in their own way. Each and every community joins in the life of the temple deities. Trumpet player, for instance, comes from the Harijan community.

M.A. Lakshmithathacharya Swami has served as the head priest of the famous Śrīvaiṣṇavite temple centre in Melkoṭe, near Mysore in Karnataka.

Vasundhara Doraswamy on Akkā Mahādevī and on Choreographing Akkā's Vacanas

Vasundhara Doraswamy

Vasundhara Doraswamy is an internationally renowned Bharatnāṭyam dancer based in Mysore, Karnataka. She is also a reputed choreographer and a venerable *guru* too. She has choreographed and performed Akkā Mahādevī's *vacana*s at various places in Karnataka. Her latest dance recital based on *vacana*s was in April 2005 in Mysore, where she danced for two-and-a-half hours transmitting the intense rhythmic passion of Vīraśaiva outpourings to a charmed audience. Following are the excerpts from a talk held with her at her dance school in Mysore.

Alka Tyagi: What inspired you to make Akkā's *vacanas*, the basis of your performance?

Vasundhara Doraswamy: There is *nāyaka–nāyikā bhāva* in her *vacanas*, which is very important in a performance and then there is this spiritual — *bhakti* — element which is the basis of all classical dance or classical arts. In Akkā Mahādevī's *vacanas* *bhakti* is the *sthāyī bhāva* and other *bhāvas* are *sañchārībhāvas* only. *Bhakti* in her *vacanas* is reflected in an intense desire for union with her chosen God — Cennamallikārjuna. In classical dance also, union (*yoga*) is the goal and the aesthetic elements are subsumed in the process of performance where the performer is constantly being led by desire for the union of *ātmā* (the individual soul) with the *paramātmā* (the Divine).

Alka Tyagi: Which are the *vacanas* that you chose to choreograph in the performance?

Vasundhara Doraswamy: I chose two *vacanas* of Akkā Mahādevī. These were: "O Parrots Prattling Away" and "Listen O Sister! (*Akkā Kelluvva*)".

Alka Tyagi: Is there any specific reason for choosing these particular *vacanas* from Akkā's oeuvre?

Vasundhara Doraswamy: These *vacanas* have a very varied range of images which can be easily choreographed. In the first *vacana,* i.e. "O Parrots Prattling Away", Akkā is eagerly enquiring the birds and beasts of the forest about the whereabouts of her Lord and Lover Cennamallikārjuna. In the second *vacana* "Listen O Sister!" the poetess is relating in great excitement, her dream about the preparations of her marriage and her strange bridegroom, to her close friend (*sakhī*).

Due to their dialogic nature and the element of drama inherent in them, these *vacanas* provide a lot of scope for my imagination as a creative performer.

Alka Tyagi: What, according to you, is the significance of Akkā Mahādevī's works for a modern woman?

Vaundhara Doraswamy: Akkā Mahādevī's life and her songs which contain the essence of her lived experience can be very inspiring for a woman living in modern world. Akkā is an example of a very strong will at work. This strong will drove her to choose and live her life in her own way. She achieved whatever she wanted to achieve, and that is what is most important for a modern woman too — to chose and then follow the choice to its logical end.

Alka Tyagi: How do you personally relate to Akkā Mahādevī?

Vasundhara Doraswamy: Akkā Mahādevī was a part of a conventional society and she lived or at least tried to live within those conventions in the beginning, but when it became difficult for her to live a life not in accordance with her inner calling, she chose to walk against the grain. She, with a steadfast and strong will, made society bend down to make way for. In spite of their initial doubts and harsh enquiries, senior *śaraṇas* could not ignore the fire of the pure soul that was shining in this young beautiful woman.

Finally she created her own identity in the *anubhava mantapa*. Society in India has not changed much since then. This kind of life-pattern relates to my own life and my growth as an individual. This is the reason why I find Akkā Mahādevī so fascinating.

Sangeet Vidvān R.S. Nandkumar on Musical Renderings of Vacanas by Vīraśaiva Saints

R.S. Nandkumar is a fourth generation musician in the *paramparā* of Sant Tyāgarāja. A natural musician of international fame, he is a research scholar as well. He has in served various capacities at Dr Gangubai Hangal Music and Performing Arts Univeristy, Mysore, and presently as

Director of Publication Wing of the University. He has also served as Member, Karnataka Sangeetha Nrutya Academy. He has worked for Unesco's intangible art forms of Karnataka. Nandkumar has submitted a doctoral thesis on the musical work and life of Śrīpadarāja, which traces the evolution of Carnatic music.

Sangeet Vidvān R.S. Nandkumar

Alka Tagi: Could you please tell us a little about your work in the field of *vacana* singing?

R.S. Nandkumar: Any musical composition of our country seeks to achieve two main goals: one, expression of the pure aesthetic and the other, to communicate an idea. To achieve both these, our music has developed various stages called forms of expression. These forms may be different for rendering in the normal human voice or instrumental in rendering the musical notes or an intertwined composition of words and musical notes.

When it comes to such a musical composition, the intension of the word — content — is very important, for, it is this that usually directs the musical flow throughout the composition. In south India, I believe, that *vacana*s of *Śiva-śaraṇa*s were the earliest available spoken and sung compositions in the dialect of the common man. The great Śiva *śaraṇa*s sought to convey many important facts and virtues of human life and endeavour in a comprehensive but simple manner that could be easily understood by the proverbial "man on the street". It is tantamount to an all-time respected aphorism "speak as you sing and sing as you speak".

Vacana is defined as "what is/can be said" (*vācanīya*). But "how" it is said and/or sung is also important. What seems to be *vācanīya*, i.e. the focal thesis or the essential idea for the creation of that *vacana* is essential for a musical rendering. In *vacana*s we find sometimes a group of ideas that work towards conveying a single idea. In fact, this single idea is the focal point. This is the punch line and not the *aṅkita* as is generally conceived.

I am always trying to analyse the formal content or in other words, the form of the *vacana*s. The form has often been negated as the *vacanakāra*s themselves seemed to defy form and structure. Basavanna's famous enunciation, "I sing as I please/without tarnishing the Śivatva (*ānu olidante ānu pāduvenu . . . ninage kīdillavāgi*)" has served as a kind of directive to the *vacana* composers. I usually find that none of the contemporary *vacana* singers put their efforts to do what can be called as a kind of musical-quantification and sing the *vacana*s either borrowing the form from the *pada* tradition (the *vacana* was originally not composed in this form, either in its literary or ideological delineation) or simply repeated the first line of the *vacana* or the *aṅkita* (*vacanakāra*'s signature-nomenclature) in the end (for the sake of "musical" convenience). However this was not very conducive to communicate the theme of the *vacana* or the central idea or the punch line of the *vacana*. So the whole purpose of the *vacana*, which is to articulate a specific idea, is defeated.

Please take a look at the *pada* format; its first line is called the *pallavī* and it is at once an introduction as well as the conclusion of the "thesis" of the composition. The main content of this thesis is usually in the most essential part, i.e. the *caraṇa*. Sometimes, these two are bridged by another segment called the *anupallavī* (*melāpaka*), thus called because it usually follows the *pallavi*. Hence, this musical form (the great Vaiṣṇava movement took this form to sing praise of the Lord and perhaps this easy and organized singing and communicating made this movement pan-Indian in its scope). Now, we can realize that most of the *vacana*'s theses were not composed on this "logic" and the musical rendition in this illogical order only makes it more confusing and sometimes incoherent. However, please take a *vacana*, think about it as a *vācanīya* thesis, find out the innermost focus, trace this focal point to its concomitant peripheral ideas in the form of other sentences hovering around this main sentence. Then sing the introductory portion of the "thesis" of the *vacana* (it can be any sentence of the *vacana*, I call this the *udgrāha khaṇḍa*) so many number of times that enshrines the central focus of this theme (this can be actually the central portion of the total length of the *vacana* — I call this the *dhruva* portion). Sing this in matching proportion to its predecessor *udgrāha khaṇḍa*. Then we come to the main punch line of the *vacana* that gives out its inner and essential meaning (I call this the *aṁśa khaṇḍa*). I can say or sing it as much as I please (refer to Basavanna's saying *ānu olidante . . .*). I can do *ālāpa* (aesthetic freestyle musical delineation), I can do *svara-kalpana* (render musical notes to or without the *tāla* or *laya*) and sing this line to many musical varieties that enshrines and enlivens this central focus of the *vacana*. Then I come to the end portion of this *vacana*, that usually contains (however, it is not always the case with all the *vacanas*) the *aṅkita* of the composer. I call this the *abhoga khaṇḍa*. Now if you see, we have four *khaṇḍas*. Depending on the type and length of the *vacana* I can sing or say these *khaṇḍas*. Some *vacanas* may not establish all these four portions at all, making it more to the point of the thesis of the *vacana*. So, on the whole, if you take the entire gamut of the *vacana sāhitya*, the musical renditions in all its variety are mind-boggling and perhaps a great challenge to a performer.

The questions that came to my mind as a singer and composer were related to creating a singing pattern that would not bring down the emphasis or misplace the emphasis. "How should one begin?", "What should be repeated?", "What is the punch line?" and "How should one end a *vacana* song?" are the major questions that have to be dealt with when you begin to work on *vacana* singing.

Considering these I evolved a way of singing in which the line that conveys the central idea is the line to end the *vacana*. I called this form *vacana saṅgati*. (*Saṅgati* is made of *saṅ*(*g*) and *gati*, where *sam* is *samyag* = comprehensive, all encompassing, combined; and *gati* is the converging point. So *saṅgati* is the combined movement to arrive at the punch line where entire focus of the *vacana* is located.)

Alka Tyagi: You did this programme called "Vacana-Pada Vaidya" for All India Radio, Mysore, which became very popular. Could you tell me a little about it?

R.S. Nandkumar: In this programme we took *vacana*s and *pada*s; specifically *vacana*s from Allama Prabhu along with some of the contemporary *vacanakāra*s and sang them in *vacana-saṅgati* format while elaborating upon the medical concepts portrayed in them. This caught on well with the *vacana* singing community in these parts.

Famous Hindustani musician from north Karnataka, Nagaraj Rao Havaldar who is a disciple (and in earlier days, disciple's disciple) of Pandit Bhimsen Joshi seems to have caught on this form and later used it in his singing.

Alka Tyagi: How, in your opinion, did the tradition of *vacana* singing evolved with time?

R.S. Nandkumar: *Vacanas* flourished from the twelfth century onwards. This was also the time when our music was not known by any distinctive categorization. Our music was just performed by our people as their music and they did not specify any name to it. This was done by others who heard it and felt the necessity to name it. I now quote an example; dichotomous nomenclature of Indian music in terms of Karnataka Music and Hindustani Music of our Indian music happened only a few decades ago. We find the earliest reference to this in work by a Pune-based Maharashtrian, Kāśīnātha Apatilāsi, who in his work *Saṅgīta Sudhākara* mentioned this for the first time. He wrote it in the year 1914. Maybe a decade or two prior to his times, this dichotomy evolved.

In my opinion, *vacanas* were as much a voice of reform as they were an expression of *bhakti*. *Vacanakāras*' primary emphasis in the *vacanas* always came upon new ways of interpreting the religious ideologies that was made more and more complex and un-understandable, which posed as a hindrance on the path of spirituality. Music and art were not their major domains. *Vacanas* were simply recited and sung as a message of religious and ideological reform and that of a movement of social evolution which believed in reinterpreting the structures of caste, class and gender. Therefore *vacanas* were basically recited and sometimes were recited in the mode of performance. Element of performance came from a very common feature found in *vacana* compositions, viz. the element of dialogism.

Alka Tyagi: You are right in pointing out the dialogic nature of *vacanas*. This is inherent in all *vacana* compositions as they were basically recited in the company of other *śaraṇas* as a part of an ongoing dialogue on various issues that concerned *śaraṇa*s. Do you think the compositions had something innately classical in them especially with regard to music?

R.S. Nandkumar: Character of Indian music is defined by the ancient Indian music Śāstras. *Vacana*s neither had the content nor the form that could be contained or adapted to the classical theories of Indian music. For instance, great musicologist Śārṅgadeva, who was a contemporary of *vacanakāra*s and who had written about all the categories of music that were prevalent in his times (he even took into account the songs that a *grahiṇī* sang while carrying out her routine chores at home), does not mention the *vacana*s as a musical category.

If we look at the two streams of tradition — *mārga* and *deśī vacana*s automatically fall into the latter. However, there have always been harmonious exchanges of various elements between these two streams. *Mārga* and *deśī* streams of music find their distinction from the range and type of instruments used. For instance, *vīṇā* and *mṛdaṅgam* go with the *mārgī* and *tamate*, and drum goes generally with the *deśī* category. While *mārga* category tends to absorb the new art forms only if they reflect or cater to the classical or elite culture, *deśī* category is more open and easily renders itself to the voices of the masses. *Vacanas* basically contained a comprehensive range of voices where there were people from highest social class like Basavanna and also people from the lowest of lower classes like Sule Sunkavva. Most significant point of concern for us is that content of the *vacana*s undermined the established structures of politics, religion and society. Due to this basic counter-theme of *vacana* poetry, they could hardly be adapted into the *mārga* stream of music. It was only some two generations ago, say, 100 years ago that the masters of classical music took up the *vacana* lore and rendered it in classical *rāga*s and *tāla*s.

Music is an art form and all art forms are a prerogative of a refined society which has taste and also the leisure to engage in that taste. If you see the context of *vacana* compositions, you will know that the society, at that time, was in the throes of stormy changes and upheavals. In that context there was hardly a moment of leisure that could be conducive to composition of classical music variety. It is true that Basavanna says about the *vīṇā* being his body and mentions the *battīsa rāgas*. However, if one sees on a larger canvas, the then "classical (*mārga*) music" was such that it necessitated a formal training and such training was possible to a very few selected who could afford both the time and resource. Moreover, then the rich used this to regain "superiority" to the extent of social abuse. The *vacanakāra*s realized this and perhaps used the *deśī* modes of expressions that could be sung by those who could and for those who couldn't, they simply said the *vacana*s. Therefore, organized music seems to have happened to the *vacana*s only as an afterthought in the early 20th century or so. Theoretically, again as an afterthought, there are two kinds of *vacana*s called as *nudi vacana*s and *svara-vacana*s. *Svara-vacana*s are those which can easily be adapted to *svara* and hence, sometimes, *laya* (rhythm). And some of these could be rendered on the lines of *pada*s.

Alka Tyagi: In recent times however *vacana* singing has touched its zenith in the hands of great maestros like Mallikarjuna Mansoor. What according to you is the scope and significance of *vacana* singing in modern times?

R.S. Nandkumar: In contemporary scenario Vīraśaiva community has evolved its own corpus of religious doctrines and rituals based on Vīraśaiva saints' definitions and ideologies. There is no doubt, whatsoever, about significance of *vacana*s being used as a major reference point in all the aspects of living in Vīraśaiva religion. *Vacana*s are carefully preserved texts which hold the status of nothing less than a sacred book for a Vīraśaiva in modern times. They look into the content of *vacana*s and draw inspiration from them regarding their religious, social and family life. Moreover, some of the *vacana*s go beyond these religious prescriptions and deal with the life itself. These are readily accepted and adopted for singing and saying by all who desire such valued nuggets of knowledge. Hence, the *vacana*s are now exposed to the world to look into and sing/say them as they please!

Now, it is natural that these texts have attracted the attention of music composers and singers, and have been sung by great maestros like Mallikarjuna Mansoor and Pandit Basavaraja Rajguru. I now have a point to say here. When it comes to "classical" music arena, we have now arrived at confusing crossroads. The purists say that strict adherence to tradition is a must and hence the *vacana*s should be sung like a traditional classical musical composition (for which it was not originally conceived). Such purists recklessly apply "heavy" *ālāpa*s and *tāna*s and (in Carnatic music: *neraval* = various musical phrases to a given word phrase) and sometimes *kalpanā-svara*s = creative *svara* patterns sung with an organized end pattern *svara*, called as a *muktāyī*. All these, in my humble opinion, only contribute to destroy the subtle mood and enshrined idea of the *vacana*. On the other hand, the revolutionaries have started by singing these *vacanas* akin to their original intension and meaning, but alas, in order to make it more and more popular, they have made it more glitzy and hence commercial too.

It is time that we took notice of these and made suitable amendments so as to render these properly to their final inheritors; the common man, the most valued and essential part of our country.

Nandini Eswer, Rohitha and Rashmi Eswer on Āṇḍāḷ, Kṛṣṇa Bhakti and Śrīvaiṣṇavism

Nandini Eswer, famous virtuoso and an extremely sincere exponent of Indian classical dance forms, is the founder director of "Rāsavṛnda". "Rāsavṛnda" is a dance repertory

Nandini Eswer with Rohitha and Rashmi Rohita

based in Mysore, Karnataka, in south India. The institute is dedicated to reveal through classical dance forms, the richness and essence of Indian spiritual tradition as expounded in our sacred texts and ancient *Śāstras*.

While Bharatnāṭyam is at the centre of major choreography projects taken up by "Rāsavṛnda", Nandini Eswer, with the support of the dynamic young couple dancers Rohitha Eswer and Rashmi Rohita, also provides training in other Indian classical dance forms to the enthusiasts and disciples from around the country. She invites eminent *gurus* to conduct workshops to impart knowledge regarding other classical art forms apart from Bharatnāṭyam.

They have used Āṇḍāḷ's poetry as well as Akkā's *vacanas* in their dance performances. They have produced dance-dramas like Gokulanirgamana, Harinābhiśaraṇa, Kerege Hara, Dasarukanda Gopī Kṛṣṇa and Sāvitrī-Satyavān. Another very siginificant dance-drama produced by them is called Krishna Bhakte Goda, which was based on Śrī Āṇḍāḷ's life story.

Being in Nandini Eswer's presence is a personal delight. Rohitha Eswer and Rashmi Srinivasan, who happen to be her son and daughter-in-law, are also very accomplished performers in their own right. The duo have been part of all the performances done by "Rāsavr̥nda" and have performed all over India as well as abroad.

Following are some excerpts from a talk with all three of them:

Alka Tyagi: I came to know that you have done an entire dance sequence on the life of Āṇḍāḷ. Could you please tell me a little more about the programme?

Nandini Eswer: One of my disciples, Manimala who is a Śrīvaiṣṇavite, was to have her "Raṅga Praveśa" back in the year 1991. Being a Śrīvaiṣṇavite, she was very familiar with the life story of Āṇḍāḷ. Together we realized that it would be a very auspicious beginning for her if she begins with the story of a saint who rose to the status of a Goddess. We consulted the material available. Kr̥ṣṇadevarāya's *Amuktamalyada* and Garuḍavāhana Paṇḍita's *Divyasūricaritam* and Pinpalakiya Perumāḷ Jiyar's *Kuruparamparāpirapavam* are the major hagiographical works which serve as a resource for information on Āṇḍāḷ's life. However, renowned Sanskrit scholar Vidvan L. Vasudeva Bhatt wrote the script in Kannada language for us and lyrics were set to music by Smt. S.K. Vasumati. It was a two-hour performance, which ran in two phases. First phase was solo performance by Manimala where she alone dealt all the characters. In the next phase, few years later, this was constructed as a dance-drama. It was a full-fledged dance-drama with complete traditional costumes. It was a very fulfilling experience to see the life of an Āḻvār woman saint brought down to the stage in front of an audience which comprised of the devotees as well as laymen.

Alka Tyagi: You have used Akkā Mahādevī's *vacana*s in your choreographies. What kind of *vacana*s fascinate you most?

Nandini Eswer: We have used a few of Akkā's *vacana*s like for the *vacana* where the poetess is asking a bird about her Lord Cennamallikārjuna.

What is significant for me in this *vacana* is the urgency felt by the *bhakta* with relation to the divine. The image of the bird, who is posited here in many roles, becomes the metaphor to convey this urgency. Bird here is invoked as a *sakhī*, as a messenger as well as in its original form as a bird itself.

Alka Tyagi: How do you inculcate a *vacana* in a dance sequence?

Nandini Eswer: Every dance sequence has a well-defined path, which is called *mārga*. In Bharatnāṭyam, various stages of *mārga* are: *alaripu; jattisvara; śabdam; padavarṇa; pādam; aṣṭapadī; devaranāma; tillana* or *tarānā* and finally obeisance to God.

It is in the seventh stage where we can bring a *vacana* or a *śloka*. *Vacana*s are usually danced in place of a *devaranāma* or after a *devaranāma* before *tillana*.

Alka Tyagi: Rashmiji I just discovered that you are a Śrīvaiṣṇavite. For me it is a joy as I would really like to know how the Śrīvaiṣṇavite religion conserves itself in the hands of young and educated. Especially when we know that our post-colonial education system feeds us on secularism at schools and college levels and only a few fortunate ones like you get a parallel education in the traditional and classical inheritance of our culture. So first of all, I would like to know, is it difficult to find a bridge between the two systems that is the modern education and the religious legacy? Then to be more particular could you please tell me, what does the story of Śrī Āṇḍāḷ mean to a classical dancer like you who is of modern times?

Rashmi Srinivasan: First, I would like to thank you; it is my pleasure to share my views and opinion about what you have asked.

I am a Śrīvaiṣṇavite being brought up in a very traditional and orthodox family. In fact it is those customs and traditions which were imbibed in my childhood have made me god-fearing and have helped me to uphold our culture. In my opinion bridging of two systems, i.e. modern education and religious legacy, is not difficult but in turn the blend of the two always gives a clarity to your vision and thought process.

Right from my childhood I am familiar with the story of Āṇḍāḷ and as a classical dancer, it has been one of my dream characters. However, to enact that role, one has to understand, visualize and realize the core philosophy, and the religious, spiritual and aesthetic content conveyed in the lyrics.

Rituals at home play a vital role; they enhance your imagination and evoke the concept of divinity, which needs to be understood and realized. This is my personal opinion as a dancer. I do not have a particular daily routine as a Śrīvaiṣṇavite. I do offer my daily prayers after my bath and perform *tulasī pūjā* regularly.

Alka Tyagi: Nandiniji, your engagements with various dance ventures at Rāsavr̥nda are unique in many ways. I realize that lot of your work is experimental in nature. At Rāsvr̥nda you have successfully worked on projects like "*Mokṣa-mārga* Philosophy-based Dance Feature"; "Compositions of Jaina Literature in Prākr̥t and Kannada Languages"; "The Essence of *Bhagavad-Gītā*"; and "Philosophy and *Bhakti* in Saint Tyāgraja's *Pañcaratna Kr̥tis*". This is just to name a few, but clearly your attempts seem to be focused on bringing all that is esoteric in Indian philosophy and spirituality to the stage in such a way that it becomes accessible to everyone — regardless of whether they are formally aware of or educated about the tradition or not.

The brochure on "Rāsavr̥nda" also states, "Its (Rāsvr̥nda's) mission is to attempt through the eternal bliss of dance to facilitate the realization of the divine spirit and true happiness [*Ānanda*] within us".

I am very keen to understand how you accomplish this task of giving a form that too a very visible emotional form with human gestures to concepts like *jñāna-yoga*, for instance.

Nandini Eswer: I have always tried to take the traditional form of classical dance a little further than merely being an expression of *śr̥ṅgāra* and *bhakti*. To work on *jñana* and to literally show that it can be transformed into *bhakti* by using the same form which is associated with *bhakti*, has been my effort at *Rāsavr̥nda*. I have deep conviction that through the structure and scheme of Indian classical dance we can convey the essence of all spiritual theories in a manner which can invoke spiritual joy in the heart of all *sahr̥dayas*. It is this conviction that makes me venture into concepts and ideas unknown in the realm of classical dance.

In *mokṣa-mārga*, for instance, we worked on the three main streams of Vedāntic thought, i.e. Dvaita, Advaita and Viśiṣṭādvaita. I was specifically talking to you about the *Bhagavad-Gītā* production. Here we used three-level stages. One to depict Dhr̥tarāṣṭra and Sañjaya, the next level, the philosophers and at the base level, Kr̥ṣṇa and Arjuna. The philosophers represented the thought process of Kr̥ṣṇa on the battlefield. They also depicted the concepts of *Bhagavad-Gītā* adopted in daily life and how a common man should see Kr̥ṣṇa's philosophy in his day-to-day life and adopt it in his living.

When we have to work on philosophical concepts we have to conceive and create new vocabulary of gestures and emotional attitudes. We have to create our own dictionary actually. We do create one and keep referring back to it. Rohitha here is my co-composer and a constant source of inspiration.

Rohitha Eswer: Yes we have to visualize and give a tangible form to all that is abstract in a lyric or script. For a dancer, visualization is all and it becomes a very big challenge if you take up an entire sequence from *Bhagavad-Gītā*.

Alka Tyagi: Rohithaji, could you please tell me again about that lyric in which you talked about the image of mother Yaśodā playing with child Kṛṣṇa?

Rohitha Eswer: The lyrics are:

adisidale yaśodā jagadodhāraṇa
anoraniyana mahatomahiyana
aprameyana adisidale yaśodhā
adisidale yaśodā = mother Yaśodā is making her child play
Jagadodhāraṇa = the one who protects the world
anoraniyana = smaller than atom
Mahatomahiyana = bigger than the biggest (universe) (*Kṛṣṇa*)

It is this Kṛṣṇa where Yaśodā is making him to "play" (here she is making the protector of the world to play). Āḻvār saints especially Viṣṇucitta Āḻvār and Tirumaṅgai Āḻvār have written verses on Kṛṣṇa's childhood with similar theme.

M.A. Jayashree on Śrīvaiṣṇavism and Musical Rendering of Tiruppāvai

M.A. Jayashree, Professor of Sanskrit, has authored many books in the fields of Sanskrit, Yoga, ancient sciences, Indian history, Indian culture and music.

She is a musician with a melodious voice, an artist in the Mysore School of Painting, delivers discourses on Purāṇas, *Tiruppāvai* and philosophy and a great teacher of spoken Sanskrit.

As a propounder of "*Śruti paramparā*" (the oral tradition), she has cut many CDs, to enable learning of Sanskrit by chanting and memorizing and to understand *Yoga-Sūtras* effectively and has a large number of overseas students to her credit.

Alka Tyagi: You have released this beautiful CD on "Ubhaya Veda", where you have sung *Gadyatrayam* of Rāmānujācarya, *Mukundamālā* of Kulaśekharāḷvār and *Tiruppāvai* of Śrī Āṇḍāḷ. Āṇḍāḷ's *Tiruppāvai* is sung in a manner that provides the listener an opportunity to learn it by heart. You underline the importance of listening here and it involves recitation and repetition. The method that you employ is easy to follow and can help the interested learners a great deal. What significance does it hold for a learner except for giving them a chance to sing these hymns?

M.A. Jayashree: Actually the method employed here comes from "*Śruti paramparā*". In ancient times disciples used to learn

M.A. Jayashree

entire texts of Vedas by heart through this method itself. Besides allowing them to sing these hymns, this kind of CD also helps them to get deeper into the tradition.

In these days of skepticism there is a belief that if any communication has to be effective we have to have logical understanding of the communication not only in terms of expression but also in terms of its language content. In this world where logic dominates over emotions only rational understanding is supposed to be valid and any emotional affectation is considered as weakness, subjective experience is suspected even if it is your own. But in this domain of faith, devotion and love, it is the domination of emotion. We do not realize the impact of emotion on us until and unless we face a traumatic experience.

So going back to the beliefs of the Indian pious minds, we know by historical evidence that words do have their impact on the psyche whether the meaning is understood or not. That is why many words are called as *mantras* which literally means, by remembering it, it will protect the person. That is why there has been so much emphasis on the efficacy of literature which is rendered by the highly evolved, for it has the force of transformation in its tonal value itself let alone in terms of meaning. So the primary impact of a good literature is by its tonal value and for this if we add melody. So it becomes all the more endearing and can capture any mind and set it on the path of spirituality. Indian system has devised methods to use all types of inducement to bring individuals on to the path of spirituality or evolution.

We all know by experience that frequent exposure to an activity induces a sense of affinity to the thing and here affinity to the tune and hence to the text and then on to its meaning and about the composer, so with least amount of effort one can enter into the spiritual path.

Alka Tyagi: In what way is Āṇḍāḷ's *Tiruppāvai* integrated in a common Śrīvaiṣṇava home and their ways of worship?

M.A. Jayashree: Every Śrīvaiṣṇava home will be having an idol or a picture of Āṇḍāḷ. Everyday as a part of *nityānusandhāna* (daily worship), *Tiruppāvai* is sung. The last two verses are integrated into "Śattumorai", a procedure where the devout Śrīvaiṣṇava offers his gratitude to all those who contributed to this system of worship and wishes that the tradition should live for hundred years more. The *Vaazi Tirunamam* of Āṇḍāḷ is chanted at the time of *tīrtha* distribution. During the month of Margazhi (December–January), everyday one verse of the *Tiruppāvai* is sung in the temples and homes early morning. Poṅgal as *prasādam* is distributed. It is said Śrī Rāmānujācārya decided in consultation with his Ayurveda physician Garuḍavāhana Paṇḍita, what offering should be prepared in different seasons and different times. So even the offerings have a rational basis behind them.

Why Āṇḍāḷ's hymns only would be a natural question. Āṇḍāḷ is revered in the provocations pantheon because of her extraordinary devotion to the Lord. She represents the epitome of the Śrīvaiṣṇva Śaraṅāgati concept of Ananyatva.

In the moth of Margazhi, there are discourses every year on the *Tiruppāvai* hymns of Āṇḍāḷ which is heard with reverence by the devout Śrīvaiṣṇvas. The commentators to the hymns have shown how her thirty compositions have in them the very essence of Śrīvaiṣṇavism, i.e., the attitude of the soul and that of God, the relationship between the master and the disciple, the components of *prapatti* and so on. All these are explained at three levels to the lay public.

Alka Tyagi: Which are the verses from *Nachiar Tirumoḷ̤i* that are generally printed on the wedding invitation cards? What is the importance of such an invocation?

M.A. Jayashree: Āṇḍāḷ has composed 143 verses in addition to thirty verses of the *Tiruppāvai* verses. *Varṇamayiram* contains the rest of the verses which are divided into fourteen sections. The sixth section which is specifically called "Vāranamāyiram", is sung during the wedding of a Śrīvaiṣṇava couple. There are ten verses in this section and the first verse starts with the word *vāranamāyiram*. Here Āṇḍāḷ describes her wedding to her friend as she saw in her dreams. She says at the end of each verse, *kenā kanden tozi nān* (O friend, I saw a dream). These verses describe the Śrīvaiṣṇava wedding procedure.

The Śrīvaiṣṇava wedding invitation cards may have one of these ten verses. Āṇḍāḷ speaks of her marriage with the Lord, her devotion as well as the grace of the Lord. So it is the message for the bride and the bridegroom, how they should pattern their relationship to each other.

"Āṇḍāḷ Talks About Love" by K. Satchidanandan

Āṇḍāḷ is the only woman among the Āḷvārs, the Vaiṣṇavite ascetics of Tamil Nadu of the post-Saṅgam period. Daughter of Periāḷvār, Āṇḍāḷ is believed to have lived in the eighth century CE. Devotion and lust appear with equal force in the poetry of Āṇḍāḷ who was a devotee of Viṣṇu from her early childhood. Legend has it that Āṇḍāḷ was adamant that she would not marry anyone else other than the One who lies on the serpent-bed in the Śrīraṅgam Temple, and that Viṣṇu appeared in dream to the priests of Śrīraṅgam Temple and commanded them to ceremoniously bring Āṇḍāḷ from Śrīvelliputtur to Śrīraṅgam for the wedding, and that as she got down from the palanquin and came into the sanctum, she disappeared into Viṣṇu's idol. She is believed to have been only fifteen then. Her chief works are *Tiruppāvai* and *Nachiar Tirumoḷi*. In this poem, I am trying to imagine how it would be if "Āṇḍāḷ Talks About Love" — The Poet.

Āṇḍāḷ Talks About Love

Thinking that if she so much as utters a word,
With the soft warmth of that word it may dissolve
Like snow — without speaking to him, and
Containing it within herself, stifled, like
The goblin that lives under water on the riverbed;
With the discomfiture of an ant whose tiny legs
Got stuck in honey; to see in the sea-eye,
Him sprouting a golden feather on the fourteenth-day moon,
Leaning the dark-rosewood-body on the blossomed cassia tree
And sniffing it and caressing it softly, hiding it from her mother;
Deeming the bed as soft as the body of a hare, as a thorny murikku *tree*
And feeling her body smarting; and turning into a karavīra *plant*
That strains its ears for a little breeze to throw down a flower on him;
And, disentangling her hair at dawn, confused that it is a bunch of tender leaves,
Heaving a deep sigh and like a mad woman whose mind does not settle down,
The long eyes smarting with pain, sitting with her chin on her palm —
This is one kind of love.
At the slope of the hill where he arrives following the tunes of the reed-flute
With the herd of cattle, his twirling eyes following the swirling whip —
Along that stream where honey flows, strewing her bangles, anklets
Ear-rings, pearl-necklesses and dresses, daily, as if unawares,
Laughing like the wild-rivers, bowing low in a dance, like

The milky moonlight on the coconut palm-fronds during an ātira *night;*
Standing in waist-deep water at the bathing ghāṭ, *at a time when he is due to arrive,*
Smearing her kayām-*flower-coloured (dark-blue-hued) body with the foaming*
Juices of uluñcikka *and tender shoots of* vellila, *and the rare* nāḷpāmaram
And the fragrant nenmeni *powder, declaring to all within earshot*
of her presence; and if by all this he somehow does not take notice,
Uprooting a sītamudi *from the banks, and tying a stone to it, and*
Hurling it right in front of him; and if even that is not enough,
Stopping the water-sports then and there, and winding a wet cloth
Around her naked body, like a mermaid, climbing on the embankment
Smearing the fine cimpāñjī *upon her two feet calloused with*
Running after her cattle, and henna *on her palms with blood-red lifelines, and*
Sitting pretty on the grassy lawn, like the bloomed aśoka *tree in the soft sun*
Waiting for the cowherd —
This is another kind of love.
As the hillock covered with flowers shakes like
The flower-bedecked kāvadi *in the sound of the* murasu,
As the water in the Kāverī goes down to the level of the sands
Shivering in fear, hearing the booming perumpara
Like the trumpeting of mad elephants; as the steeds,

Elephants, the army, chariots all, raising their pennants
And standards, and bursting crackers, rush on, bent on battle —
As the clouds of billowing dust form a giant wall
Separating man from his adversary, imprison him
In the dark, stinking of blood — at that moment,
Adorning her husband with the tilaka *for battle*
With the lifeblood flowing from her sundered heart
And throwing around his neck kāñci-*flower-garlands*
And crowning him with vañci *flowers, and handing him*
The sword, and accompanying him till the threshold of
Their nuptial chamber smelling of akil *smoke;*
Then following him till the small courtyard where
Mango-blooms lie strewn; then, till the bathing pond
Where, in the cradle of the petal of the white-water lily
The mañcadikkuru *fallen, swings; then, till the clump of bamboos*
Whose skin is peeled by the creeping bean-vines; then till the path
Where spreads the silken carpet of the mayilellu *flowers; then till*
The jowār *fields — following him thus and finally covering him with*
*The blue-*kūvla-*flower-garlands of her unceasing gaze;*
Then, turning back and as if afraid to look back, rushing —
Like deluvial waters and storm, along the same mud-dyke
She had come on coy steps like ebbing water once, as a newly-wed bride —
And falling like a corpse at the threshold:
That is yet another kind of love.
As time passes, as bamboos flower, as in the vales where bloom
Screw-pines, silk-cotton trees, karuñoci, indam, bakula, curappunna

Payini, vāṇī, cerupūla, punali, punna, *as the mind and body*
Are awakened in the bird-calls in which flow the memories of honeymoon,
Like a sleep-walker, without anyone knowing, following the tunes of a flute,
Under the shade of a big veṅga *tree, like the rays of the full moon embracing*
The raincloud, dissolving in him, and then, the kājala *running down her eyes*
And with the bindi *brushed away, her fine clothes now sticking with*
Sand-grains and tiny grass-seeds, and the sliver of a peacock feather
Got entangled in her hair, with the marks of a pair of blue lips
Wandering all over her body, with welts here and there that sprout
Sweet memories, with a mind battling out good and bad,
With a body fatigued by bearing intense pleasure
With lips on which rise the Madhurāṣṭakam,
With thoughts burning and churning as to what the taste of the sin
of the lone, separated one — whether it is sweet,
Sour, salty, astringent, smarting hot — with bent head and walking slowly,
Reaching home and without anyone noticing,
Changing her clothes furtively —
This too is another kind of love.
Turning body into an infinitely sacred temple
With nine doors, having sculpted Him with the chisel of meditation
on the soft stone of dream, washing Him with my tears
And installing Him in the sanctum of my heart with

Eight kisses, and daily waving the āratī *of my flaming eyes*
And offering the soft petals of my lips
And adorning Him with the deep-blue silk cloth
of my tresses washed in the breeze from Kāverī
And smearing the sandal paste of marrow from my bosom
Where only love blossoms; like the anklet
That strains its ears for the tunes of the flute
Like the hoods that rise in the Yamunā, yearning
For the flowery-feet dancing on them,
Turning the entire body into ears, with palms folded,
Holding my breath, thinking that each fish is He,
He, the turtles, tigers, boars, the dwarfs that pass
Through the street, He the hill-tribes wearing bows and arrows,
Labourers who go with hoes and axes slung across their shoulders,
He, the cowherd blowing on his reed-pipe,
He, the soldier wearing the sword —
Seeing the puruṣa *who took ten incarnations in*
Each being thus, and paying Him obeisance,
And untouched by thirst, hunger, lust,
Unaware of rain or shine or mist
Unmindful of hairs turning gray, and
Body aging, sitting at the base of
The ancient kadamba *tree and*
Doing penance —
This is my kind of love.

— tr. A.J. Thomas

Akkā Speaking

— K. Satchidanandan

O Śiva O Cennamallikārjuna
Open the door

I have come, Word, all naked
Yours, all my hidden fire,
The coconut flower in my body
Yours, this offering, the crescent moon
of my dreams. Yours,
The divine Gaṅgā of my words
Yours too, the kālakūṭa *venom*
That I drink everyday
So is the ḍamaru *of my* prāṇas
So too the dance of time that my feet,
Freed from anklets dance
Yours, too, this minute
Born in countless yonis,
Having seen countless worlds,
Having traversed hells
I have come
Like a shepherd grazing many
Magical worlds greeted by the unripe mango
of joy, afraid, I began searching
For you in mountains and forests,
Unaware of your being in my womb-vessel
Without giving out even a little finger
Silent, like the fragrance of campaka,
Like the glow inside gold
Like pungent taste in the chilli,
Unaware that you pervaded me
I dressed myself in countless coral
Beads of Kailāsa,
I became all alone, yet not alone,
In the world
For me, kalpavṛkṣas, *all trees*
Sañjīvanies, *all plants*
Śivaliṅgams, all stones
Holy places, all my destinations,

Amr̥ta, *all drinking water*
Kalyāṇa saugandhikas, *all flowers*
So long as my Beloved is within me
You glow inside me without flames
Penetrating me without bleeding
You ecstasy of union without copulation
Taking me, without slightest movements,
Beyond planets
Sprouting without sowing
You, parrot's eye and nest,
The nest and the flowering tree,
Tree and the forest,
Forest and earth,
Earth and the (fivefold) world, the world and dream
The mind-stuff the dream inhabits
O Hara! O Mallikārjuna!
I have shut the door
I am coming step by step
Lightenings are bathing me
Floods are decking my hair with jasmines
I, standing, naked, clothed with morning sunlight
Come O blue-throated one
With your snake-garland
I hear the echoes of hooves of your ox
In the ghāṭs
I see your crescent glow
Turning into emerald the sandal leaves
Filling the breeze with Gaṅgā
No more the smoke of kitchen fire
Or the daggers of the wicked eyes
Embrace me with your blue arms
Put out my awareness
Suck my life out with just a kiss
From now on, just the two of us

In eternity's waves
My life-breath will sing blue
Against which the elephant has rubbed its body
— tr. H.S. Shivaprakash

Popular Depiction of Āṇḍāḷ as a Goddess

Āṇḍāḷ's Dream from Nachiar Tirumoli

Performed by Delhi based Bharatanāṭyam dancer
Anjana Rajan

Depiction of Āṇḍāḷ in Contemporary Performances

"Pavai Nonbu" a dance ballet based on Āṇḍāḷ's *Tiruppāvai* performed by Bharatnāṭyam dancer Padma Subramaniam at Vani Mahal, Chennai, on 31 December 2005.

Saint Āṇḍāḷ and Saint Hildegard

An exploration of mystical, musical poetry by two saint-poetesses — Āṇḍāḷ of eighth century, India, and Hildegard von Bingen of eleventh-century Germany — set to a haunting, evocative score that uniquely pairs medieval and south Indian classical vocal styles by contemporary dancers from India and Germany.

Popular Renderings of Akkā Mahādevī's Life in Film, Calendar and Painting

Pictures from Madhusree Datta's Film on Akkā Mahādevī

1. Celebration of Akkā Mahādevī janmatithi
on the last fullmoon day on the month of Chaitra (March-April)
at Udutadi village in Shimoga district, Karnataka.
(Still from film Scribbles on Akka, directed by Madhusree Dutta, 2000)

2. Painting on Akkā Mahādevī by Nilima Sheikh.
(Still from film Scribbles on Akka, directed by Madhusree Dutta, 2000)

3. Painter Nilima Sheikh in her studio, in front of
her work-in-progress painting on Akkā Mahādevī.
(Still from film Scribbles on Akka, directed by Madhusree Dutta, 2000)

Appendices

Appendix A

Bhakti Poetry and Bhakti Experience

A State of Mind and a Way of Being

Bhakti Poetry and Bhakti Experience

BHAKTI is an experience and *bhakti* poetry is an expression of that experience. Poetry is a category of art and to that extent *bhakti* poetry also is a category of art. In Indian aesthetic theories art experience is described as something very close to the spiritual experience. It is *brahmānanda sahodara*. According to Prof. R. Sathyanarayana:

> Art experience is non-referential; that is, it has no referent in the phenomenal world even though its symbolic stuff is derived from physical material. Art experience is different from all other forms of experience and is thus unique. It is perhaps nearer to spiritual experience than to others and is hence sometimes claimed to be coeval with it; this is why it is described in Indian aesthetics as *brahamānada sahodaraḥ*. However it differs from spiritual experience in following ways: It is transcient and endures only as long as the stimulating art form is present but disappears when the latter ceases to exist. The experience of *mokṣa* or *Brahman*, on the other hand, is by definition, permanent.
>
> — Sathyanarayana 2006: 7

Bhakti poetry is very intense in its expression as it is an effect of a spiritual experience into an art form. In fact, the compositions of all saint-poets inhere within themselves, at least, four conceptual categories — poetry, *bhakti*, self-realization (*ātma śākṣātkāra*) and liberation (*mokṣa*). These categories are not exclusive of each other. However, except for poetry, the rest of the three categories are non-discursive fields. That is why the vocabulary available to talk about these concepts becomes less and less objective. Amongst these four categories, poetry is most accessible to the conscious mind because in poetry objective reference points in terms of name and form are available which help to fathom the depths of a poetic tradition and thereby help to create a poetic context. This is so because poetry is always embedded in a particular culture and that same culture provides the reference points to understand it and helps to generate meanings out of it. The other three categories are not verbal categories. They are more of mental states than mere words and meanings, or signifiers and signifieds. In fact, in all the four categories, consciousness seems to assume a kind of modality, which is different in terms of intensity and expansion of awareness.

Consciousness generally operates on rational and non-rational, verbal and non-verbal or discursive and non-discursive (representational) levels. In discursive consciousness, a logical sequence of words or even that of events is followed while in representational consciousness, which is more emotive, all the experience is presented to the mind at the same time. For instance, when we watch a painting, a picture, a landscape or even when we listen to a piece of classical music, the effect or experience is felt in a single stroke or a flash which is much more intense than any linguistic feature can capture.

All spiritual and mystical experiences including devotion and *bhakti* in the final sense are non-discursive and non-rational. In order to express these experiences in linguistic signs, the language has to continuously break into signs that are ever pregnant with unlimited possibilities.

Here it is important to note that categories of *bhakti*, mysticism and self-realization or (*mokṣa*) have most often used poetry as one of the important communicative vehicles. Poetic discourse, through its capacity to allow condensed symbols in its structure, provides an appropriate model, which can convey intense and wide-ranging experiences. Therefore, *bhakti* poetry evidently inheres in its body the other three categories. *Bhakti* poetry seems to be a very suitable tenor to put across the modes of experience of devotion, self-realization and that of liberation or even mysticism. Indira Peterson says something to this effect when she talks about the *bhakti* poetry of the sixth-century Tamil Śaivite saints:

> Poetry is the *bhakti* experience made palpable. The hymn is the embodiment of the unification of emotion and ritual, interior (*akam*) and exterior (*puram*) — the experience of love and its expression; . . . — Indira Peterson 1989: p. 40

It is for this reason that all the sacred classical texts in India from Vedas through Upaniṣads to the epics have a chanting or singing tradition associated with them. The theoretical models evolve only after poetry has done its function of sieving down into the cultural consciousness through its intense simplicity.

On the other hand, in spite of the fact that *bhakti* poetry has always been deceptively simple in that it always talked to masses in their idiom, it has without exception invoked very esoteric readings from religious scholars. The perspectives, which these scholars/theologians bring to *bhakti*, are often limited to finding mythological parallels in the poems or to reading the poems as symbolic representation of some school of religious philosophy. There had hardly been any attempt to understand or to explain the experience independently of religious ideology, which respective devotional songs apparently convey.

It is important here to mention the work of the poet, critic and translator A.K. Ramanujan, who has made a successful attempt towards a secular reading of *bhakti* poetry in his essays that accompany his translations of Tamil classical as well as *bhakti* poetry. A.K. Ramanujan attempts to relate *bhakti* poetry to an unbroken classical poetic tradition, thereby ascribing to it a discursive field which is rooted in a register that is not necessarily religious. Especially in his "Afterword" to *Hymns for the Drowning,* Ramanujan relates the special poetic features of the *bhakti* and describes how *bhakti* poetry draws from the classical tradition. According to him, "Not only the personae, but the landscapes and the situations of classical Tamil love poetry (and heroic poetry) are enlisted as signifiers" for a new "signification". His lucid list of the signifiers, which are used in *bhakti* poetry, is worth quoting:

> 1. Vedic/Upaniṣadic concepts and symbols.
> 2. Buddhist and Jaina elements.
> 3. Purāṇa mythologies.
> 4. Love poetry and heroic poetry in Tamil (or Sanskrit poetry, for later *bhakti*) and in other regions.
> 5. Earlier notions of *bhakti* from the *Gītā*, *Paripatal* and *Tirumurukarruppatai.*
> 6. Folk religion, folk meters, motifs and genres.
>
> — Ramanujan 1981: p. 160

Besides enumerating the common signifiers and references that feed the content of *bhakti* songs, Ramanujan also talks about those features of *bhakti* poetry, that make it different from other traditional genres of poetry. Among these features, the chief characteristic is that all *bhakti* poetry is subjective and intensely personal. *Bhakta* is the poet, the speaker and the character. The second feature is that while traditional Indian poetry aims at achieving *rasa* (aesthetic emotion), *bhakti* poetry claims no such thing and experience or *anubhava* is the means as well as the goal. In Ramanujan's words "we have here a poetics of *bhāva* (feeling), not *rasa*, a poetics of personal feeling whether aesthetic or not". The next feature of *bhakti* poetry is that in *bhakti* as in "Vedic and epic texts" *phalaśruti* (religious end, lit. fruit) is supposed to be the function of the song rather than the aesthetic function. Another characteristic of *bhakti* is the use of everything, which is common and popular in the vocabulary. This is a very important feature of *bhakti* poetry and due to this, *bhakti* poetry and *bhakti* movements became major mass movements in Indian history. And it is due to this particular feature that *bhakti* poetry played a very significant role in shaping the regional languages in different parts of the country. According to Ramanujan:

> To the extent that the poetry espouses *bhāva* or "natural", "spontaneous" feeling, it tends to draw on the common stock of speech, local dialect, colloquial tones, and turns away from the standard literary language or poetic diction — though *bhakti* poets will use anything that is sufficiently common and will develop conventions of their own, a rhetoric of their own, a rhetoric of spontaneity, a complex stance of simplicity. Beginning with a first language, they may construct a second. — Ramanujan 1981: 164

Bhakti Poetry: Towards a Poetics of Experience

Taking off from exactly where Ramanujan left stating that *bhakti* involves a poetics of *anubhava* (experience) rather than a poetics of aesthetic enjoyment or *rasānubhūti*, this section is an attempt to arrive at some explanation about the experience of *bhakti*.

Ramanujan's work on Tamil *bhakti* poetry has been a significant move towards the creation of a "new poetics" or a poetics that can provide a perspective which is more literary and hence different from usually adopted religious perspectives on *bhakti*. But this was not a complete project, as it emphasizes more on content, i.e. on the nature of what is expressed than on the nature of the experience itself. The reason behind this may be the incomprehensive nature of the experience of *bhakta* and its rich direct ecstatic expression in the songs that flow from him/her. For instance, we do not find any explanation in these theoretical attempts for the experience of ecstasy, something similar to the biblical concept of "epiphany".[1]

When studying the poetry of Akkā Mahādevī and Āṇḍāḷ, I was often questioning myself about what was unique to these poems. Apparently they are also, like all love poetry, narratives of desire for the beloved and like all *bhakti* poetry they happen to be extremely simple narrations of this love for the beloved. What is the difference except that the beloved here happens to be God? What is it that makes them the source of intense ecstasy? Is it some different state of being which gave rise to these expressions? What was going on in their mind when these songs came forth? It often seems to be a different state of being, not accessible to a common mind, which was the source of these ecstatic compositions which are so powerful that they have become a part of the cultural consciousness of an entire race.

Bhakti: A Transcendental State of Consciousness

Here I propose to submit my thesis that *bhakti* emerges from a holistic state of consciousness which is called *turīya* in ancient Indian philosophies of consciousness. It is a very desirable state of being where one transcends the material bases of life and is able to live on a plane that is beyond material and is full of *ānanda* (bliss). A *bhakta* in the advanced stages of *bhakti* experiences awareness which is more expansive than the individual consciousness in general. This state of awareness takes the *bhakta* through a range of experiences that are not comprehensive to our normal state of consciousness. Poetry that comes out of this experience gives us a glimpse of their state of consciousness.

---

[1] This concept is very aptly used by British novelist, James Joyce in his novel *Portrait of an Artist as a Young Man* to represent artist-protagonist's experience of a sudden flash of illumination.

Indian theories on consciousness provide very comprehensive models of consciousness. These models, if studied carefully, can provide an appropriate framework to study and understand *bhakti* phenomenon and its effulgent poetic expression.

To begin with, I am trying to suggest that *bhakti* is an experience which happens only when the consciousness is operating at a higher level of awareness. Poetic expression of this *bhakti* experience is only one phase in a series of various phases that constitute the process of human expression as such. Speech is the most important manifestation of human expression and communication. Indian theories of cosmogony ascribe a very important status to the concept of "speech" (*vāc*) as it is called in Sanskrit. Mid-eleventh-century Kāśmīrī scholar Ācārya Abhinavagupta, who is the famous exponent of Kāśmīr Śaivism and is the author of *Tantrāloka*, has expounded the theory of *vāc*. Accordingly *vāc* is a manifestation of Divine Principle, which is conceived as Śiva in all forms of Śaivism including Kāśmīr Śaivism in the creation. *Vāc* is conceptualized as Goddess or Śakti (lit. power) itself. To quote Motilal Pandit, a modern scholar on Kāśmīr Śaivism:

> Śakti which is the essential nature of Śiva, expresses itself through five functions. These five functions correspond to the four hierarchical manifestations of the word (*vāc*), which are: the transcendent (*parā*), the visionary (*paśyantī*), the middle (*madhyamā*) and the gross (*vaikharī*). The transcendent and the visionary stages of the word represent perfectunity, whereas the middle denotes the stage of unity in diversity (*bhedābheda*) and the gross embodies complete diversity (*bheda*). The five functional powers that are associated with the four stages of manifestation of the word are consciousness (*cit*), bliss (*ānanda*), will (*icchā*), knowledge (*jñāna*) and action (*kriyā*). The first two functions — consciousness and bliss — correspond to the transcendent stage of pure unity, and so are not at all considered to be a

> manifestational stage. As this is the stage of unity, so consciousness and bliss are equated with Śiva and Śakti. Also at this stage of pure creation no manifestational activity takes place. Accordingly this state or stage has been termed as that of pure "I" (*aham*), and not of "I am This" (*aham idam*). In so far as the other three functional powers of the Absolute are concerned, they are seen to be related to the manifestational process of creation. These powers are will, knowledge, and action, and they emerge or become operative when the process of impure creation begins.
>
> — Pandit 2003: 184

In other words, in the above paragraph, we are dealing with the philosophy of creation itself. In Śaivism, creation is a downward movement, a descent of the divine energy (Śakti). This Śakti which is an undetachable aspect of Śiva is complete and effulgent in itself before the act of creation and this state of being is of complete unity (*abheda*). Here the *vāc* or the expression is transcendent (*parā*) and visionary (*paśyantī*). After this when the *ichhā* (will) to create emerges in Śiva, then the expression manifests in middle (*madhyamā*) phase and after the *ichhā,* comes the *jñāna* (knowledge) and then *kriyā* (action) takes place to effect the creation. At this final stage, the expression is gross (*vaikharī*). Here the idea of creation gets a tangible form and shape in the spatial dimension.

just as the creation expresses itself in the cosmic macrocosm, it also expresses itself in the microcosm of human consciousness in the same manner, the major means of expression being the same — *Vāc Śakti*.

Bhakti is an experience of complete unity with the cosmic self (*abheda*) which is *parā* and *paśyantī*. As it comes down to tangible expression of, for instance, a poetic form, it undergoes what has been called above as manifestational process where the consciousness relates to *madhyamā* level and finally to *vaikharī* level of expression.

Now it becomes important to understand the nature of consciousness and the role it plays in the life of an individual. How does consciousness behave when it undergoes different modes of experience? Does *bhakti* poetry provide us with a window to those states of consciousness which are far beyond the gross sense-experience?

Human Consciousness

Indian philosophy does not conceive of the individual self as an isolated entity, independent of creation that is effected by cosmic consciousness. It claims that individual self is not able to connect and envisage its role in the cosmic plan due to layers of impressions on its awareness. This is the classic *avidyā* (ignorance). Alain Danielou describes this idea about limited faculties of the individual and expansive nature of the cosmic principle with reference to Śaivite cosmogony as follows:

> According to the evolution of the cycles, man's pride rises against his instinct, creating artificial mental constructs which oppose his perception of the subtle world. Subsequently the disastrous grandeur of the human species develops on a material level, until Śiva (the prime cause and source of life) appears and teaches men three ways of knowledge and realization, which are Sāṁkhya (cosmology), Yoga (the mastery of subtle man), and Tantra (initiatory and magical rites and practices). Sāṁkhya explains the structure of the world and the system of the creation, the parallelism and interdependence of the various aspects of matter, life and species, and the fundamental oneness of macrocosm and microcosm of the universe and the living being. . . . Yoga is a technique in which by means of introspection, man learns to know himself. He is able to silence the digression of his thought, to pass beyond the limits of his senses and go back to the deep sources of his life. Contact is made with the invisible powers hidden within himself, as in all aspects of the created, which constitutes

> the deepest nature of the living being. The body, including the mental and intellectual faculties is only its support; a sort of clothing. Tantra is the link between Sāṁkhya and Yoga. It teaches the initiatory and magical methods through which man can enter into direct contact with the secret nature of things of the invisible and mysterious world of gods and spirits. — Danielou 1992: 140

Individual consciousness is intimately connected with the workings of cosmic consciousness. Knowledge of this correlation of individual consciousness with higher consciousness and its scheme of things in creation is decided by the sensitivity and expansion of awareness of the individual consciousness. Individual consciousness can be enlightened by various means. *Bhakti, jñāna, yoga* and Tantra are some of the major paths revealed in Indian philosophical system. The poets under study use at least three means in their journey to self-realization. While Āṇḍāḷ is purely a *bhakta*, Akkā Mahādevi is a *bhakta*, a *yoginī* as well as a tāntric. Akkā had been exposed to all the esoteric practices of Yoga and Tantra and she did her *sādhanā* (spiritual practices) along these lines. This is clearly revealed in her works especially in *Yogāṅga Trividhi* which is an exposition of the experiences of *kuṇḍalinī yoga*, a part of Tantra.

Indian philosophy (Darśana), as it is rightly called, describes the composition of human being by relating it as a microcosm of the bigger macrocosmic Consciousness. Therefore, all the elements found in creation as a whole are also found subtlely strewn in the physio-psychic complex of a human individual. Interrelations between these principles are revealed sometimes in tacit and sometimes in explicit ways from Upaniṣadic tradition onwards.[2] Tantras relate the descent

2 Hence the famous expressions from Upaniṣads like *aham brahmāsmi* (I am *Brahman*), *tat tvam asi* (You are That) and *soham* (I am Him). *Mānṇḍūkya Upaniṣad*, for instance, says *ayamātma brahma* (This Ātmā is *Brahman*).

of divine consciousness into human consciousness, revealing a very complex yet structured relationship between various elements in the creation and their corresponding threads in the human complex (see table on p. 222). Here, for the purpose of expositing *bhakti* poetry and *bhakti* experience, only the interconnections that are useful are hinted. To validate this same argument, Alain Danielou (1992: 145) quotes French author J. Evola and also *Muṇḍaka Upaniṣad*:

> The basis of Yoga is the analogical–magical correspondence of macrocosm and microcosm. All the powers which are manifested and operating in the world are present and active in the body. — J. Evola, *Le Yoga Tantrique*, p. 215
>
> Further than the farthest, it is very near in the body. For those who are enlightened, it is there in the hollow of the heart. — *Muṇḍaka Upaniṣad* III.1.7

Human being is conceived as a uniquely structured dynamics of various energies, which can be tapped by expanding the level of consciousness from gross to subtle, and then to psychic and cosmic states. When the awareness starts entering into higher levels, there is more and more harmony between individual self and cosmic or transcendental self. *Bhakti* is considered to be the easiest and the most accessible path to this kind of liberation.

Bhakti (keeping in mind that it is said to be a means, a goal as well as a state of mind), *yoga* and Tantra offer a well-defined path, which makes the experience of different aspects of cosmic consciousness possible in human being. This condition, state or concept is known by various names as *ātmā* or *AUṀ* or *turīya* state. Āṇḍāḷ's *Tiruppāvai* and Akkā Mahādevī's *Yogāṅga Trividhi* and her *vacanas* offer clear examples of this path as well as this condition.

These saints, like all saints, were enlightened beings, who were trying to express the experiences of this cosmic state (*turīya*)

Interconnections Between Elements in Human Complex and Cosmic Complex*

Human Physio-Psychic Complex	*Human Consciousness*	*Human Experience*	*Human Expression*	*"Cosmic Complex"*
Sthūla (gross body)	*Jāgṛti* (conscious state)	Related to senses, gross and at material plane	*Vaikharī* (gross, physical speech)	*A* (sound of the first syllable. *A* has frequencies that relate to conscious state)
Śūkṣma (subtle body)	*Svapna* (sub-conscious state)	Mental-related to thoughts and thought constructs	*Madhyamā* (word in its subtle form as existing in *antaḥ-karaṇa* prior to its gross manifestation)	*U* (sound of the second syllable. *U* has frequencies that relate to dream state)
Kāraṇa (psychic body)	*Suṣupti* (unconscious state)	Completely unconnected with senses. Experience of perfect stillness	*Paśyantī* (going forth; seeing)	*Ṁ* (sound of the third syllable. *Ṁ* has frequencies that relate to subconscious state)
Ātman (cosmic or transcendental body)	*Turīya* (transcendental state)	Unity with cosmic consciousness *(bhakti* experience falls in this category)	*Parā Vāc* (spiritual logos in the form of *nāda*)**	*AUṀ* (primal sound of *AUṀ* has the frequencies of sound which relate to transcendental *Māṇḍūkya Upaniṣad*.

* All the entries across the columms are interrelated.

** According to Swami Satyasangananda (1984 : 90): *Nāda* (primal sound) is one of the first manifest forms of creation. Even Bible begins with the statement, "In the beginning was the word". In Indian philosophy, this word is known as *oṁ*, which is the eternal *nāda* or cosmic *mantra*. In the *Māṇḍukyopaniṣad* there is a very clear explanation of the *mantra oṁ* and how it stimulates and expands the different levels of consciousness.

of awareness in some form and they found poetry or song compositions to be the most suitable medium to affect that.

Māṇḍūkya Upaniṣad recognizes and describes four states of consciousness — *jāgṛti, svapna, suṣupti* and *turīya*. In the West, nineteenth-century Viennese psychologist, Sigmund Freud, studied the composition of human mind and defined three dimensions of consciousness. Freud's three divisions of conscious, subconscious and unconscious states of mind can be said to be quite in correspondence with the first three states of *jāgṛti* (waking), *svapna* (dream) and *suṣupti* (sleeping) states as prescribed by Indian sages.[3] And the fourth stage of *turīya* (superconsciousness) is an extraordinary state of consciousness, in which the individual self becomes fully aware of all the three states of consciousness simultaneously.[4]

Human consciousness is intimately connected with various components of the human mind.

---

3 It is interesting to note that while Freud studied and conducted research on human subjects that were abnormal or mentally sick, Indian sages were interested in the super normal states of awareness in much evolved human beings such as *ṛṣis* and *yogīs*.

4 Swami Nirañjanānanda Sarasvatī, in a very comprehensive text on *yoga*, says: Once the *nidrā* (*suṣupti*) has been perceived and there is an extension of the field of awareness, encompassing all three states of *jāgṛti, svapna* and *nidrā*, the broad awareness is known as *turīya*. Some people describe *turīya* as super mind, but it does not mean this. *Turīya* means "simultaneous awareness of all three states" which takes us closer to the state of enlightenment. And further:

"*Prajñā*, the all-knowing, self-contained consciousness, abides in deep sleep, in which all things have vanished. Here, when it is said that things have vanished, it refers to duality ceasing, including the concept of you and me, the body and the experiences of the body. It also means that all the experiences related to name, form and idea, disappear. When everything disappears, one experiences the Advaita aspect, unity with the individual soul."

— *Yoga Darśana*, p. 263

Tantra philosophy describes four components of individual mind, which are collectively known as *antaḥkaraṇa* (lit. *antaḥ* means "inner", *karaṇa* means "instrument"). *Antaḥkaraṇa* is the instrument of consciousness in an individual. And different states of consciousness described above are a result of the workings of *antaḥkaraṇa*. *Antaḥkaraṇa* or individual mind functions through its four dimensions — *manas* (thought constructs), *buddhi* (intellect), *citta* (memory) and *ahaṁkāra* (ego). To quote Swami Satyasangananda:

> The *antaḥkaraṇa* functions through the conscious, subconscious and unconscious realms, creating gross, subtle and causal experiences. As the *antaḥkaraṇa* has evolved out of a combination of the three *guṇas*: *sattva*, *rajas* and *tamas*, the quality of experience is largely determined by the pervading influence of these cosmic principles. *Manas*, *citta*, *buddhi* and *ahaṁkāra* behave differently under the sway of *sattva*, as opposed to *rajas* and *tamas*, and thus manifest differently in the three states of awareness.
>
> — Satyasangananda 1984: 51

Manas and *citta* work in the conscious and subconscious states of mind and hence influence the actions and thoughts in *jāgṛti* and *svapna* states. *Buddhi* and *ahaṁkāra* are present in varying degrees in all the three states and so influence the workings in all the three states including *suṣupti*.

Levels of Human Experience

The physio-psychic complex or the human body is described as a very sensitive index, which inheres different levels of experiences. It has been divided into *sthūla*, *sūkṣma* and *kāraṇa*. These three components are significant, as they go into making sense of the individual self in the external material world. Here, I would like to add that there is a fourth stage also that we can call cosmic body or transcendental body which is named as *ātman* in the classical texts. *Ātman* is a holistic state of experience which pervades and watches over the whole being. These states relate to various levels of experiences that are possible for a human being in the body.

To come back to *sthūla*, or gross level this is the physical level of senses and their respective objects where the experience of reality is limited. Limitations in perception arise because of the fact that the information about the outside world is perceived through five sense faculties, which have their own limitations. This level relates to *jāgṛti* or conscious state of consciousness. In this state, experience is limited only to the visible or material world of senses.[5]

The second — *sūkṣma* or subtle body — is subtler than the physical component. This relates to the mental state and state of *svapna*. This subtle body experiences the reality through *manas* and *citta*. These are subtle tools of the being, which are used to process "vibrations of thoughts, feelings, desires, motivations and actions". The experiences or, in other words, the objects, which the awareness is able to perceive through this state, are invisible as they relate more to the world of energy than the world of matter. In other words, the experiences in this state are subtle and have no material shape or form. The thoughts, ideas, emotions, feelings and desires, which form the realm of subconscious, are energies working subtly in the *sūkṣma*. This state of being is described as *svapna*.

The third state of being is the *kāraṇa*, where psychic dimension is active. This state is associated with *suṣupti* level. Here, the senses get completely disconnected from their objects. Therefore, all processing in terms of thoughts and thought constructs stops. The experiences in this state are

---

5 *Jñānendriyas* (five sense-organs — ear, nose, eyes, tongue and skin) and *karmendriyas* (five organs of action — hands, feet, mouth, reproductive and excretory organs) are the major feeders of information to the individual operating at gross level of being.

psychic. In this level of being, there is absolutely no movement or activity, there is perfect stillness.

The fourth state of being, which can be called as cosmic body or transcendental body relates to *turīya*. The awareness in this state is named as *ātman*. Experience in this state is of perfect enlightenment as the awareness here has become so expansive that it can simultaneously comprehend all the other levels of being, i.e. *jāgr̥ti, svapna* and *suṣupti*. In other words, *ātmā,* the seer, at this level is able to perceive the entire range of experiences belonging to the other three states simultaneously. This is the transcendental state, where consciousness gains cosmic dimensions and flows as a continuous stream connecting all creation.[6]

Māṇḍūkya Upaniṣad relates *ātman* to the primal sound of oṁ (*AUṀ*), the *praṇava* and other three states of being to

---

[6] *Māṇḍūkya Upaniṣad* describes these four states as follows:

"*Brahman* is all and *ātmā* is *Brahaman*. *Ātmā,* the Self, has four conditions.

The first condition is the dreaming life of outward-moving consciousness, enjoying the seven gross elements. The second condition is the dreaming life of inner-moving consciousness, enjoying the seven subtle inner elements in its own light and solitude. The third condition is the sleeping life of silent consciousness when a person has no desires and beholds no dream, that condition of deep sleep is one of oneness, a mass of silent consciousness made of peace and enjoying peace. This silent consciousness is all powerful, all knowing, the inner ruler, the source of all, the beginning and end of all beings. The fourth condition is *ātmā* in his own pure state: the awakened life of supreme consciousness. It is neither outer, nor inner, nor inner consciousness, neither semi-consciousness, nor sleeping consciousness, neither consciousness nor unconsciousness. He is *ātman*, the spirit himself, that cannot be seen or touched, that is above all distinction, beyond thought and ineffable." —*Māṇḍūkya Upaniṣad* various syllables of *AUṀ* as in *A*, *U* and, *Ṁ*. To quote from an English edition of the Upaniṣad:

> This self, though beyond words, is that supreme word *oṁ*; though indivisible, it can be divided in three letters corresponding to the three conditions of the self, the letter *A*, the letter *U*, and the letter *Ṁ*.
>
> The waking condition, called the material condition, corresponds to the letter *A*, which leads the alphabet and breathes in all the other letters. He who understands gets all he wants; becomes a leader among men.
>
> The dreaming condition, called the mental condition, corresponds to the second letter *U*. It upholds; stands between waking and sleeping. He who understands, upholds the tradition of spiritual knowledge; looks upon everything with an imperil eye. No one ignorant of spirit is born into his family.
>
> Undreaming sleep, called the intellectual condition, corresponds to the third letter, *Ṁ*. It weighs and unites. He who understands, weighs the world: rejects; unites himself with the cause.
>
> The fourth condition of the self corresponds to *oṁ* as One, indivisible word. He is whole; beyond bargain. The world disappears in Him. He is the good; the one without a second. Thus *oṁ* is nothing but self. He who understands, with the help of his personal self, merges himself into the impersonal self; He who understands.
>
> — "At the Feet of the Master Mandooka (*Māṇḍūkya Upaniṣad*)", in Shree Purohit Swamy and W.B. Yeats, *Ten Principal Upanishads*, p. 61.

Consciousness and Awareness

It is important here to understand the concept of awareness and also to see the difference between consciousness and awareness. In fact, awareness is the mirror, which makes levels of consciousness visible to the being. Consciousness just is. As said earlier, it is like a continuous stream without a beginning and an end, and awareness is like a beam of light, which enlightens this endless stream of being. Paramhaṁsa Swami Niranjanananda Saraswatī uses the following diagram to describe the relationship and notion of consciousness and awareness:

Jāgr̥ti (A-H) (Wakefulness)	*Svapna* (I-S) (Dream)	*Nidrā* (R-Z) (Deep Sleep)
Conscious Mind	Subconscious Mind	Unconscious Mind
Gross (*sthūla*)	Subtle (*sūkṣma*)	Causal (*kāraṇa*)

A B C D E F G H I J K L M N O P Q R S T U V W X Y Z

Anādi Cetanā (Endless Consciousness)
— *Yoga Darshan,* Swami Niranjananda Saraswati

For the sake of analysis, Swami Niranjanananda has created twenty-six points on this unending line of consciousness dividing them into three sections. Each section relates to a particular dimension of awareness. According to the diagram, our experiences in *jāgr̥ti* state might range from A to H, for instance. In this state, we are fully awake and the experiences are generally gross and relate to senses. *Svapna* is the state when we are dreaming and subtler experiences flow. This state ranges from H to Q. *Nidrā* or *suṣupti* state is when we are completely cut-off from the material world and enter into a state of deep sleep. This state ranges from Q to Z.

Normally we are aware of only one point at a time in this stream of consciousness until something draws our awareness to itself. This way our awareness is constantly moving from one point to another point. We are not able to expand our awareness enough to take full experience of even *jāgr̥ti* state, leave alone the *svapna* and *suṣupti* states in one lifetime. However, expansion of awareness is possible by adopting specific yogic/*bhakti sādhanā*. In fact, all our soteriological theories of *mokṣa* and salvation are nothing but description of means to expand the awareness. As, when the awareness has become as expansive as to enlighten all the points from A to Z, from *jāgr̥ti* to *suṣupti,* then the self becomes the image of the Divine. This is a state of *mokṣa* that is also understood as a release from binaries such as self/other, pleasure/pain, subject/object, etc. a state called as the state of *jīvan-mukti* in *bhakti* terminology.

Hence with reference to *bhakti* poetry and *bhakti* experience, we may say that both happen at a high level of awareness. While poetry might be an effect of *jāgr̥ti, svapna* or *suṣupti* state of mind, *bhakti,* mysticism and *mokṣa,* are a product of *turīya* (super-conscious) state of the consciousness. *Bhakti* poetry then can be taken to be emerging from a very expansive awareness that appears to be mystical to the common mind.

Experience of *bhakti* clearly seems to be associated with the fourth state of awareness, i.e. the state of *turīya* where all the dualities cease to exist and the *bhakta* becomes a reflection of the cosmic or divine consciousness.

Appendix B

Tiruppāvai
The Sacred Vow

by Āṇḍāḷ

1

On the full-moon day of Mārkaḷi month
Come, let's bathe in the pond. You,
Little beauties from cowherds' shire
Full of wealth beyond all bounds!
Nandagopāla's sharp-speared mighty son,
The kind-eyed Yaśodā's little lion cub
Nārāyaṇa will himself give us boons. Bathe
And be praised. Hail! Our vow!

2

O girls who will gain great fortune!
Listen to our tasks during the vow:
Singing of Lord prone on the milk sea
We will drink no milk or ghee,
Will wear no flowers in the braid,
And give up driveling and mischief.
Listen! We will give bountiful alms
And think of the higher path. Hail! Our vow!

3

The lofty god who measured the worlds!
If we praise him and keep the vow,
Evil will end; it will rain thrice a month;
Carps will leap from lush rice fields
And bees rest among lilies' clumps
Just hold and squeeze hard udders

And cows will yield pots of milk!
O ceaseless fortune! Hail! Our vow!

4

Come down, O impeccable rain!
Plunge into the ocean and rise with water
Thunder, dark-hued, like First One
Blaze forth like discus in the long-armed
Padmanābha's hands. Fall non-stop
Like the downpour of *śārṅgya* shafts.
Come! Rescue the world when we
Bathe in Mārkaḷi. Hail! Our vow!

5

That great wonder from north Mathurā,
The dweller on the Yamunā's bank,
The diamond born into the cowherd's clan!
Dāmodara that lit up mother's frame!
If, pure in body, we dwell on him
Sing his praises offering flowers, all our sins
Of past and now will burn like cotton wool
In yawning flames. Hail! Our vow!

6

Listen to birdsong! Can't you hear the boom
Of white conch from Bird-king's temple?
Rise! Sages place in their hearts Him,
The Seed on the snake bed in the ocean,
Who sucked poison from Pūtanā's breasts,
Who kicked the demon Śakaṭa,
And repeat sweetly: "Hari, Hari",
Our souls are soothed. Hail! Our vow!

7

Listen! The warble of skylarks! Can't
You make out their wondrous speech
You, crazy? O lovely one! When *gopī*'s

Are churning the buttermilk, the pearls and disks
Of their necklaces swing. Can't you
Hear and see O best of women
Nārāyaṇa's name and Keśava's form?
Open the door! Hail! Our vow!

8

The east is bright. Buffalo calves have
Left for grazing. Stopping the girls
On their way to the holy bath, we have
Come to wake you. Wake up!
O wise girl! Beat the drum!
If we serve king of gods who beat
The mighty demons and split up the horse,
He will grant us all. Hail! Our vow!

9

Look! The lamps around jewelled house!
Ah, the fragrance! Still on bed,
O cousin girl? Open the diamond door
Wake her up! You, silent aunt!
Is she dumb, deaf or just lazy?
What drug can cause such sleep?
"O Magician O Mādhava O Vaikuṇṭha!"
We go on repeating. Hail! Our vow!

10

You observed vows and reached heavens
O mother! Dumb, these doors shut!
Hurt by the basil-decked Nārāyaṇa,
Giver of everyone of our boons,
The defeated Kumbhakarṇa has sent
You such strange sleep. Does sleep
Still cling to you? O precious pearl!
Unlatch the door. Hail! Our vow!

11

O golden shoot of the impeccable cowherd
Clan that milk countless cows
And strike down hoards of foes!
Why cower like a snake in its whole?
Turn into a wild peahen. While girls
Come thick into your backyard singing
Of the pearl-hued, why be still and silent?
Why such slumber? Hail! Our vow!

12

Hearing the plaintive bleating of calves
The milky udders of buffalos leak by themselves,
Wetting the floor of the house. O sister
Of such a rich house owner, can't you
Rise? When snow has started falling,
Right on your threshold they are
Singing of the slayer of Laṅkā's king.
"What sleep!" wonder your kin. Hail! Our vow!

13

Singing of the slayer of Baka, the demon bird
And of the worst of monsters, little girls
Have already reached the holy pond.
Except the morning star, the rest have dimmed
O doe-eyed girl! O bee-eyed girl!
Why are you lying down and not
Bathing? The moment is precious.
Throw out sleep, the thief. Hail! Our vow!

14

Look! Lotuses have bloomed and lilies,
Folded up in your backyard garden well.
Saffron-clothed sages with shining teeth
Are walking to the golden temple!
"I will wake you up", you had lied.
Wake up sister. Shame on your tongue!

Sing of the lotus eyes of the lord
Of conch and discus. Hail! Our vow!

15

"Hey, little parrot! Still asleep?"
"Don't disturb. Go on. I will follow"
"I know you have a lying mouth"
"Yes, you surely know. I am like this"
"Get up, you! What fortune is greater?
"Have others gone?" "Come see for yourself"
Sing of the loftiest miracle man
Who has quelled mighty foes. Hail! Our vow!

16

O Nandagopāla's watchman!
O keeper of gates with flags and buntings!
Unlatch the diamond gate!
The pearl-hued one had promised
He would give his drum to us,
Us the simple cowherd girls. Here we are
Singing to wake him up. Don't shout!
Open the mighty gate. Hail! Our vow!

17

O generous giver of food, drink and clothes!
O master! Wake up. O Nandagopāla!
O crown of women! O light of the clan!
Our lady! Wake up. O Yaśodā!
O supreme of sky god who grew
Taller than the sky and split the sky!
O golden ankleted Baladeva! Wake up!
Wake up your younger brother. Hail! Our vow!

18

O Nappinnai! O daughter-in-law of Nandagopāla
The unfailing hero strong as elephant!
You of fragrant hair! Open the door.

Listen! The crowing of cocks! The song
Of *koil* birds from among *mādhavī* creepers!
How shapely your fingers! As we are singing
Of your lord, come, come quick.
Come tinkling your bangled hands
Open the door with glee. Hail! Our vow!

19

On the breast of Nappinnai on soft bed
Of smooth cotton in the lighted house
You are asleep, garlands on your chest
Speak up! O woman with shaded eyes!
Can't you be away from your lord?
Is that right? Can't you keep away
From him even for half a moment?
Not proper at all! Hail! Our vow!

20

O dispeller of fear who went beyond
Thirty-three gods! Wake up, O strong one
O affluent, candid lord! O conqueror
Of enemies! Wake up! O purity!
O Nappinnai with big breasts, slender waist
And red lips! Wake up! O sister!
Give us fans and mirrors! Drown us
In water with your lord, hail! Our vow!

21

O son of the rich owner of generous cows,
Which, when the pot is held up, melt down
To yield abundant milk, wake up!
O protector of your seekers! You who appeared
In this very world! Wake up from sleep!
Just as, terrorized, your foes come crowding
To your threshold to touch your feet,
We have gathered to praise you. Hail! Our vow!

22

Like shamed kings crowding your courtyard,
We have come to stand beneath your cot
All of us, together, here and now.
Those lovely eyes half-open like lotus!
Won't they fall on us even for a while?
If only you look at us with lovely eyes
Bright like the sun and the moon put together,
All our curses fall away. Hail! Our vow!

23

Like, in terrible rain, the brave lion asleep
In a mountain cave waking up, his eyes spitting
Fire, his mane erect, swaying and stretching
His spine and darting out roaring, you too,
O bloom-eyed, issuing out of your palace,
Come rushing towards us. Take
Your lion-seat. Ask of us as to what
We are here for. Hail! Our vow!

24

Hail! The feet that measured whole earth!
Hail! The art that won splendid Laṅkā!
Hail! The feet that kicked Śakaṭa!
Hail! Hands that flung the demon Kaṁsa!
Hail! The virtue making an umbrella of the hill!
Hail! The spear that strikes down foes!
Beating drum, we have come singing of you
Bless us all. Hail! Our vow!

25

Born as one mother's child, the same night
You grew up as another's child
You rose like a volcano in the heart
Of Kaṁsa envious of you, to quell
His great jealousy. O Lord! We have
Come chasing you. If you fulfil our wishes

We will sing of your beauty and strength
What a feast! Hail! Our vow!

26

O pearl-hued highest one! If elders ask
What joys we got from bathing in Mārkaḷi,
Here they are: Milk-white conches resembling
Your *Pāñcajanya* sounding so loud
That the world trembles; the drums
To announce your glories; the singers
Of your benediction; lamps and flags.
Grant these from *pīpal* leaf bed, hail! Our vow!

27

O great Govinda! O conqueror of the reluctant!
These are joys following beating drums
And singing: Wearing fabulous jewels —
Bangles, bracelets and ear-rings —
That wins the whole world's praise,
We play. And then pour so much ghee
Into the milk-rice that it drips from elbows
And enjoy the feast together. Hail! Our vow!

28

We that follow cattle into woods and eat . . .
We have no sense, the children of cowherds.
Still blessed enough to beget you,
O Govinda free from all faults!
Not even for a while can we leave you
We know nothing, cowherd girls calling
You as we like. Don't frown, O king!
Grant us our wish. Hail! Our vow!

29

Worshipping you at dawn, we love
To think of your lotus feet. Listen!
You born of those who make a living

Out of tending and grazing cattle!
Don't go without granting our wish.
We ask of nothing paltry. Listen!
In every birth we will be with you
As your bonded slaves to serve you
Burn other wishes. Hail! Our vow!

30

O Keśava! O Mādhava who churned the ocean!
Godā, of lovely Puduvai, blessed by Bhaṭṭanāthar,
The *japa* bead in cooling lotus,
Has sung, as if by moon-faced beauties,
These thirty stanzas in Saṅga Tamil. To whoever
Repeats these lines Mountain-armed Lord
Tirumal of lovely eyes and face
Will grant peace. Hail! Our vow!

— tr. H.S. Shiva Prakash

Appendix C

Akkā Mahādevī's Vacanas

1

Hills have no sap in them, they say
Tell me, sir, how else are trees born there?
Charcoal has no liquid in it, they say
Tell me, sir, how else does iron melt in it?
I have no body, they say
Tell, me, sir, how else does Cennamallikārjuna live in me?

2

Look, all of you
All the Vedas, Śāstras, Āgamas, Purāṇas
Are the grit and husk
From the beaten paddy.
Why beat it? Why strike it?
Once you purge the mind
From flowing here and there,
Pure light dawns,
Cennamallikārjuna.

3

You parrots, chirping on by rote!
Have you seen him? Have you?
You, *koel*s, singing aloud!
Have you seen him? Have you?
You bees swooping, sporting!
Have you seen him? Have you?
You swans sporting on lake's edge!
Have you seen him? Have you?
You hunting men and women
Sporting among hills and vales,

Have you seen him? Have you?
Where is he,
Cennamallika, my god?
Tell me, won't you,
If you have seen . . .

4

The deer on earth and the hare in the moon —
What good is there love
If they can't mate?
If your eyes lust in vain
It is like a mango tree
Bearing fruits
Standing in a flood.
O Master Cennamallikārjuna,
I came into a world I shouldn't have come into
For I fell in love with the one too far away.

5

When in passion
Do what you like, O Master
When in passion
Cut off the locks, O Master
When in passion
Bite off the fingers, O Master,
O Master Cennamallikārjuna
Heap miseries on me
If I ever grumble in pain.

6

Don't hole me. Don't
Stop me. Let go
Of my hand, the hem
Of my *sāṛī*. Don't
You know of the worst hell
For those that break
The promise made in black and white?

You shall be doomed
If you touch the woman
Married to Cennamallikārjuna.

7

O Sister, listen sister dear
I dreamt a dream. I saw
Rice, betel and coconut
I saw, O dear.
A gorava boy
With short-matted locks of hair
And shining teeth
Coming home for Alms
I went chasing him
Going beyond all boundaries
And held his hands
Seeing Cennamallikārjuna,
I opened My eyes.

8

Guru became kin,
Liṅga, the bridegroom
And I, the bride.
The whole world knows:
The uncountable devotees are my parents
Who gave me in marriage
Finding the ideal groom
Cennamallikārjuna is my husband,
No one else
O Brother.

10

Like treasure hiding in the earth
Like taste hiding in the fruit
Like gold hiding in the stone
Like oil hiding in the sesame
Like fire hiding in the tree

No one else can see Cennamallikārjuna —
The Brahman hiding in the yearning.
— H.S. Shivaprakash, 2010, *I Keep Vigil of Rudra*,
New Delhi: Penguin Books

Bibliography

Arthur, Avalon (Sir John Woodroffe), 1953, *The Serpent Power: Being the Ṣaṭ-Cakra Nirūpaṇa and Pāduka-Pañcaka, Madras:* Ganesh & Co.

Ayyar C.V. Narayana, 1974, *Origin and Early History of Saivism in South India,* Madras: University of Madras, 1939 rpr.

Bailey, G.M. and I. Kesarcodi-Watson, eds., 1992, *Bhakti Studies,* New Delhi: Sterling Publishers.

Basavaraju, L., ed., 2004, *Śivagaṇa Prasādi Mahādevīakkana Prabhudevara Śūnya Sampādane,* Gulberga: Sharana Basaveshvara Vidyavardhaka Sangha (Kannada Text).

Basham, A.L., 1964, *Studies in Indian History and Culture,* Calcutta: Sambodhi Publications.

Bharti, Srirama, 1999, *Araiyar Sevai: Theatre Expression in Śrī-Vaiṣṇava Worship,* Mumbai: Bhartiya Vidya Bhavan.

———, 2000 *The Sacred Book of Four Thousand,* Chennai: Sri Sadagopan Tirunarayanswami Divya Prabandha Pathsala.

Bhattacharyya, N.N., 1999, *History of the Tantric Religion,* New Delhi: Manohar.

Bhoosnurmath, S.S. and Armando Menezes, eds., 1968, *Śūnyasampādane,* vols. 2 and 3, Dharwad: Karnatak University.

———, 1970, *Śūnyasampādane,* vol. 4, Dharwad: Karnataka University.

Blake, Michael, R., 1992, *The Origins of Vīraśaiva Sects: A Typological Analysis of Ritual and Associational Patterns in the Śūnyasampādane,* Delhi: Motilal Banarsidass.

Chaitanya, Vinaya, tr., 2005, *Songs for Śiva: Vacanas of Akkā Mahādevī,* U K: Alta Mira Press.

Champakalakshmi, R., 1981, *Vaiṣṇava Iconography in the Tamil Country,* New Delhi: Orient Longman.

Champakalakshmi, R. and S. Gopala, eds., 1996, *Tradition Dissent and*

Ideology: Essays in Honour of Romila Thapar, New Delhi: Oxford University Press.

Chandler, David, 2002, *Semiotics: The Basics,* London and New York: Routledge.

Chenchiah, P. and Raja M. Bhujanga Rao Bahadur, 1988, *A History of Telugu Literature,* Madras and New Delhi: Asian Educational Services.

Collinson, Diane, Kathryn Plant and Robert Wilkinson, 2002, *Fifty Eastern Thinkers,* London and New York: Routledge.

Coomaraswamy, Ananda, 1997, *The Dance of Shiva,* New Delhi: Munshiram Manoharlal.

Danielou, Alain, 1987, *While the Gods Play: Shaiva Oracles and Predictions on the Cycles of History and the Destiny of Mankind.* (Translated from the French by Barbara Baily, Michael Baker, and Deborah Lawlor.) Rochestor, Vermont: Inner Traditions International.

———, 1984, *Gods of Love and Ecstasy: The Traditions of Shiva and Dionysus,* New York: Inner Traditions.

Davy, G.N., ed., 2002, *Indian Literary Criticism: Theory and Interpretation,* Hyderabad: Orient Longman.

Dehejia, Vidya, 1988, *Slaves of the Lord: The Path of the Tamil Saints,* Delhi: Munshiram Manoharlal.

———, 1990, *Antal and Her Path of Love: Poems of a Woman Saint from South of India,* Albany: State University of New York Press.

Devotional Poets and Mystics, Part I, 1991, New Delhi: Publications Division, Ministry of Information and Broadcasting, Government of India, 1978 repr.

Dharwadkar, Vinay, ed., 1999, *The Collected Essays of A.K. Ramanujan,* New Delhi: Oxford University Press.

Dubianski, Alexander M., 2000, *Ritual and Mythological Sources of the Early Tamil Poetry,* The Netherlands: Egbert Forsten.

Dwivedi, Mukund, ed., 1981, *Hazariprasad Dwivedi Granthavali,* vol. 4, New Delhi: Rajkamal Prakashan.

Elgood, Heather, 1999, *Hinduism and the Religious Arts,* London and New York: Cassell.

Eliade, Mircea, 1982, *A History of Religious Ideas: From Gautama Buddha to the Triumph of Christianity,* vol. II, tr. Willard R. Trask, Chicago: University of Chicago Press.

Fausboll, V., 2003, *Indian Mythology: According to the Mahabharata, in Outline,* Varanasi: Bharatiya Vidya Prakashan.

Haberman, David L., 2003, tr. with Intro. and Notes, *The Bhaktirasāmṛtasindhu of Rūpa Gosvāmin,* Delhi: Indira Gandhi National Centre for the Arts and Motilal Banarsidass.

Hardy, Friedhelm, 1983, *Viraha-Bhakti: The Early History of Krishna Devotion in South India,* Delhi: Oxford University Press.

Hart, George, 1999, *The Poems of Ancient Tamil: Their Mileau and Their Sanskrit Counterparts,* New Delhi: Oxford University Press.

Heehs, Peter, ed. 2002, *Indian Religions: The Spiritual Traditions of South Asia,* Delhi: Permanent Black.

Ishwaran, K., 1992, *Speaking of Basava: Lingayat Religion and Culture in South India,* USA: Westview Press.

Iyengar, Masti Venkatesh, 1969, *Bhaṭṭara Magaḷu,* Bangalore: Jeevana Karyalaya (Kannada text).

Jairaman, P., 2003, *Bhakti ke Āyāma: Kṛṣṇa Bhakti Sāhitya,* New Delhi: Vani Prakashan.

Jaishetty, Bhalchandra, 1998, *Vacana,* Banglore: Karnataka Sahitya Akademi (Hindi text).

Johnston, William, 1977, *The Still Point,* London: Harper and Row.

Jung, C.G., 1995, *Jung on the East,* ed. with an Intro. J.J. Clarke, London: Routledge.

Khandelwal, Meena, 2004, *Women in Ochre Robes: Gendering Hindu Renunciation,* Albany: State University of New York Press.

Lorenzen, David, N., ed., 2004, *Religious Movements in South Asia 600-1800: Debates in Indian History and Society,* New Delhi: Oxford University Press.

Mahadevi, Mate, 2005, *Taraṅgiṇī,* Bangalore: Suyidhana Sugrantha Male, 1975, 8th edn. 2005 (Kannada text).

Majumdar, R.C., 1954, gen. ed., *The History and Culture of the Indian People: The Classical Age,* Bombay: Bharatiya Vidya Bhavan.

Marulasiddaiah, H.M., ed., 1998, *Dimensions of Bhakti Movement in India,* Mysore: Akhil Bhartiya Sharna Sahitya Parishat.

Murali, S., ed., 1998, *South Indian Studies,* New Delhi: B.R. Publishing Corporation.

Nagabhushanswamy, O.L., ed., 1996, *Harihara,* Bangalore: Karnataka Sahitya Akademi (Kannada text).

———, 2007, *The Sign: Vachanas of the 12th Century,* tr. O.L. Nagabhushan Swamy, Lakshmi Chandrasekhar and Vijaya Guttal, Hampi: Karnataka University, Prasararaṅga.

Nandimath, S.C., L.M.A. Menezes and R.C. Hiremath, eds., 1965, *Śūnyasampādane,* vol. I, Dharwad: Karnatak University.

Pandey, Kanti Chandra, 1950, *Comparative Aesthetics,* vol. I: *Indian Aesthetics,* Banaras: Chowkhamba Sanskrit Series Office.

Pandit, Motilal, 2003, *The Trika Śaivism of Kashmir,* New Delhi: Munshiram Manoharlal.

Parimoo, Ratan, ed., 1987, *Vaiṣṇavism in Indian Arts and Culture,* New Delhi: Books and Books.

Parthasarthy, Indira, 2002, *Vaiṣṇavisam in Tamil Literature: Between the 7th and 9th Centuries,* Chennai: International Institute of Tamil Studies.

Parthasarthy, R., tr. 1993, *The Cilappatikaram of Ilanko Atikal: An Epic of South India,* New York: Columbia University Press.

Perumal, V., 1982, *Glimpses of Tamil Culture,* West Germany: Berlin Tamil Sangam.

Peterson, Indira Viswanathan, 1989, *Poems to Siva,* United Kingdom: Prinston University Press.

Pollock, Sheldon, 2007, *The Language of the Gods in the World of Men: Sanskrit, Culture, and Power in Premodern India,* Delhi: Permanent Black.

Ramanujan, A.K., 1985, *Poems of Love and War,* Delhi: Oxford University Press.

———, tr., 1981, *Hymns for the Drowning: Poems for Vishnu by Nammalvar,* Princeton, New Jeresy: Princeton University Press.

———, tr. and Intro., 1973, *Speaking of Siva.* England: Penguin Books.

Rao, Chimakurti Seshagiri, comp. & ed., 1995, *History and Cutlure of the Andhras,* Hyderabad: Telugu University.

Sadarangani, Neeti, M., 2004, *Bhakti Poetry in Medieval India: Its Inception, Cultural Encounter and Impact,* New Delhi: Sarup and Sons.

Sakhare, M.R., 1978, *History and Philosophy of Lingayat Religion,* Dharwad: Karnatak University.

Sampathkumaracharya, V.S., 2006, *The Place of Srivaishnava Community in Karnatic Music,* Mysore: Vedantic Charities.

Sastri, K.A. Nilakanta, 1963, *The Culture and History of Tamils*, Calcutta: Firma, K.L. Mukhopadhyaya.

Sekkizhār, 2004, *Periya Purāṇam: A Tamil Classic on the Great Śaiva Saints of South India*, tr. G., Vanmikanthan, Madras: Sri Ramakrishna Math.

Sen, Geeti and Maully Kaushal, eds., 2004, *Journeys: Heroes, Pilgrims and Explorers*, New Delhi: India International Centre, Penguin, Viking.

Sharma, Raghu Nath, 1996, *Bhakti in the Vaiṣṇava Rasa-Śāstra*, Delhi: Pratibha Prakashan.

Sharma, Krishna, 1987, *Bhakti and the Bhakti Movement: A New Perspective*. New Delhi: Munshiram Manoharlal.

Sharma, T.R.S., chief ed., 2000, *Ancient Indian Literature: An Anthology*, vol. 3, New Delhi: Sahitya Akademi.

Shendge, Malati, J., 1997, *The Language of the Harrappans: From Akkadian to Sanskrit*, New Delhi: Abhinav Publications.

Shilbrack, Kevin, ed., 2002, *Thinking Through Myths*, London: Routledge.

Silburn, Lilian, 1988, *Kuṇḍalinī: The Energy of the Depths*, Albany: State University of New York Press.

Sivaramkrishna, M. and Sumita Roy, eds., 1996, *Poet Saints of India*, New Delhi: Sterling Publishers.

Sri Andal: Her Contribution to Literature, Philosophy, Religion and Art, 1985, A compilation of lectures during All India Seminar on Andal, 13-15 August 1983, Madras: Sri Ramanuja Vedanta Centre.

Sri Basavesvara: Eighth Centenary Commemoration Volume, 1992, Bangalore: Government of Mysore, 1967, USA: Westview Press.

Śrīmad Bhāgavad-Gītā, Gorakhpur: Gita Press.

Staal, Frits, 1996, *Ritual and Mantras: Rules Without Meaning*, Delhi: Motilal Banarsidass.

Subramanian, S.V. and R. Vijayalakshmy, eds., 1983, *Philosophical Heritage of the Tamils*, Madras: International Institute of Tamil Studies.

Sundaram, P.S., tr., 1992, *Tiruvalluvar: The Kural*, New Delhi: Penguin.

Swami Chinmayananda, 1968, *Love Divine: Nārada Bhakti Sūtra*, Uttarkashi: Sri Tapovan Kuti.

Swami Niranjanananda Saraswati, 1993 (rpt. 2002), *Yoga Darshan: Vision of the Yoga Upanishads*, Bihar: Yoga Publications Trust.

Swami Satyasangananda Saraswati, 1984, *Tattva Śuddhi*, Bihar: Yoga Publications Trust.

Swami Sivananda Saraswati, 1957, *Nārada Bhakti Sūtras*, UP, Himalayas: The Divine Life Society.

———, 2002, *Essence of Bhakti Yoga*, Rishikesh: The Divine Life Society.

———, 2005, *Kuṇḍalinī Yoga*, Rishikesh: The Divine Life Society, 12th edn.

Swamy, Shree Purohit and W.B. Yeats, (1937) *Ten Principal Upanishads*, London: Faber and Faber. Mcmxxxvii.

Thipperudra Swamy, H., 1968, *The Virsaiva Saints: A Study*, S.M. Angadi, Mysore: Rao and Raghavan.

Tulpule, Shankar Gopal, 1984, *Mysticism in Medieval India*, Wiesbaden: Harrassowitz.

Vadhan, Amar Singh, 2006, *Tamil Sahitya aur Sanskriti*, Delhi: Abhishek Prakashan.

Vanmikanathan, G. tr., 1985, *Periya Purāṇam: A Tamil Classic on the Great Śaiva Saints of South India, by Sekkizhaar*, Madras: Shri Ramakrishana Math.

Varadachari, V., 1982, *Āgamas and South Indian Vaiṣṇavism*, Madras: M. Rangacharya Memorial Trust.

Varadachari, K.C., 1966, *Āḻvārs of South India*, Bombay: Bharatiya Vidya Bhavan.

Varadarajan, Mu, 1988, *A History of Tamil Literature*, New Delhi: Sahitya Akademi.

Vedavalli, M.D., 1983, "Message of Sri Andal's Tiruppavai to the Modern World", in *Sri Andal: Her Contribution to Literature, Philosophy, Religion and Art*, Madras: Sri Ramanuja Vedanta Centre.

Velliath, S.J., Cyril, 1993, *The Mysticism of Ramanuja*, New Delhi: Munshiram Manoharlal.

Verma, Rajinder Singh, 1996, *Singer Saints of India: A Study and an Anthology*, New Delhi: A Sterling Paperback.

Woodroffe, Sir John, 1956, *Introduction to Tantra Sastra*, Madras: Ganesh & Co., 3th edn.

———, 1978, *Principles of Tantra*, pt I, Madras: Ganesh & Co., 5th edn.

Yaravintelimath, C.R., tr., 2006, *Vachanas of Women Saints*, Bangalore: Basavasamithi.

Zide, Arlene R.K., ed. 1993, *In Their Own Voice: The Penguin Anthology of Contemporary Indian Women Poets*, New Delhi: Penguin Books India.

Index

Abhinavagupta, Ācārya, 26, 29, 221

abhoga khaṇḍa, 182

Absolute, awareness of, 30

Absolute Consciousness (Śiva), 53

ācāraliṅga, 43

adbhuta(m), 25, 29

ādhāra cakra, 138

Advaita aspect, 192, 227

aesthetic enjoyment or *rasānubhūti*, poetics of, 219

Āgamas, 6-7, 9

Āgamic ritual worship, ancient system of, 36

Āgamic rituals, 35

agnosticism, modern times of, 160

aham poetry, 34, 77

Aikya Sthala, 45

Ajaganna, 117

Akkā,
- human dimension of, 154
- image of, 168
- spiritual journey of, 160
- struggles of, 167

Akkā's journey poems, rewriting of, 159

Akkā's life,
- message of, 166
- mythologization of, 167
- theme of, 166

Akkā's *vacanas*, humanized reworkings of, 159

Akkagaḷa Pīṭhike, 117

Akkammā, Śaraṇeya, 51

ālayāśritagrāma, 176

All India Radio, Mysore, 183

all *sahṛdayas*, heart of, 192

Āḻvār(s), 17, 20
- *bhakti*, 18
- literature, 39
- personal gods of, 53
- poetry, 18
- poetry of, 94

Āḻvār saint(s)/goddess, 21, 24, 31, 33, 68, 174-75, 193
- hymns of, 39
- lives of, 97
- status of, 69

Ammaiyyar, Karaikkal, 35

amṛta, 135-36, 204

aṁśa khaṇḍa, 182

Amuktamalyada, 96-97, 189

an adolescent, immature love of, 107

Anādi Cetanā, 232

anāhata cakra, 137

ānanda, 15, 220, 221
Ananyatva, Śrīvaiṣṇva Śaraṅāgati concept of, 196
ancient Draviḍians, religion of, 5
ancient Indian music Śāstras, 185
ancient Sāṁkhya philosophy, cosmogonies of, 11
Āṇḍāḷ Kauthuvam, 110
Āṇḍāḷ,
  life story of, 189
  Saint, 208
  spiritual power of, 102
  story of, 101
Āṇḍāḷ's merger with Lord Raṅganātha, 102
Āṇḍāḷ's miraculous birth, episode of, 99
Andhra Pradesh, 49, 112
aṅga, 42
  union of, 47
aṅga is *jīva*, 139
aṅkita, 53, 117, 181
annadasoha, 52
antaḥkaraṇa, 228
anubhava mantapa, 114, 118, 120, 146, 149, 155, 179
  idea of, 52
  leading *śaraṇa*s of, 146
anubhava, joy of, 128
anuloma vivāha, 10
Appār, 33-34, 36, 39
Araiyar Sevai, 103, 105
āratī, 108, 202
arcā, 103
arcadevatā, 176
arcāmūrti, 175
arcana, 32, 89, 91
arcāvatāra, 175
Arjuna, 16, 27-28, 192
arpaṇa-kriyā, 45
art, genres of, 96
Aryan(s), 14
  culture, 7-8
  influence, 7
  sects, 9
ascetic-wanderer(s), 9, 114
aṣṭopacāra, 44
asura culture, 7
asura Pralamba, 81
Aśvamedha Yajña, 9-10
Ātmā, 226, 230
ātma śākṣātkāra, 215
ātmā with *paramātmā*, union of, 178
ātman, 226, 230
ātmanivedana, 89-90
attaining *mokṣa* in Śaivism, natural way of, 6
Attuḷai, 99-100
Avadhāna, 45
avataraṇa, 21
avatāras, 3-4, 90, 93
avidyā, 45, 223
Avvaiyar, 35, 100
awareness, three states of, 228
Ayarpadi, 88, 93
  girls of, 89
Ayyar, Narayan C.V., 38

Badardinni, Ashok, 165
Bahinābāī, ix

Bakāsura, 91
bāla līlās, 28
Basava Dal, 155
Basavanna, 114, 117-18, 126, 128, 132, 142, 146-47, 149-50, 153, 164-65, 181-82, 185-86
Basavaraju, 147
Basaveshwara, Jagatjyothi, 100
Bāsaveśvara, prime minister, 49
bathing, ritual of, 86
battīsa rāgas, 186
beḍagina vacanas, 132
beḍagu, conventions of, 132
beḍagu mode, incredible imagery of, 140
Bedara Kannappa, 100
Bhagavad Viṣayam, 173
Bhagavad-Gītā, 9, 16, 18-19, 21, 30, 122, 192, 218
  contemplation of, 106
Bhāgavata Purāṇa, 18, 21, 23-25, 32, 64, 79-80, 88
Bhagawatar, Tyagaraj, 100
bhakta(s), 28, 32, 40, 41, 46, 72, 82, 87, 99, 120, 137
Bhakta Kanakadasa, 100
bhakta sthala, 44, 46
bhakta-sādhaka, 133
Bhakte, Krishna Goda, 189
bhakti, 6, 22, 31, 33, 39, 57, 59, 63, 68, 73-74, 76, 85-86, 121, 140, 175, 178, 224, 233
  ancient texts of, 18
  arts of, vii
  aspect of, 16
  attitude of, 17, 175
  awareness of, 87
  beginnings of, 9
  categories of, 216
  chosen path of, x
  convergence of, 132, 140
  early phases of, 40
  elements of, 122, 133
  eleven ways of, 24
  emergence of, 5
  expression of, 184, 192
  feature(s) of, 134
  final stage of, 20
  freedom, impulse of, 41
  history of, 92
  ideal of, 85
  literature, centre of, 19
  phenomenon of, 18
  poetics, 82
  poets/poetess, vii-ix, 60-62, 67, 77
  post-institutional phase of, 40
  praxis of, 41
  sādhanā, 232
  Śāstras, 32
  songs, content of, 218
  spirit of, 17
  symbol of, 86
  terminology, 233
  texts, 65
  tradition(s), 30, 66, 82
  traditional modes of, 91
  Vaiṣṇava schools of, 64
  values, consolidation of, 34
  way of, 121, 127
  world-view, 100
bhakti and Tantra philosophy, 138
bhakti bhāvas, 26

all forms of, 27
bhakti cults, 31
bhakti culture, institutionalization of, 38
bhakti euphoria, initial phase of, 39
bhakti experience(s), xii, 96, 164, 226
  motto of, 164
  advanced stages of, 220
  infinite variety of, 141
bhakti expressions,
  indebtedness of, 65
  leitmotiv of, 102
Bhakti movement(s), vii-viii, 30, 34, 37, 40, 54, 58, 65, 68, 92, 219
  consolidation of, 35
bhakti paraphernalia, 85
bhakti phenomenon, 59-60, 221
bhakti philosophy, 30
  broader political base, 41
bhakti poetry, ix, 24, 59, 63, 215, 217-20, 223
  diction of, 57
  feature(s) of, 218-19
  secular reading of, 217
Bhakti saints, 4
  popularity of, 36
Bhakti-Sūtras, 18, 32
bhakti-yoga, 20, 122, 132
  course of, 95
  heights of, 20
  love as form of, 80
Bhāraśivas, 34
Bharata Muni, 29, 105
Bharathiyar, Subrahmanya, 101-02
Bharatnāṭyam, 109-10, 177, 188, 190, 209
Bharti, Srirama, 27-29, 62, 65, 71, 75, 78, 81, 84-86, 89-94, 104-05, 113
Bhaṭṭara Magaḷu, 98
Bhavānī, 147
bhāvas, *bhāva* of, 29
Bhoosnurmath, 115, 127, 146, 149
Bhūdevī, 69
Bible, 226
Bijjala (King), 10, 49
  murder of, 10
bindu cakra, 136
Biswas, Seema, 169
Black Faces, 5
blue-throated one, 204
Bommaiah, 153
Bommayyā, Kinnarī, 125, 146-48, 169
Brahma Purāṇa, 18, 79-80
Brahman, 215, 230
brahmānanda sahodara, 215
brāhmaṇas, authority of, 10
bridal mysticism, 29, 70, 74, 117, 174
  expression of, 77
bridal-mystic *bhakti*, 78
Buddha,
  contemporary of, 9
  gospel of, 15
  philosophies of, 33
Buddhism, 10, 15, 33
  life-denying values of, 33

Buddhist
  elements, 218
  religions, 16
  texts, 63

Caitanya Sampradāya, 31
Campantar, 37
Candragupta, 11
Caṅkam (Saṅgam) anthologies, 87
Caṅkam poetry, hallmark of, 77
caraṇa, 182
celebration of life and its mysteries, religion of, 4
Cennabasavanna, 48, 117, 146, 153
  holy feet of, 48
Cennamallikārjuna (Lord), 48, 53, 114-17, 121, 124-25, 127-31, 141, 143-44, 149, 159, 161, 169, 178, 190, 202
  empire of, 157
  heart of, 156
cerebro-spinal axis, 136
Chaitanya, Vinaya, 121, 124-25
Chamarasa, poet, 146, 154, 165
Champakalakshmi, R., 36-37, 39-40
changing sociology and psychology, 161
characteristics of
  arcana, 90
  bhakti, 20, 111
  five love *tinais*, 76
  oral poetics, 141
  vandana, 90
Chinmayananda, 22-23
Chosen God, 117
Chosen One, 70, 74, 85, 133
Christ, 13
Christian bride, 169
Cilappadikāram, 14, 26, 33
classic tāntric terms, 139
classical
  rāgas, 185
  tālas, 185
classical *aham* (love) poetry, 75
classical *bhakti*, 18
  discourse, 59
  literature, 59
classical form(s) of
  bhakti, 18
  dāsya, 31
  mād, 31
  sakhya, 31
  vātsalya, 31
  yoga, 20
classical
  Indian music, theories of, 185
  music, masters of, 185
  poetic tradition, unbroken, 218
  poetic vocabulary, 29
  Tamil love poetry, 75, 218
  tāntric discourse, 137
collective unconscious of
  all *bhaktas*, 19
  people, 144
  whole race, 63
compassion, symbol of, 174
compassionate omniscient energy, 46
compositions,
  mādhurya-centred, 73

compositions of
 bhakti tradition, 142
 Nāyaṉmārs, 35
concept(s) of
 avatāra, 19, 21
 awareness, 231
 Bhagavad-Gītā, 192
 kāyaka, 50
 māyā, 131
 Pavai Nonbu, 87
 ṣaṭsthala, 42
 Vaiṣṇava *bhakti*, 18
conceptions,
 cosmological, 6
 metaphysical, 6
 ritual, 6
consciousness,
 extraordinary state of, 227
 holistic state of, 220
 levels of, 231
 light of, 156
 normal state of, 220
 three states of, 227
 turīya state of, 96, 133
contemporary
 dancers from India and Germany, 208
 Indian woman, 166
 Kannada poetesses, 168
 karnatic classical music, singers of, 111
 of John the Baptist, 10
 of *vacanakāras*, 185
 Tamil culture, 112
cosmic
 body, 228
 complex, 226
 consciousness, 41, 223-24
 dimensions, 230
 mantra, 226
 Self, 96
 state (*turīya*), 225
cosmic principle(s), 4
 expansive nature of, 223
cosmogony, theory of, 42
cultural consciousness, 217, 220
cultural transmigration, evidence of, 13

Dakṣiṇāpatha, 13
ḍamaru, 162, 203
Dāmodara (Lord), 90
Danielou, Alain, 4-5, 8, 10-11, 223-25
darśana, 20
Daśanāmī Nāgās, 9
dasoha, 50-51
 spirit of, 50
dāsya, 26-27, 32, 89-90
 bhakti, 27
 bhāva, 27
Dehejia, Vidya, 24-25, 76, 87-88
deity, Sumerian, 5
deśī vacanas, 185
desire, body of, 130
Devi, Rukmini Arundale, 110
devotional ecstacy, 33
dhāraṇā, 20
Dharwadkar, 31
Dhr̥tarāṣṭra, 192
dhruva portion, 182
dhyāna, 20, 106
Divine Being, 22

divine consciousness, 45, 225, 233
divine energy (Śakti), descent of, 222
divine principle,
  consciousness of, 43
  manifestation of, 221
divine *śṛṅgāra*, 175
Divine Will, 46, 60
Divya Prabandham, 35, 75, 105
Divyasūricaritam, 189
Doraswamy, Vasundhara, 177
dramatic anthology, 145
Draviḍian civilization, influence of, 5
Draviḍian culture, an agrarian culture, 3
Draviḍian deity, 4
Draviḍian God, 3, 8
dṛṣṭi, synthesis of, 45
Dubianski, M. Alexander, 76
Dutta, Madhusree, 165, 211-12
Dwivedi, Mukund, 66

early *siddhas*, 40
ecstatic compositions, 220
effulgent poetic expression, 221
eight kisses, 202
eikya, 137
eleven Āḻvārs, 29, 35, 69
elevenfold *bhakti*, 23
Eliot, T.S., 160
emotional *bhakti*, 19-20
emotional *bhakti* poetry, 31
epiphany, 220
Eric, J. Lott, 72
Eswer, Nandini, 187-88
Eswer, Rashmi, 187-88
Eswer, Rohitha, 187-88, 193
eternal *nāda*, 226
etymological meaning of *parai*, 72
ever expansive Cosmic Consciousness, 122
Evola, J., 225
existence of *vacanas*, mode of, 141
experience and expression, context of *bhakti*, 67
experience(s) of
  awakening *kuṇḍalinī śaktī*, 133
  bhakta(s), 83, 219
  bhakti, 71, 219, 233
  ecstasy, 220
  mokṣa, 215
  śaraṇa, 139
expositing *bhakti* poetry, purpose of, 225
extreme longing, ecstatic songs of, 74

favourite *bhakti* sense, 20
female principle, 173
feminine consciousness, 174
fertility god, 3
fertility ritual, pre-Vaiṣṇavite, 65
first ice age, 5
fivefold *bhakti*, 26
  aegis of, 31
Freud, Sigmund, 227
Friedhelm Hardy, 24

Gadyatrayam, 194
Ganeshan, Shivaji, 101-02

Gaṅgā, 163, 203-04
garbhagṛha, 83
garlands of thirty and 143 *pāsurams*, 69
Garuḍavāhana Paṇḍita, 189, 196
Gautama Buddha, 10, 35
ghana guru, 134
Giriya Navilu, 154
goal of *sādhanā* is enlightenment, 132
God,
  higher consciousness of, 87
  realization of, 82
God Murugan, 61
Godāvarī (river), 13
Goddess, status of, 189
Goggeśvara, 66
Gokula, 21, 25, 78
Gokulanirgamana, 188
Gopala, 37, 40
Gopī Kṛṣṇa, Dasarukanda, 188
gopikā(s), 25, 72, 79, 95
  bhakti attitude to Kṛṣṇa, 92
  ecstasy in *rāsa* dance, episodes of, 25
gopikā episode, 79, 91
gopikās to Kṛṣṇa, relationship of, 91
Goṣāla, 10
  disciple of, 10
  religion, 9
Goswāmī, Jīva, 32
Govardhana, 62
grāmāśritālaya, 176
great universal appeal, poetess of, 161
gross sense-experience, 223
gross senses, level of, 129
Guheśvara's *śaraṇas*, 127
Guheśvaraliṅga, 127
Gulura Siddhavīranārya, 146, 148
Gummalapura Siddhaliṅgeśa Śivayogī, 146
guru, 45, 52, 127, 134-35, 140
Guru Tantra, 134
guruliṅga, 43
guru–śiṣya relationship, 140

Haḷegeyadeva, 125, 146-47
Hampī, 118
Hanumān, 16
Haṛappā, 5-6
Hardy, Friedhelm, 80
Haridas, 100
Harihara, 115-16, 118, 149-50, 153-55, 164-65
Harinābhiśaraṇa, 188
Harivaṁśa Purāṇa, 18, 25, 79
Harṣavardhana, reign of, 12
haṭha-yoga, practices of, 11
Havaldar, Nagaraj Rao, 183
hegemony, construction of, 58
Herculean valour, 126
herdswomen, round dance of, 26
heroism, non-ascetic values of, 34
Hindu culture, 174
  spirit of polytheism, 4
Hindu society, socio-historical evolution of, 50
Hinduism, 8, 15

liberation in, 6
Hindustani Music, 184
Hindustani musician, 183
Hiremath, 54
His Supreme Godhead, 90
house with nine doors, 136
human consciousness, 226-27
human individual, physio-psychic complex of, 224
human physio-psychic complex, 226
human psyche, psychological aspects of, 84
human *śṛṅgāra*, *bhāva* of, 175

idea of
- *bhakti*, 105
- creation, 222
- fertility, 3
- God, 19

ideological delineation, 181
Ilaṅgo Aḍigaḷ, 14
immanence, awareness of, 94
incomprehensive Absolute, 30
independence, Akkā's spirit of, 166
Indian classical dance, exponent of, 187
Indian
- classical singers, 109
- culture, 193
- history, mass movements, 219
- music, 193
- mythological tradition, 21
- Paśupati, 5
- philosophical system, 224
- philosophies of consciousness, 220
- philosophy, 191, 223-24, 226
- spiritual tradition, essence of, 188
- spirituality, 191
- spirituality, two distinct strains of, 122
- subcontinent, 5
- theories of cosmogony, 221
- theories on consciousness, 221

individual consciousness, expansion of, 96
Indra, 4, 6, 64
Indus civilization, 7
Indus Valley, 5
infatuation, temple of, 130
infinite Śakti, 47
intellectual *bhakti*, 19-20
intense
- *bhakti* sentiment, 74
- *bhakti* song, 95
- love for Kṛṣṇa, 25

intersemiotic
- contemporary performances, translations of, 142
- dimensions, 132
- transformations of Akkā Mahādevī's life, 166
- transformations, 57, 59-60, 78, 144, 146, 154, 169
- translation(s), 64, 168

intertextual dimensions, 132
Isaippa, 103
iṣṭa devatā, 175
iṣṭaliṅga, 43
Masti Venkatesh Iyengar, 100
Iyengar, Ariyakudi Ramanuja,

111
Iyengar, Malathi, 110
Iyengar, Masti Venkatesh, 98

Jacobson, Roman, 63, 141
jāgṛti, 226-27, 229-30, 232-33
Jaina(s), 14
  elements, 218
  poetry, 87
  propaganda, 38
  religions, 16
  texts, 63
Jainism, 10, 15, 33
  life-denying values of, 33
Jairaman, P., 26
Jaiswal, K.P., 12
Janaka, 99
jaṅgama(s), 11, 45, 50, 52, 115
  guru, 139
  sthala, 46
jaṅgamaliṅga, 43
Javali, V.K., 50
Jayadratha, 28
Jayashree, M.A., 111, 193, 195
Jayasudarshana, Bhagya, 157
jealousy, cloak of, 130
jīvan-mukti, 46, 233
jñāna, 22, 221-22, 224
jñāna-yoga, 122, 192
Jnanapeeth award, 98
Jñānendriyas, 229
Jnaneshwar, Sant, 100
Jñānī, womb of, 147
jogī, 48
Joshi, Pandit Bhimsen, 183
Judaic traditions, 66

Kabīr, Saint, 30, 66, 109
Kabīr Pantha, 31
Kadalī, 159
  description of, 155
  womb of, 156
Kadaḷīvana, 120, 155
Kailāsa, 150, 155, 162
Kalabhras, rule of, 33
kālakūṭa venom, 162, 203
Kālāmukha(s), 5, 9, 11
Kālāmukha Śaivism, 11
Kalyāṇa, 52, 114, 117-18, 120, 146, 148-49, 153-54
  city of, 49
  journey to, 129
Kalyāṇa is Kailāśa, 153
Kalyāṇa saugandhikas, 162, 204
Kalyāṇa Utsava, 103
kāma, emotions of, 32
Kāmadeva, 77
Kannaḍiga Vīraśaivas, 40
Kannagi, legend of, 14
kānta, 26
Kāpālikas, 9
kāraṇa, 226, 228-29, 232
karma, 22, 130
karma-yoga, 44, 122
karmendriyas, 229
Karnataka, 12, 39, 42, 49, 112, 144, 173, 177
  literary history of, 50
  playwright of, 164
  Music, 184
Kāśīnātha Apatilāsi, 184

Kāśmīr Śaivism, 221
Kathakali, 64
Kattimani, Basavaraj, 154
Kausala, 13
Kaushal, Maully, 119, 126
Kauśika (King), 116, 123, 126, 148, 151-53, 155
kaustubha, 98
Kāverī, 108, 199, 202
Kāyaka philosophy, essence of, 51
kāyakave kailāsa, 50
Kerege Hara, 188
kīrtana, 32, 89, 91
Kodaṇḍa Rāma, 62
Kodhai's Dream, 110
Kothai, 113
Kothari, Sunil, 110
Krānti Kaḷian, 165
Kranti Kalyāṇa Series, 154
kriyā, 221
Kṛṣṇa('s), 4, 16, 21, 27-29, 67, 70, 86, 88, 93, 95, 106, 192-93
  avatāra, 21, 90
  Carita, 79, 81, 91
  consciousness, 87
  episode, 79, 91
  heart of, 112
  house, 140
  myths, 78
  name, miracle of, 90
  names, 91
  of Viṣṇu, *avatāra*, 68
  personality, 86
  praises of, 95
  songs of, 18
  stories, episodes of, 64
  thought process of, 192
Kṛṣṇa *bhakti*, 89
  evolution of, 19
  goal of, 88
  literature, Hindi, 26
Kṛṣṇa with *gopīs*, celebrated *rāsa* dance of, 24
Kṛṣṇadevarāya, 96-97, 189
kṣapaṇa, 48
Ksheer Sāgara, 93
Kulaśekharāḷvār, 194
Kumārasambhavam, 150
Kumatturkknnanār, 61
kummi, 105
kuṇḍalinī, 136
  ascent of, 137-38
  awakening of, 139
  rising of, 137
  śakti, 45, 136
  yoga, 133, 136, 224
kuriñci, 76
kuriñci theme, 77
Kurukṣetra, 21
kuruṇḍu tree, 105
Kuruparamparāpirapavam, 189
Kuṣāṇas, 11-12

Lakkammā, Ayadakki, 51
Lakṣmaṇa, 16, 105
Lakṣmī, 100
Lakulīśa, 9-11
  cult, 11
langue, 58
Laṅkā, 61

later
  bhakti literature, 30
  bhakti, scholars of, 26
  bhakti, theologians of, 26
  medieval hagiographic accounts, 154
  siddhas, 40
laya, 182, 186
Lemuria, 5
liberated soul (Buddha), 15
life story, Śrī Āṇḍāḷ's, 189
life-negating values, 15
Lilian Silburn, 137
liṅga, 3, 42, 45, 52, 115-16, 138
  union of, 47
liṅga is Śiva, 139
liṅga-aṅga saṁyoga, 138
Liṅgāyata community, 144
Liṅgāyata religion,
  framework for consolidation of, 119
  message of, 155
Liṅgāyata tradition, 156
  first woman Jagadguru of, 155
literature, efficacy of, 195
Lord, *darśana* of, 106
Lord of
  Animals, 5
  Govardhana, 76
  Śrīraṅgam, 98, 106
  Veṅkaṭa (Viṣṇu), 97
  Yadu, 98
Lord Viṣṇu, twelve *avatāras* of, 21
Lord Viṣṇu's gift, 102
Lott, 73
love for Divine, 32
love, non-ascetic values of, 34
lyrical evocation of Akkā's journey, 161

macrocosmic Consciousness, 224
Mādhava, 93
Mādhāvacārya, 11
mādhurya, 25-28, 32
  bhakti, 28-29, 69-70
  bhāva, 25, 28-30, 69, 73-74
mādhurya bhāva in classical *bhakti* poetics, 91
madhyamā, 221-22, 226
Madivala, 129
Mahābhārata, 16, 18, 21, 27, 63, 88, 175
  epic tradition of, 18
Mahadevan, K.V., 101
Mahādevayya, 147
Mahadevi, 156
Mahadevi, Mate, 155
Mahādeviyakkana Rāgaḷe, 115, 118, 153-55
mahāliṅga, 43
Mahāmane, 52, 147
  idea of, 52
mahārāsa, 80
Mahāvīra Jaina, 10, 35
  contemporary of, 9
Mahendravarman, 34
Maheśāni, 135
Maheśvara, 47
  devotee of, 12
  sect, 12
  sthala, 44, 46

Māheśvarī, *sthala* of, 138
major hagiographical works, 189
major Upaniṣads, 8
Makkhali Goṣāla, 9
Mala, Vyjayanthi Bali, 110
Mallikārjuna, 163, 204
Mallinātha, 116, 153
Mālwā, 12
Manmatha, 98
Mannār, 99
Mansoor, Mallikarjuna, 186-87
Mantragopya, 132
man–woman relationship, 15, 74
Māṇḍūkya Upaniṣad, 226-27, 230-31
Maṇikavasagar, 33, 35
Maṇimekalai, 14-15, 33
Marayya, Śaraṇa, 51
mārga, 186
  vacanas, 185
Mārgaḷi/Margazhi, 72, 112, 196
  bath, purification of, 89
  bathing ritual, 85
  festival of, 65, 86
  rite, 102
mārgī, 185
Māri, 135
Marrayya Priya Amareś-varaliṅga, 51
Marxists, 58
Master of Ubhaya Vedānta, 173
Mathurā, 21, 25
māyāvilāsaviḍambanā sthala, 43-44
medieval period, *bhakti* traditions of, 64
Meenakshi, K., 37, 41
melāpaka, 182
Melkoṭe, 173, 176-77
Menezes, 54, 115, 127, 146, 149
metaphorical journey to Kalyāṇa, 153
metaphysical transcendence, principle of, 158
Milk Ocean, 89, 93
Mīrā, 109, 116
modern Kannada poetesses, 156
modern Kannada women's poetry, 165
Moheṅjo-Dāṛo, 5-6
mokṣa, 120, 122, 135, 215-16
  desire for, 59
  soteriological theories of, 232
mokṣa-mārga, 192
mokṣa-mārga Philosophy-based Dance Feature, 191
mother Yaśodā, image of, 193
moving *liṅgam*, 41
mṛda-bhakti, 152
Muktayakkā, 117
Mukundamālā, 194
mūlādhāra cakra, 136-38
mullai, 76
Muṇḍaka Upaniṣad, 225
music,
  deśī streams of, 185
  mārga stream of, 185
Muslim invasions, 12, 176
mystic union, 164
mystical
  Absolute, 30
  being, state of, 30

experiences, 216
framework, 103
Gokula, infusion of, 93
Gokula, space of, 88
rites, 9
mythopoeic imagination, 147

Nachiar Tirumoḻi, 18, 25, 31, 69-71, 74-78, 104, 106, 109-11, 113, 143, 175, 196-97
Nagabhushanswamy, 151
Nagarajan, A.P., 100-02
Nagiah, V., 100
naked *yogī*, 11
nakedness, concept of, 158
Nālāyira-Divya-Prabandham, 17-18, 38-39, 75-76, 78, 94, 103
Nammāḷvār, 20, 27, 29, 62, 174
Nandagopa, 88, 91
Nandalāla, 102
Nandanār, 38
saint, 38
Nandimath, S.C., 43, 45-46, 54, 145
Nandkumar, Prema, 68
Nandkumar, R.S., 179-80
Narada, 18, 22-24, 32, 84, 98
Nārāyaṇa (Lord), 69, 71, 91
Nāthamuni, Śrī, 103
first Śrīvaiṣṇava ācārya, 17, 38
National School of Drama, 165
Nāṭyaśāstra, 29
navadhā bhakti, 23-24, 26, 42-43, 89
stages of, 23
Nāyaṉmār(s), 17, 20, 68
bhakti, 33, 53
hymnists, 40
hymns, 39
lives of, 35
personal gods of, 53
saints, 33
saints, hymns of, 39
saints, period of, 33, 36, 42, 111
saints, poetry of, 33
nāyaka–nāyikā bhāva, 15, 178
Netunceralatan, Imayavarampan, 61
new *bhakti* tradition, 36
new poetics, creation of, 219
nidrā (*suṣupti*), 227, 232
nine *sthalas*, 42
nirahaṁkāra, 45
nirākāra, 30-31
nirguṇa, 31, 66, 141
bhakta, 30, 65
bhakti, 30, 65
panthas, 132
Nirmalaṅga, 147
nirveda bhāva, 26, 29
nityānusandhāna, 196
non-Aryan priestly class, 11
non-theistic Absolute Brahman, 9
nudi vacanas, 186
Nūtana Purātanara Rāgaḷegaḷu, 150

pada
format, 181
tradition, 181
Padagaḷu, 117
pādasevana, 32, 89, 91

Padmanābha (Lord), 65, 86
pādodaka, 115
Painting, Mysore School of, 193
palai, 76
pallaṇḍu, 72, 84
Pallava kings, 34
Pallava–Pantiya (Paṇḍya) period, 37
pallavī, 181
palm-leaf manuscripts, 7-8, 145
Pampa Śātaka, 150
pāñcajanya, 72, 84
Pañcaratna Kṛtis, 191
Pandit, Motilal, 221
pan-Indian Sanskrit, 142
Pāṇini, grammarian, 8
Parā Vāc, 226
Paraśivaliṅga (Lord), 47
Parātriṁśikā, 137
paratva, 31
Parimoo, 110
Paripatal, 87, 218
parole, 58
Parthasarthy, R., 26
Pārvatī, 5
paścima cakra, gate of, 156
Pāśupata, 9
    ancient religion of, 11
    religion, 11
Paśupati, Lord, 8
pāsurams, 68
paśyantī, 221-22, 226
Patañjali, 20
path(s) of
    Āṇḍāḷ, 123
    bhakti, 83, 121-22
    devotion, 6
    idealization, 156
    liberation, 122
    sādhanā, 134
    spirituality, 195
    Tantra and Yoga, characteristic of, 140
    transcendence, 160
patriarchal household, shackles of, 126
patriarchal mores, 161
Pattanshetty, Hema, 158
Pavai, 65
    vow of, 87
Pavai Nonbu, 110, 209
pavai theme, essential components of, 87
Peirce, 57
Periāḷvār, 82, 197
Periya Purāṇam, 35, 38
Periya Tirumoḻi, 94
personal god, idea of, 9, 21
Perumāḷ, Pinpalakiya Jiyar, 189
Peterson, Indira, 217
phalaśruti, 133, 218
philosophy of
    bhakti, 32, 81
    creation, 222
    Śaiva Siddhānta, 34
    Vaiṣṇavism, 97
physio-psychic complex, 228
piṇḍa sthala, 43
piṅgalā, 136
poetic
    biographer, 149

tradition, 216
poetics of
anubhava, 219
bhāva, 218
personal feeling, 218
poetry,
convergence of, 140
traditional genres of, 218
poisoned breasts, Pūtanā, 93
Poṅgal, 196
Poongothai, 113
post-Saṅgam
age, 15
period, 197
pot with nine holes, 136
Potana, 100
poṭarāja, 48
prabandham, major features of, 96
Prabhu, Allama, 46, 53-54, 65-66, 114, 117, 120, 126-28, 132, 142, 145-50, 153-54, 183
Prabhudeva, 118, 129, 149
Prabhuliṅgaḷīḷe, 146
Prākṛt, 63
prāṇaliṅga, 43, 47
praṇaliṅgī, 137
sthala, 45, 47
prāṇas, 162, 203
praṇava, 230
prāṇa-vāyu, 156
prāṇāyāma, 106
prapatti, components of, 196
prasāda, 45, 115
prasādaliṅga, 43
prasādam, 52, 167, 196
prasādī, 137
sthala, 45-47
pratyāhāra, 20
Prauḍhadevarāya I, 150
pre-Aryan cultures, 5
prema bhakti, 32
pre-marital love, 76-77
primal God Śiva, 67
process(es) of
complete withdrawal, 20
mythification, 154
mythologization, 150
senses, withdrawal of, 20
signification, 60
temple administration, 39
propitiousness of eternal Paraśiva, 46
Purāṇa mythologies, 218
Purāṇas, 6, 193
Purāṇic literature, historical authenticity of, 21
Purāṇic lore, 21
Purātanara Rāgaḷegaḷu, 149
purātanas, 149
Purohit Swamy, Shree, 231
puruṣa, 202
Puttaswamayya, B., 154, 164

rāgānuga bhakti, 32
Rāgaḷe, 150
rāja-yoga, 20
Rajguru, Pandit Basavaraja, 187
Rajkumar, Dr, 100
Rājpūtānā, 12
Ram Carita, 81
Rāma, 4, 88
Rāma *avatāra*, 21, 90

Rāma stories, episodes of, 64
Rāmalīlā, 63
Rāmanaṭṭam, 64
Ramanna, saint, 67
Rāmānuja, Ācārya, 174, 176
Rāmānujācārya, Śrī, 38-39, 112, 194, 196
Ramanujan, A.K., 20, 31, 42, 62-63, 75, 77, 141, 161, 217-19
Rāmāyaṇa, 16, 18, 21, 63-64, 88, 175
Rāmeśvaraliṅga, 51
Rangacharya, T.K., 111
Raṅga Praveśa, 189
Raṅganātha (Lord), 175
Raṅganātha, Śrī, 106
Raṅganātha, statue of, 175
Raṅganāyakī, 100
  avatāra of, 100
rāsa-nṛtya, 26, 79
Rāsavṛnda, 188-89, 191-92
Ratnam, Anita, 110
Rāvaṇa, 91, 94
Rāya, Prauḍhadeva, 53
rebellion, fascinating symbol of, 160
Reddy, Sujata, 98
religion of celebration of life and its mysteries, 4
religio-political atmosphere, 9
religious cults, 9
religious perspectives on *bhakti*, 219
religious philosophy, school of, 217
Renugopala, 176
representational consciousness, 216
Ṛgveda, 4, 8, 13
River Goddess, 89
rudrakaṇikā, 147
Rudra-Śiva, 8
Rudra-Śiva's dual form of protector–destroyer, 9
Rukmiṇī, 88

sacrificial *yajñas*, 9
sādhaka, 82-83, 85
sādhanā(s), 73, 82-83, 85, 88, 119, 136
  esoteric forms of, 52
  esoteric ways of, 120
sādhana rūpa bhakti, 32
sādhya rūpa bhakti, 32
Sage Bhaṭṭa, 99
saguṇa, 31, 66, 141
saguṇa and *nirguṇa bhakti*, difference between, 140
saguṇa bhakta, 30
saguṇa bhakti, 30-31, 65
ṣahasrāra, 139, 156
Sahitya Akademi Award, 165
Saint
  Āṇḍāḷ, 208
  Basavanna, leadership of, 42
  Hildegard, 208
  Kabīr, 30, 66
  Nandanār, 38
  Ramanna, 67
  Tirumular, 34, 39-40
  Tyāgraja, 191
saint-poet(s), 92, 119, 165
saint-poetess(es), 42, 59, 161, 169

consciousness, 220, 233
jīvan-mukti, 134
mokṣa, 20, 32, 233
saṁbhoga, 29
svapna, 229
turīya, 233
union or self-realization, 139
yogī, 135
Sthalabalabrāhmī, 48
Sthalabrahma Nirabhari, 48
*sthalabrāhmī*s, 47-48
Sthavara Liṅgam, 41
sthāyī bhāva, 178
sthitaprajñayatā, 16
sthūla, 226, 228, 232
story of
Attuḷai, 99
mythology, 156
Śrī Āṇḍāḷ, 191
Viṣṇucitta, 97
Strī, religion of, 173
structuring spiritual practice, two ways of, 140
Subbalakshmi, M.S., 100
subconscious, realm of, 229
Subramaniam, Padma, 110, 209
śūdra Nayanar, 38
sujñāna, 45
Sukathā Prasaṅga, 145
sūkṣma, 226, 228-29, 232
Sumerian Goddess, 5
Sundarambal, K.P., 100
Sundarār, 33, 35
Śūnya Sampādane, 46, 114, 117-18, 125, 127, 145-46, 149, 153-55, 164-65
Supreme
Consciousness, 139
God, 3, 8
Goddess, 89
reality, two aspects of, 30
saguṇa aspect of, 30
Supreme Being, 20
incarnation of, 79
Sūrya, 6
śuṣumnā, 45, 137
suṣumṇā nāḍī, 136, 138
suṣupti, 226-27, 229-30, 233
Sutta Nipāta, 13
svādhiṣṭhāna cakra, 138
svapna, 226-27, 230, 232-33
svara
kalpana, 182
vacanas, 132, 186
Śvetāśvatara Upaniṣad, 8-9
Swami Lakshmithathacharya, M.A., 173, 177
Swamy, Thipperudra, 6, 11
Śyāma, 97
systematic compilation of *śaraṇa* literature, 53

tāla(s), 103, 182
tamate, 185
Tamil
Āḻvār, 53
Āḻvār saints, 16, 26
aham poetry, devices of, 78
bhakti poetry, 219
classical resources, 76
cultural values of, 33
culture, 13-16

Divyaprabandham, 39
history, 34
inscription in Brāhmī script, 13
literature, 34
Nāyaṉmār saints, 16
Śaivite compositions, 64
Śaivite saints, 217
Śrīvaiṣṇava temples, 103
Siddhas, 40
Vaiṣṇava saints, 87
Tamil land, 13, 15, 26, 76, 112
fertility God of, 65
Tamil love poems,
classical form of, 77
mythology form of, 77
Tamil Nadu, 12, 17, 35, 39, 58, 64, 71, 112
bhakti, origin of, 16
Nāyaṉmārs of, 149
Nāyaṉmārs saints in, 36
Tamil Saṅgam, 61
Tamil Saṅgam period, 33
literary works of, 87
Tantra, 11, 122, 132, 223-25, 228
convergence of, 140
esoteric techniques of, 120
Tantra sādhanā, beginning of, 138
Tantrāloka, author of, 221
tāntric
facet, 122
philosophy, 138-39
psychic physiology, 140
sādhanā(s), 120, 122
sādhanā, convergence of, 132
sādhanā practitioner, 139
tradition, lines of, 135
tradition, texts of, 132
vocabulary of *cakras*, 137
yogic symbols, 135
tāntric discourse, 136
inherent part of, 133
tāttvika, 136
Tayar, 103
ten principal Upanishads, 231
Tevaram, 35, 39, 64, 67
textual fidelity, 64
theistic Brahmā, status of, 8
theological symbolism, 80
theories about the origin of *bhakti*, 17
Thipperudra, H. Swamy, 5, 11
thirty and 143 *pāsurams*, garlands of, 69
thirty-three Śiva *Śaraṇeyas*, 52
Thomas, A.J., 106, 109, 202
three Nāyaṉmārs saints, 101
tīrtha
distribution time, 196
pada, 133
sthalas, 36
yātrās, 36
Tirumal Perumai, 101
Tirumandiram, 34
Tirumaṅgai Āḻvār, 29, 94, 193
tirumañjanam, 104
Tirumular, 39-40
saint, 34
Tirumurai, 33
Tirumurukarruppatai, 218
Tirunārāyaṇa (Lord), 176
Tirunavukkaracar (Appār), 37
Tirunilakanta Yalppanar, 37
Tiruppanāḷvār, 38

Tiruppāvai, 18, 25, 31, 64, 69-72, 77-78, 83-93, 95-96, 102, 110-12, 133, 140, 174, 194, 196-97, 209, 225
  Āṇḍāḷ Goṣṭhī of, 104
  musical rendering of, 193
  teachings of, 174
Tiruttoṇḍattogai, 35
Tiruvaraṅganuḷa, 176
Tiruvarutselvar, 101
Tiruvasagam, 35
Tiruvilaiyadal, 101
Tiruviliyadalpurāṇam, 101
Tontada Siddhaliṅgeśvara, 146
traditional *bhakti*
  ritual, 90
  dimensions of, 90
tranquillity, blissful state of, 45
transcendental state of consciousness, 220
transluscent *vacanas*, 132
true *bhakta*, sacred space of, 41
Tukaram, Sant, 100
tulasī grove, 68, 101
tulasī pūjā, 191
turīya, 220, 225-27, 230
  product of, 233
twelve Āḻvārs, works of, 17
twelve poet-saints, 17
Tyāgraja, Saint, 191

Ubhaya Veda, 194
udgrāha khaṇḍa, 182
Udutadi, 115, 147, 152, 165, 167, 169
  temple of, 168
ulaṭīyabhāsā, 132
union, ecstasy of, 163, 204
Universal Consciousness, 96
Unmanifest Supreme, 84
Upaniṣad(s), 7, 9, 13, 16, 19, 30, 217, 231
Upaniṣadic tradition, 224

Vaazi Tirunamam, 196
vāc, 221-22
  Śakti, 222
  theory of, 221
vacana(s), 114, 117, 120-21, 127, 130-31, 142-44, 177-78, 181, 184-86
  composers, 181
  content of, 187
  dialogic nature of, 184
  kinds of, 186
  literature, 51, 141
  lore, 185
  punch line of, 181
  purpose of, 181
  Pada Vaidya, 183
  subject matter of, 50
  sāhitya, 183
  saṅgati, 183
  song, 183
  texts, 67
  verbal texture of, 141
vacana compositions, 184
  context of, 186
vacana movement, narrative of, 154
vacana poetry, counter-theme of, 185

vacana singing, 183
  field of, 180
  tradition of, 184
vacanakāras, 117-18, 184, 186
vacana-saṅgati format, 183
Vadaperumkoil, 88
Vaidehi, 168
vaidhī bhakti, 32
Vaidyanathan, Rama, 110
vaikharī, 221-22, 226
Vaikuṇṭha, 81
Vaiṣṇava(s), 31
  devasthānams, 39
  movement, great, 182
  position, 73
  tradition, 98
Vaiṣṇava *bhakti* poetry, evolution of, 21
Vaiṣṇavism, 3, 6, 12, 34-35, 64, 174
  harmonious coexistence of, 4
  prominence of, 12
Vaiṣṇavite
  devotional rite, 65
  saint, 38
Vākāṭaka(s), 12, 34
Vāmana, 61
vandana, 89, 91
Vāṇī, 98
Varṇamayiram, 71, 113, 197
varṇāśrama dharma, 38, 41
  menace of, 50
Varuṇa, 6
Vasanta Kumari, M.L., 111
Vasudeva Bhatt, L., 189
Vasumati, S.K., 189
vātsalya, 25-28, 32
  attitude of, 28
Vatsāsura, 62
Vedāntic thought, streams of, 192
Vedas, 7, 13, 16, 217
  supremacy of, 7
Vedavalli, R., 111
Vedic
  culture, 13
  family system, 49
  karma-kāṇḍa, 10
  language, 8
Vedic religion, rigid ritualism of, 10
Vemana, 100
Viennese psychologist, 227
Vijaya, K.R., 101-02
Vijayanagara, 96, 145, 150
vīṇā, 185-86
viraha bhakti, 29, 70
  aspects of, 80
viraha-bhāva, 70
Vīraśaiva
  aṅkitas, 53
  beliefs, 120
  bhakti, 33, 53
  community, 186
  concepts, 120
  outpourings, 177
  path, 123
  philosophy, 42, 117, 119, 138-39, 158
  poetry, 149
  poets, 30, 67
  proposition, 119
  renaissance, 150
  saint-poets, 142

socio-political agendas of, 50
spiritual agendas of, 50
Vīraśaiva faith, 42-43, 117
characteristics of, 46
Vīraśaiva movement, 41, 49, 164
evolution of, 33
facets of, 52
rise of, 10
Vīraśaiva religion, 186
development of, 115
Vīraśaiva saints, 141, 150, 179, 186
canonization of, 150
lives of, 150
vacanas of, 145
Vīraśaiva sect, philosophical tenets of, 53
Vīraśaiva texts of Karnataka, 65
Vīraśaiva tradition, achievements of, 145
Vīraśaiva women writers, lives of, 49
Vīraśaivism, 11, 31, 33, 48, 137, 139
aegis of, 54
convergence of, 140
important tenets of, 42
major tenets of, 120
movement of, 49
tenets of, 48, 114
Vīraśaivism Liṅgāyata, popular name of, 43
Vīraśaivism of Basavanna's time, 11
Vīraśaivite saint-poetess, 12
Vīraśaivite woman saint, 114
virginity test, physicality of, 147
Virūpākṣa (Lord), 150
Viśiṣṭādvaita, 173, 192
Viṣṇu (Lord), 3-4, 6, 35, 64, 79, 93, 197
and his *avatāras*, legends of, 68
bhakti, 9, 42, 87
devotee(s) of, 17, 197
important Purāṇas of, 21
legend of, 24
mythology, 18, 75
mythology, gamut of, 78
oneness of, 4
stories, episodes of, 64
temple of, 93-94
twenty-two *avatāras*, 21
Viṣṇu Purāṇa, 18, 21, 24-25, 64, 79-80
Viṣṇucitta Āḻvār, 27-28, 68-69, 79-82, 98, 102, 193
Viṣṇucitta, story of, 101
von Bingen, Hildegard, Saint, 208
vratas, 94
vrātyas, 6
Vṛndāvana, 21, 78-79

Wema Kaḍphises, 12
woman, clandestine love of, 107
woman in love, ecstasies of, 120
woman's freedom, ultimate symbol of, 157
women
śaraṇas, 52
vacanakāras, 52
Woodroffe, Sir John, 134-36
worship, Āgamic modes of, 37

Yadugirināyikā, 176
Yajurveda, 8
Yamunā, 95, 108, 202
Yāmunācārya, 38
Yaravintelimath, C.R., 48-49, 51-53, 114, 116, 121, 124, 128, 144
Yaśodā, 193
    perspective of, 28
Yeats, W.B., 231
Yoga Darshan, 232
yoga, 19, 22, 105, 224-25, 227
Yoga, 6, 122, 132, 223-24
    convergence of, 140
    esoteric techniques of, 120
yoga-mudrā, 6
Yogāṅga Trividhi, 117, 120, 122, 132-34, 136-40, 224-25
    tāntric aspects of, 134
Yoga-Sūtras, 20, 194
yogī(s), 93
    great, 6
yogī sitting in lotus pose, 6
yogic
    discourse, 136
    facet, 122
    sādhanā, 120
yoginī, 139, 224

Zide, 157